CRYPTO ASSET INVESTING IN THE AGE OF AUTONOMY

CRYPTO ASSET INVESTING IN THE AGE OF AUTONOMY

JAKE RYAN

WILEY

For general information on our other products and services or for technical support, please contact our Customer Care Department within the United States at (800) 762-2974, outside the United States at (317) 572-3993, or fax (317) 572-4002.

Wiley publishes in a variety of print and electronic formats and by print-on-demand. Some material included with standard print versions of this book may not be included in e-books or in print-on-demand. If this book refers to media such as a CD or DVD that is not included in the version you purchased, you may download this material at http://booksupport.wiley.com. For more information about Wiley products, visit www.wiley.com.

Library of Congress Cataloging-in-Publication Data is Available:

ISBN 9781119705369 (Hardcover)
ISBN 9781119705444 (ePDF)
ISBN 9781119705376 (ePub)

Cover Design: Wiley
Cover Image: © KTSDESIGN/SCIENCE PHOTO LIBRARY/Getty Images

SKY10022424_111220

Contents

PART III
CRYPTO INVESTMENT STRATEGIES   155

12 A Primer on Crypto Asset Investing   157
13 Quantitative Analysis Frameworks   176
14 Understanding Crypto Asset Classes   198
15 Investment Themes   209
16 Building an Investment System   223

Notes   245
Further Reading and Resources   255
Appendix   259
Index   265

Acknowledgments

There are many people without whose involvement this book would not have been possible. I'd like to thank and acknowledge them all for their contribution. First, I'd like to acknowledge and thank my mom, Pam Skersick. Not in just the "mom" sense, though I thank her for that, too. My mom was instrumental in encouraging me to stay on track and write a third book proposal after my first two attempts at getting a book deal failed. She was a tireless supporter of my writing. She was also my proofreader through the entire writing process of the manuscript. Words cannot express how thankful I am for her support.

I would also like to thank my business partner, James Diorio. Thank you for helping and supporting the project from day one and for helping to write most of Chapter 8 to meet the deadline. Thanks for believing in the Age of Autonomy investment thesis and especially for believing in me. I'd also like to thank RT Moreno. It's been a journey to get this book published. I want to acknowledge you for your commitment to "transform the money, transform the world."

I would also like to thank my wife, Onkar, for supporting my writing efforts. It's been a sacrifice and I appreciate all you do for me and for our family.

I would also like to thank my dad, John Ryan, for always having conviction in my investment pursuits. He's always been an early investor.

I would like to thank Nels Paine and Rob Cone for being advisors to my crypto fund and providing me direction about the world of institutional investment.

I would also like to thank my literary agent and initial editor, Herb Schaffner. Without your help, direction, and expertise, there is no way this book would have been published. It was a pleasure to work through the initial drafts with you and I'm so glad I found you to help edit, create, and network this book into existence. I hope we work together again soon.

I would also like to thank my editor, Bill Falloon, and the entire team at Wiley, including Purvi Patel for editing and Samantha Enders for cover art. Thank you for your contribution to this book. A special thanks as well to Kinga Toth for helping proofread and edit the early manuscript.

I have a special thanks to Joshua Hong for being an instrumental believer and supporter of the *Age of Autonomy*™ thesis. He led and financially supported the Autonomy2040 conference in Tulum, Mexico, getting some of the top minds in blockchain, robotics, IoT, and AI together at one conference. It's that inclusion of several revolutionary technologies under one roof that's going to make the difference.

Finally, I'd like to extend a special thanks to so many out there in the VC, tech, financial, and crypto investment community. You provided me with ideas, guidance, and advice, and I appreciate you – Gordon Mattey, Joshua Hong, Ric Edelman, Anuraag Shah, Travis Kling, Brock Pierce, Coburn Hawk, Otto Penzato, Tom Shaughnessy, Kevin Kelly, Tyrone Ross, Chris Paine, Tiffany Asakawa, Plan B, and many others. You've helped me directly or indirectly with this book and inspired me along the way.

Author's Note

I started writing the manuscript for this book in late 2019. A lot has changed in the world from the time I started to the time I finished. A global pandemic has come and upended the world. An economy already in trouble has been thrown into further turmoil. Central banks around the globe are expanding monetary policy and using exotic instruments to try and stabilize their economies. In 2020, in the United States alone, public debt ballooned an estimated 80% in one year. Chaos abounds.

Through it all, the crypto markets have survived and thrived. If ever there was a macroeconomic case for Bitcoin, the time is now. Investors all over the world are concerned about inflation. In fact, the #1 debate in finance is whether inflation or deflation is coming. The debate is happening all over the world. It's this analysis from which all investment strategies are born.

I have been an investor for a long time. I bought my first mutual fund when I was 15 years old. I bought my first stock when I was 18 years old. I learned how to trade options when I was 22 years old. While finance has never been my profession, investing has always been my passion. My profession for the first half of my career was in software technology. I graduated from the University of Texas at Austin with a degree in computer science. I had a specialization in the field of artificial intelligence. My first job out of school was as a VisualBasic developer for a Fortune 100 company, having never seen or programmed in VisualBasic. Eventually, I started my own software consulting firm, the Venice Consulting Group, and served clients like SAG-AFTRA, FOX Sports, and Lexus. In 2014, I started angel investing in early stage equity of AI and fin-tech start-ups. In 2015, I invested in seed stage equity of my first blockchain company. In 2016, I started investing in bitcoin – I think my first price paid was around $450. I love the crypto space because it sits at the intersection of technology, economics, and finance.

While I've read a lot of books on economics, I am not a formally trained economist. There may be debates going on in economics that are beyond the scope of this book. Too, there are times that I make analogies and don't represent all of the technical detail due to my commitment to the audience for book readability. There are cases where I make more generalizations that don't go into the full detail of specifics and that may not fully represent the technology that's going on in the background. I've found in writing a book that covers this much in scope that I have to set priorities and boundaries in certain places to make the crux of the book the focal point.

As a community, I think we've done an okay job conveying the monetary value of bitcoin. We've conveyed the concepts of digital gold, digital scarcity, a hedge against central bank monetary manipulation, and a new digital reserve asset. However, I don't think we've done a good job as a crypto-community conveying the transformative nature of smart contracts and the utility value created with them. With this book, I aim to fix that. If you're going to create a new digital capital system, money is the first building block. It's required, but not sufficient. This book illustrates what comes after money in a new digital capital system.

I wrote the precursor to this book back in 2018. It was an article on *Hacker Noon* titled "Crypto's Role in the Age of Autonomy." It was my first attempt to provide an economic thesis about what is happening with crypto and the world around us. It outlined the basic premise of this book.

I am committed to being an educator and expanding the field of study around crypto asset investing. I am committed to making a difference. I think I can do that by getting more people involved in the next great technological revolution of our time. Transform the money: transform the world. With all that said, I do hope you enjoy the book.

Introduction – Why This Book and Why Now

In the middle of difficulty, lies opportunity.

— Albert Einstein

Speech, content, math, code, and money are converging. They are mental constructs humans symbolize as characters on a page or a screen. We take this symbolic transmutation of cognitive concepts into value for granted, but in fact each of these is the same thing at one level – abstractions of human design. Before, we saw code, math, and speech converging in software applications, cryptography, and web design. Now, money is fully converging with this construct. As a result, many of us are rethinking how we view the digital life of money.

I view the two most important factors of successful investing to be great timing and strong, educated conviction. Sometimes the timing aspect of investing is lucky. No one wants to rely on luck when managing their money. If you want to incorporate timing into a systematic investment thesis, create great timing through smart, impactful research. Watch for what's going to be successful in the future instead of trying to invest in what's worked in the current past. Markets change over time. As conditions evolve, successful strategies lose their advantages. If you are analyzing current returns and are following a strategy that is producing outsized returns, then I think most of the time you are too late. I see so many investors in the equities markets searching for mutual funds with a strong 12-month performance in beating the market benchmark. But if you're a new investor getting in at that point, it's already too late. Outsized returns have been made. This is why I never want to analyze past returns as a part of my decision-making process for a future investment strategy. Instead, I want to understand market cycles to figure out where we are and then where we're going. This book will show you how finding and following market cycles is key to producing outsized returns.

The second important aspect to exceptional investing is to have conviction in what you're investing. Especially when it comes to understanding new innovation or technology, you gain conviction by learning, researching, and digging deeper into a particular domain to gain expertise. In this book, you will learn why cryptoasset investing is so transformational and how to invest using systems and processes that remove emotion from the equation. I will explain the world of crypto markets and lay out easy-to-understand strategies and tactics for investing in crypto assets while showing you, the investor, what risks to manage and how to manage them.

We Are Marching Toward Two Worlds

Right now, the majority of the world is walking into a trap. They're walking into a world where every single action they do, online or offline, is being monitored, tracked, and surveilled. The tools are becoming better and better and the amount of data tracking the population is staggering. If you have Google's Gmail, they are reading your emails and the emails you send to others in an effort to better target advertising. They use Google Maps for location data. Your phone is spewing out geolocation data to more third parties than most even realize. And there are data aggregators that are collecting all this information to sell to anyone for a price. Your privacy is going the way of the dinosaur.

It's worse in some other countries. In China, they have a social scoring system that tracks all aspects of your behavior and your financial life. If you are using your mobile phone for payments through Alipay and other services, every single financial transaction is being tracked by the government. They know where you are. They know what you purchase. They know vast amounts of medical information about you. In China, this can affect whether you can buy a train ticket or upgrade to first class or not. There are over 50,000 cases of Chinese citizens who couldn't book travel because they had outstanding debts. Depending on where you live, a comfortable, lazy approach will land you living in a world of surveillance capitalism or a world of a surveillance state.

There are Chinese citizens who are having the sum of all their public actions reduced to a social score. There are American citizens who have their email surveilled to improve e-commerce opportunities for companies willing to pay. Google partnered with Mastercard, so now

Google can view all your financial transaction data. It's the aggregation of all your health, online, and financial data that's bringing about a future I suspect none of us truly want. What I am describing is only the beginning. You have a choice.

Do you want to own your own data or are you going to let it own you? Blockchain and crypto assets allow for us to create a different future. One where you own and control your own data. One where you cannot be tracked, at least not as easily. One where you could get paid for allowing access to your data. These technologies provide tools for anyone to reclaim their privacy. In this book we offer a reason and a way for taking back control of your financial life such that your life is farther away from a surveillance state and closer to financial autonomy.

Where We Are in the Current Economic Cycle

The globe is currently in a tricky spot in the current economic cycle. In 2020, we're in a transition period. Countries are laden with debt. The United States has $28 trillion in public debt with $123 trillion in unfunded liabilities that include Social Security and Medicare.[1] We are currently in a period of slowing growth coupled with the potential of inflation – and this is driving global central banks to take a dovish stance as they are worried about deflation. We are transitioning into slower growth as the potential of inflation starts to accelerate and so this changes the market dynamic. Global central banks will start to take a more neutral monetary stance as they worry about stagflation. This all drives toward the next aspect of the cycle that I think we're all most worried about, which is the next major recession or downturn in the market. When the next major downturn comes, the Federal Reserve and all global central banks will not have any ability to increase stimulus in the system. No traditional monetary solutions will be available to governments because they've been used up and not replenished. Quantitative easing (QE) has been used for too long. Interest rates are already low or zero, depending on the country. Many developed nations have negative-yielding sovereign debt, so what are they going to do? Push rates even lower? This means that our governments' only option will be fiscal reform, but that takes time, especially in the polarized political world we live in today. The easiest option will be to print more money and give it directly to the people. At the end of all this, we're going to see a public debt crisis – this is an opportunity for those who are informed about alternatives.

Investing in the New Technological Revolution

My investment thesis is based on 100 years of proven economic theory. As we've learned, short-wave economic cycles, those 5- to 10-year cycles, are driven by credit, but the long-wave economic cycles, those 50- to 60-year cycles, are driven by technological revolution. We've had five cycles over the past 200 years – the Industrial Revolution, steam/railways, electricity/city electrification, oil/autos, and the last wave, which was the Age of Information with the Internet.[2] These long-wave economic cycles drive market forces and investment over decades. Being able to spot them early is advantageous.

Artificial intelligence (AI), the Internet of Things (IoT), robotics, and cryptocurrency are converging to deliver a new technological revolution. We've already seen evidence of this. For the past 10 years AI, IoT, and robotics have been delivering new solutions that drive automation. That has been valuable, but it has not been transformational. There has been no driving force requiring a paradigm shift in how businesses operate.

Cryptocurrency was the last piece of the puzzle. It allows for generating, processing, and transferring economic value without the need for human intervention. As these technologies converge, they are bringing about a new age, what I call the *Age of Autonomy*™. Once this technological innovation reaches a tipping point, businesses around the world will push to reconstitute themselves, once again, just like they did during the last technological revolution in the Age of Information (aka the Internet Age). It's that competition that's a key driver to technology adoption and the force that drives global adoption. In the future, businesses and organizations that do not have autonomous operations simply will not be able to compete with those that do because *autonomy is the ultimate competitive advantage*. In this book I will show you why cryptocurrency is the mechanism that will unleash the wealth-building value of these technologies in our digital age and how you as a crypto investor can prosper.

The Push Toward Autonomy

With the advent of blockchain technology, we've begun a new long-wave economic cycle driven by a new technological revolution. Individuals, corporations, and organizations are pushing for greater autonomy, agency, and sovereignty. Management analysts, political gurus, and trend watchers all agree that AI is the tech frenzy of our time. Companies are feverishly developing AI for improvement in all sorts of systems, from e-commerce to customer support to robotics. We see AI helping improve our lives, from suggesting a new book to read based on past history to helping our search on Google. There is an underlying trend developing everywhere to help people improve their knowledge and therefore decision making, from GPS data helping with optimal routes home to removing one extra step in choosing a movie theater based on current location. The trend is to provide more agency and sovereignty to people by removing rote tasks and it's happening by giving more autonomy to software and robots to operate on our behalf.

Investment is pouring into start-ups and initiatives that use robotics to minimize human intervention in rote physical tasks. Investment in AI systems will top $98 billion by 2023, says a new IDC report.[3] According to Gartner, global business value derived from AI will reach a staggering $3.9 trillion by 2022[4].

I expect this revolution to reach the automobile by way of autonomous driving, which would revolutionize one of the biggest industrial sectors in the economy, starting in 2022 with long-haul trucking. We are looking at the greatest macro shift of our time and blockchain technology is going to take it one final transformational step further.

Even money itself is looking to become self-sovereign. Every time a government-backed currency has come off a commodity or gold standard, it fails. One of the first examples is Rome in the third century AD, where the amount of silver in coinage went from 100% silver per coin a hundred years earlier to 0.02% at the end of the Roman Empire. Another example is John Law and France's failure of its state finance in the early eighteenth century, through a series of missteps, creating crippling inflation of 13,000%. Another example in modern history is the hyperinflationary period of the Weimar Republic in the 1920s, which killed the German mark. Historically, fiat currencies fail as a store of value, always. Money gains its value by declaration and agreement, not by any intrinsic value. Money that can be enforced without the need of human intervention could be the most valuable money created to date.

Bitcoin was the first killer app of blockchain technology. Bitcoin brought forth something innovative by creating a global system to digitally transfer and store value. It does this through its design by using decentralization, immutability, and incentivization in novel ways that allow commerce transactions without the need of a trusted third party (i.e. like a bank). Moreover, the next generation of cryptocurrencies brings forth the capability of smart contracts (i.e. programmable money). These capabilities are new, and they will spark an entire wave of technological improvement centered around how we globally generate, store, and transfer value.

Innovations That Make the Age of Autonomy Possible

There are many innovations under the crypto umbrella. Crypto is not just one invention, but a set of ideas and innovations that have settled into a paradigm shift in what's possible with money and finance. Today – and it's completely unbelievable that it's true – the fastest way to get a transfer of money is still to fly it physically to its destination and settle the transaction in physical cash. You might say, "That's not true, I can just wire the money and it's there in a few hours." That's actually not the case. Currently the entire financial system is built on trust and it's the trust between those banks that allows it to look like the transaction is settled in a few hours. Behind the scenes, ACH, SWIFT and IBAN, and BIS all work to settle transactions in a network of banks, intermediaries, and legacy-based software to clear and settle transactions in what takes days, not hours. This is because all that legacy technology is built on 50-year-old paper-based processes. There is only a digital veneer. However, many innovations have occurred over the past decade to make true digital finance a reality.

Many innovations now exist from several inventions that have come from Bitcoin and blockchain technology. These inventions, when combined together, provide for capabilities previously not possible. Collectively, *they are revolutionary.*

Blockchain and the Proof-of-Work Consensus Mechanism

Blockchain technology is a system of creating and maintaining a decentralized network of servers that maintain a decentralized, distributed public ledger (i.e. a blockchain). At its core, a blockchain is just a decentralized public ledger. Blockchain is the underlying technology that allows cryptocurrency to function. A blockchain allows digital information to be recorded and distributed but not edited. It does this through a consensus mechanism called "proof of work," which is a fundamental invention in a blockchain. This innovation solves the Byzantine Generals

Problem, which allows systems to gain consensus among two or more nodes without requiring a trusted third party.

In the past paradigm, the financial system required trust to securely operate. The system required a trusted third party to settle accounts, form capital, issue credit, and conduct almost any commercial transactions. Bitcoin safely eliminated that requirement, reducing time and friction of all commerce transactions and creating permissionless, trust-minimized financial transactions. This is transformational.

For the first time in history, peer-to-peer consensus allows us to transact globally without the need of a trusted third party. With Bitcoin, it's the blockchain that provides certainty that one coin cannot be double-spent. To prove that no attempts to double-spend have occurred, the blockchain uses a proof-of-work consensus mechanism to agree upon and distribute every transaction, which we'll discuss in detail later in the book. With Bitcoin, all transactions are publicly communicated to all nodes in the network. With this architecture, opacity is removed from the financial system and users can trust the accuracy of the ledger.

Decentralization

Decentralization is a design principle by which the activities of an organization, particularly those regarding planning and decision making, are distributed or delegated away from a central location, group, or authority.[5] The value of a decentralized architecture, especially for public infrastructure and open protocols, is that it's not centrally owned or controlled. The benefit of decentralization is that there is no single point of failure in either the administration or execution of the system. This concept is outlined eloquently in the book *Antifragile* by N. N. Taleb,[6] which we discuss later in this book. This principle is at the heart of designing the next digital financial system of the future. A decentralized system cannot be co-opted or manipulated by a single participant. This becomes critically important when you look at money and the history of money.

Permissionless Access

One of the biggest breakthroughs with blockchain technology is that one does not need an account or permission from anyone to access it. Users do not have to have an account or request permission to use this public infrastructure. Permissionless access to public blockchains fundamentally transforms the architecture of how we design financial transactions and financial system infrastructure.

Bitcoin software runs as a virtual machine on thousands of servers across the world called miners. They get paid in the form of a chance to win mining rewards of bitcoin, to run the Bitcoin software and maintain the Bitcoin blockchain. Anyone who knows how to correctly access the Bitcoin blockchain can buy or sell or complete a variety of transactions without permission and that's transformational. Talk about egalitarian; this alone could change the world.

Immutable Records

Blockchains work in such a way that present work is built on top of past work. Therefore, there is no way to edit or alter past transactions. Public blockchains record immutable transactions in their blockchains, which means that once a transaction is recorded, it can never be changed or undone. This is securely enforced by the blockchain system itself, which is why we no longer require trust to conduct financial transactions. With a database, there's always a capability of deleting a record or transaction, which is why trust is so important in how legacy financial systems operate. With blockchains, being able to store a record that you know can never be changed is transformational and it brings forth new capabilities. Immutability is a cornerstone for how blockchains can be maintained without a trusted third party; we'll see later why that's important. Being able to record a transaction forever, that anyone can read and verify, lends itself well to areas like money and stores of value.

Trust-minimized Transactions

Our financial system is based on trust. If you want to go to the store to buy some organic, gluten-free bread, first you need to trust that the store deals with distributors to supply it. Then, you need to trust the label on the bread that it's organic. Then, you need to trust the store that they've competitively priced it. Then, you need to trust your credit card to debit the right amount. Then, you need to trust your bank to cover the charge. Then, you need to trust that your bank will hold your money and not steal it. And on and on and on. Right now, financial transactions require a whole lot of trust and trusted third parties to conduct financial transactions, but that's about to change.

With cryptocurrency, through the use of blockchain technology, a trusted third party is no longer required to complete a financial transaction. Transactions now can be *trust-minimized*. This changes the nature of how many people can now participate in financial transactions – think of the four billion people who don't have a bank account. It also reduces the cost within financial transactions. With crypto, vastly more people will be able to make financial transactions, and what they can transact and how much is a paradigm shift from the past.

Autonomous Execution

Another innovation in cryptocurrency is smart contracts or autonomous contracts. Smart contracts are chunks of code that live and run on permissionless global servers. Each blockchain has its own ecosystem of servers and miners that get paid to manage, maintain, and secure the blockchain. Smart contracts live on a set of global servers and they can always be accessed and executed – and they're permanent.

A smart contract is a self-executing contract, with the terms of the agreement written into programmable lines of code. The code and the agreements exist across a decentralized blockchain network. Smart contracts can have conditions before a transaction occurs. It can send a partial transaction if and only if a certain event occurs, like an escrow service. All business contracts, like buying a house or transferring a title or creating a trust upon death or any standard business contract, can now be expressed in a smart contract. Smart contracts move all the logic from a business contract out of paper into the digital world. In this book, I will show how the idea of programmable money will alter what's possible in the future.

Autonomous contracts are a type of smart contract. They are smart contracts that are designed to be event-driven and do not require human intervention. They are to legal agreements what digital currency is to paper money. Smart contracts allow agreements between two parties, whether that's an organization, a person, a contract, or a wallet address, to be executed without permission and without needing human intervention. The legal system exists to govern conflict. As these crypto smart contract platforms evolve, they will bring more transparency, consistency, uniformity, and autonomy to maintaining, executing, and processing legal contracts while also reducing friction, cost, and time.

Autonomous contracts open a new world of what's possible. Now, a decentralized autonomous organization (DAO), which is a collection of members who agreed to be represented by rules encoded as a computer program that is transparent, controlled by owners, and not influenced by a central authority, can be set up with cryptocurrencies as resources. They can provide goals, constraints, and actions that the DAO can deliver on without the need for human intervention. What makes this possible is the set of autonomous contracts and the infrastructure, a blockchain, to run them. Resources can be purchased and transferred based on a set of rules and logic. No humans required. This digital market infrastructure makes it possible to deliver unprecedented agency, sovereignty, and autonomy.

The Age of Autonomy – Welcome to the Future

This new age will alter every aspect of how a business or organization will go about producing goods and services. Throughout the globe, each industry, community, and government will begin building autonomous agents to produce work and generate value, then transfer and store value. These actions will be created and enforced by software – agents and bots implementing smart contracts through cryptocurrency platform networks. Robotics will achieve any movement in the physical world. The IoT will provide the sensors and networks to measure and communicate data. Artificial intelligence will provide the judgment, expertise, and evaluation within a closed system. And decentralized cryptocurrency platforms will provide movement across organizations via the smart contracts to govern and enforce the transfer and storage of value from the work produced.

This will also restore balance between the individual and the group. Autonomous agents working in a decentralized world will allow people to invest and work on projects they're interested in and be paid or rewarded for their contribution. Earning tokens through work or investing in crypto assets you believe in allow the benefit to be restored back to the individual. No longer will there be a rent-seeking intermediary like Facebook, Uber, Google, or any other to extract value from the whole. Central organizations will no longer accumulate all the benefit. The power is restored to the individual because they will be able to vote within the "on-chain" governance systems without politics and without an intermediary circumventing the will of the collective individuals.

The Ideal Investment Profile

If I were to build a profile of one of the best types of investments, it would have the following characteristics. First, the investment would have a big defensible moat; that is, it must be hard to compete against and hard to replicate. You can think of the social network Facebook as having a defensible moat. If you remember Google+, which in many ways was far superior in technology and feature set, it could not break into the social network space. People had already uploaded their photos and built their friends networks on Facebook, which made it very hard for any competitor to come and disrupt Facebook. Second, the investment should generate asymmetric returns; that is, it should be able to perform nonlinearly and produce outsized returns relative to the risk taken. Third, it should be as close to a monopoly as legally possible. Fourth, it would be antifragile, that is, it would improve in complex, chaotic circumstances. And finally, the timing should be such that the investor is early, before a huge wave of adoption is about to transpire. Crypto assets, the right ones, provide all these characteristics.

Investing in Crypto Assets in the Age of Autonomy

What if you could have invested in the Internet protocols in the 1990s? I'm talking about the Internet protocols like HTTP, SMTP, FTP, TCP/IP, SSL, and so on. Every time a web page was requested via HTTP, your fractional ownership of the protocol would generate a small return in some form. Imagine how valuable those investments might be. That wasn't possible then, but it is possible in this next digital financial revolution. Certain crypto assets represent and approximate to fractional ownership of these public blockchains. Public blockchains are permissionless, as described earlier; you need no one's permission to access or use them. If one (or many) of these blockchains really takes off and becomes widely adopted, how valuable would that fractional ownership be? That's what we're talking about in this book – an innovative investor's ability to obtain fractional ownership of public financial infrastructure that will power the next long-wave economic cycle and an investment that has all the ideal characteristics we've described.

Putting It All Together

The *Autonomous Revolution* has begun. Artificial intelligence, the IoT, robotics, and cryptocurrency are converging to deliver a new long-wave economic cycle. Soon, there will be a global race to build autonomous operations. Businesses and organizations will be in ever-more cutthroat competition to build autonomous operations that allow them to take advantage of more real-time opportunity and build systems for continuous real-time improvement.

Understanding the long-wave economic cycle and what the key technological innovation is will make you a better investor. If you could have been early in the Age of Information investing in Internet infrastructure, you would have delivered superior returns as an investor. Understanding the technological revolution and where we're at in the cycle would have kept your investment "true north." Likewise, this new long-wave cycle will be about autonomous operations. Autonomy is the ultimate competitive advantage by reducing operational cost and increasing potential leverageable opportunities. Investors and entrepreneurs who focus their strategy on building autonomous infrastructure will reap the rewards. Those that don't will be left behind.

PART I
THE HISTORY OF
ECONOMIC CYCLES
AND MONETARY POLICY

History doesn't repeat itself, but it often rhymes.

— Mark Twain

It's important to remember that the global financial market has been here before in some form. I would say almost everything in nature moves in cycles. There, too, are economic cycles. Global central banks over the past two decades have been trying to stop the economic cycle from progressing. The powers that be don't want a recession. They don't want deflation. They are doing everything in their power to change the shape of an economic cycle from a circle to a diagonal line that just continues to go straight up. But no matter what they do, they are fighting the natural order of things and they will not succeed. History has shown this time and time again. When the state tries to intervene in the economic cycle, it has always ended badly.

Understanding where you are in the economic cycle, as well as other cycles, along with understanding what monetary policy regime you're under will go a long way to improving your returns as an investor. One of the most important factors in developing an investment strategy, when in a credit-backed currency regime, is to figure out whether the economy is about to go through inflation or deflation. Part I of this book helps set the context for you the investor to be able to answer these questions for yourself. I intend to show you that the current system is fraught with risk and what you didn't see before now becomes apparent for all who pay attention.

1

The Fed and You: A Brief History

I was reading in the paper today that Congress wants to replace the dollar bill with a coin. They've already done it. It's called a nickel.

— Jay Leno

It may feel like you have no relationship with any federal entity. But, if you're using money to transact business or if you're investing in the stock market for your retirement, you have a deep relationship with at least one – the Federal Reserve. It's ironic, too, because the Federal Reserve (the Fed) isn't a public body nor is it an official part of the government. The Fed is a private bank with the superpower of managing the country's money. The Fed has a dual mandate – to maintain full employment and to keep prices stable. However, it's this one power of managing the money supply through the setting of interest rates and the printing of money that allows it to have massive influence the world over.

How It Was versus How It Is

During the post–World War II period job security, pension security, and health security were relatively more stable than has been the trend since the 1990s. You could save money in an account that generated a decent return and you were able to maintain purchasing power in part because

Figure 1.1 Productivity versus Compensation
Source: Economic Policy Institute.

you had US currency that was also money. It was a store of value because it was backed by gold. If you wanted to get a higher return, you could buy government or municipal or corporate bonds and, for risk-adjusted returns, you were doing quite well. There wasn't any need to take big risks in the stock market or to start your own business if you wanted to lead a middle-class life.

Until the early 1980s, the gap in income between blue-collar and white-collar workers was relatively stable. Moreover, the average multiple between the highest paid person at a company (like the CEO) and an average worker was between 10 and 20 times difference. There was more equality within the income system, which favored being an employee in the risk/reward calculus as productivity was shared across the organization. In 2016, the US CEO-to-worker pay ratio was 276 to 1. We see productivity continuing to increase (see Figure 1.1) while pay has remained stagnant. Therein lies the opportunity. Start a business and take advantage of productivity to increase your personal income return.

The tax structure was also completely different. Back in the 1950s and 1960s the highest tax bracket for earned income was 90%! Can you imagine that? This influenced lots of decisions. One was the risk-versus-reward ratio of trying to start a business. If you could only keep 10% of your earnings after taxes, would it be worth it to take outsized risk? Probably not.

In the twenty-first century, many companies don't expect to keep their employees for 10 or 20 years. Employers let workers go through reduction in forces (RIFs), layoffs, or a variety of other means. Due to the Employee Retirement Income Security Act (ERISA), a law enacted in the 1970s, the government made a huge change to retirement and how we go about saving and investing for retirement. Like so many laws, the law enacted did the exact opposite of what its named implied. It did not secure employee retirement income. It converted risk from the employer to the employee by moving from a defined-benefit plan to a defined-contribution plan. This was an enormous change.

Now we have defined-contribution plans like a 401(k) or a 403(b) where the risk and onus of a person's retirement lie squarely with the employee. That was not the case under a defined-benefit plan. Today's savings accounts do not produce any real return. You're lucky if you can get 0.1% interest rate per year. The US dollar is not maintaining its purchasing power like it did in the olden days. This happened in 1971 when Nixon took us off the gold standard. He turned our US dollar from a commodity currency to a credit currency. The US dollar is now good for being a medium of exchange but not good as money that is a store of value. Inflation eats away at purchasing power over time. While we're conditioned to think 2% inflation is healthy, inflation is actually a stealth tax that hits every American. It is disproportionately worse for the poor because they pay the same tax of inflation as the rich at the same rate. Moreover, they are more likely to use savings accounts versus investing if they have any wealth at all to save.

So how is it that our pillars of middle-class security were shaken by these megatrends in monetary policy, demographics, technology, and the global economy?

Monetary Policy – The History of the Federal Reserve

In search of an answer to this question, I start with a week-long discussion with my friend Dax about the Federal Reserve (the Fed). It was a few years ago when we both read an article about the Federal Reserve and it sparked a discussion about whether the Fed is harmful or helpful. Our conversation focused on an article written by a former Fed advisor, Danielle DiMartino Booth, "How the Fed Went from Lender of Last

Resort to Destroyer of American Wealth."[1] Dax was skeptical of the article and wanted to discuss its positions. Dax (DH) started the conversation with this question:

DH: *One of the recurring complaints I hear from some fiscal conservatives is about the Federal Reserve and how evil it is. I'm trying to understand why and have been doing a little research. I have read a lot of people complain about the era of "cheap money" and how it is having a terrible effect on the real US economy despite all the traditional markers like the unemployment rate and the Dow looking really good. Is it justified?*

JR: Consider this. If I offered you a $100 bill or $100 in gold, which would you take? What if I made the same offer to you in 1913 when the Federal Reserve (the Fed) was established? Which option would provide you with more purchasing power today? The answer is $100 worth of gold in today's currency. The US dollar has lost over 95% of its purchasing power in 100 years. One hundred dollars' worth of gold in 1913 would now be worth over $2,000 in today's currency.

The Fed decided to situate the entire economy on top of an abstraction of the monetary system. The abstraction, decoupling the money system from real assets, allows them immense and unchecked power. Most people are not aware of it. The Fed does not answer to Congress. They are not audited by our government. The Federal Reserve is a private corporation. By targeting 2% inflation, you're targeting a 2% "tax" on the entire economic system and it's a regressive tax. With that target, we are all agreeing to reduce our purchasing power by 2% per year. Every percentage point of inflation erodes everyone's purchasing power *by design*. And, this "tax" affects the poor most.

The Fed has helped the US dominate the world economy by using many levers and tools. We can import or export inflation as needed by many Fed maneuvers. It has been great for US citizens, but the rest of the world has caught on and they are tired of it. They are tired of the US dollar reigning supreme as the world reserve currency because it allows us to force our country's debt on the whole world. If they hold US dollars as reserve assets and the purchasing power of the US dollar diminishes by 2% per year, they are losing value. This does not include the other Fed tools used to create negative real return for bondholders. We can *monetize our debt*, a phrase that was typically reserved for developing nations.

We've been able to do this because of the Bretton Woods agreement after World War II. It tied the US dollar to gold and then all other major currencies, like the yen and the British pound, to the US dollar. This probably would have been fine if Nixon hadn't pulled us off the gold standard in 1971. It is this move that changed everything. Nixon was forced to do this, however, because the US government was spending way more than it had and there was a currency war going on with France. Charles de Gaulle et al. knew the US couldn't back every one of its dollars with gold, so he kept exchanging dollars for gold until Nixon was forced to act.

An economy is ultimately based on trust and we are at the end of that ride. The beginning of the end becomes a game of musical chairs in the form of a currency war. In fact, it's already begun. We are in the beginning of a currency war with China. You will see a lot more in the coming years. There are going to be winners and losers.

You will see more gold repatriation in the coming years, as Germany and other countries have already initiated. You've seen the list start to grow. Now countries that have begun repatriating their gold include Venezuela, the Netherlands, Belgium, Switzerland, Austria, India, Mexico, Bangladesh, Romania, and Hungary. The list is only increasing as trust continues to slowly erode.

You will see continued quantitative easing by the Fed because it cannot allow interest rates to spike as it becomes difficult to find buyers for US Treasury bonds. The US Treasury is buying more and more bonds. It's like the serpent who eats its tail. One of the main reasons these developments have not accelerated is that other major developed economies are still manipulating their own currency through quantitative easing (QE) and zero/negative interest rate policies (ZIRP/NIRP).

To answer your question, "cheap money" has us focused on financial leverage (in the form of borrowing) instead of productivity. Now, cheap money adds volatility and risk into the economic system and that's why you see greater and greater booms and busts. These are getting bigger and more severe. If our money was backed by something, like gold, there would be constraints within the system. We would not be able to print currency out of thin air. That would force the government to make better choices along the way. Capital would have to be more efficient because it would be competing against all the other ways it could be deployed more productively.

When the US was in the middle of the Industrial Revolution, we had sound money because it was backed by gold. We didn't have a central bank tweaking the economy by changing the price of borrowing. We had different problems back then. The country's wealth grew on the back of productivity, not borrowing. One reason for that was because the government couldn't borrow more than the amount of gold they owned or reasonably borrowed constrained by market forces. A core reason why the Founders didn't want the US to have a central bank was that they didn't want the government to have the power of currency manipulation.

We are not doing as "well" as you think. We have the Dow higher in dollar terms, but the purchasing power of those dollars has been greatly diminished. The average family doesn't have the same purchasing power as they did 50 years ago. Or even 20 years ago. You hear about it every day in the stories about how average families are barely making it in America. There are many reasons for this, but one reason is our debasement of our currency. Social disruption and revolt will continue as more and more people get more marginalized by the financial system.

DH: *What I want to know is, what would happen with the alternative to this? What if the Fed had not pushed the federal funds rate to zero? What would have happened? And is this writer just being unnecessarily inflammatory and political?*

JR: Well, there is no real way to *know* what would have happened. However, the Fed's best option at the time was to push the interest rates to zero for a short period of time while there was systemic risk. That was what was called for during a time when we could have lost the whole system. However, interest rates should not have stayed there for years. This manipulated the price of borrowing money and distorted the financial markets. The Fed should have allowed the cycle to naturally oscillate – we needed to take our lumps. While we can debate the need to bail out the banks, I don't think we should have allowed the bank equity holders to keep their equity. This introduced moral hazard. We should not have transferred the expense and risk from past banking malinvestment onto the government's balance sheet. That's actually a form of socialism by privatizing the gains and socializing the losses. Bank equity holders took the risk and they should have been wiped out.

We didn't fix the systemic issue of overleveraging using derivatives and creating a clearinghouse for derivatives so we could have transparency. There are financial "weapons of mass destruction" out there because the derivative market is 20 times bigger than the underlying equity market. As of 2020, there are $692 *trillion* in currency and credit derivatives in the markets with most of them opaque. We cannot see (or backtest) how all these derivatives are interrelated. The transparency into this market was not addressed, so this will be a major problem we have to deal with in the future.

We also didn't fix the fiscal policy through enacted legislation. The Fed was forced to act because the legislative branch was politically weak and couldn't enact required fiscal changes. If they did act, Members of Congress ran the risk of being ousted from office during the next election cycle. The Federal government cannot continue on a path of deficit spending. More than ceasing deficit spending, we also need a payment plan. Due to promised entitlements, the people of the US owe $27+ trillion ($27T) in debt and another $120 trillion ($120T-plus) in unfunded future liabilities. Every year of the twenty-first century, we continue to spend more than we take in, even in the boom years. We have continued deficit spending. That is not sustainable.

Without fixing both our monetary and fiscal policy, the monetary system, in particular the value of the US dollar, is going to collapse, like always, slowly at first, then all at once. If deficit spending wasn't allowed, budget adherence was forced, indiscriminate government spending was curbed, and we didn't use the Federal Reserve to paper over the deficit, then we might grow slower, but we wouldn't have the severe booms and busts. Moreover, *the people would have more control over their government.* If you don't have to worry about a budget, then it's easy to spend $680 billion-plus on "defense." You can buy all the drones and surveillance you'd ever want, but we run the possibility losing our privacy and freedom someday because of this unchecked ability for the government to spend as much as they want on whatever they want. This is about control and who has it.

DH: *What WOULD have happened if we hadn't bailed out the banks? Would that have been better? Wouldn't it have led to a second Great Depression?*

JR: What would have happened is that all insolvent banks' shareholders would have been wiped out, the debt holders of the bank would have taken over, and most of the management would have been ousted. That is the appropriate outcome when capital is deployed inefficiently. The risk should be shouldered by the shareholders of the banks, not the American citizens. If a bailout is required, the equity needs to be wiped out. All of the clean assets would have been put onto the balance sheets of reorganized banks that get a new capital structure and issue new shares. Then, the federal government could support the process where it was needed. The FDIC would sort out the depositors, where needed. Granted, we would have had a major recession while all this happened, but we would have taken our lumps and we would have been able to continue on growing a real economy on solid ground instead of what we have today.

If there was systemic risk to manage, then the US government is the lender of last resort. While the severity may have been greater, the systemic nature of the issues would have been addressed. We would have been forced to fix the issues within our banking system. And it would have been shorter in duration because the systemic problems would have been addressed and uncertainty would have been removed from the system. The anemic growth we've had after 2008 is a direct result of the actions of the Fed to "fix" the financial system. If the pain is so great, then we should make the changes to the laws so it never happens again. Instead we papered over the problem and nothing systemic was fixed. *The rich got bailed out. Not only is that not a capitalistic idea, it is also a moral hazard.* It's corporatism. Now the banks are bigger than ever. What happens next time?

DH: *Most people who lament the existence of the Fed, for the reasons you state, seem to paint a dire picture. I hear the complaint loud and clear – our money is a fiction, tied to nothing of real value, our purchasing power has been destroyed, and so on.*

JR: According to the Congressional Budget Office (CBO), mandatory spending will increase from $2.2 trillion in 2014 to $3.6 trillion by 2023. The pandemic has drastically altered that equation even more negatively. In 2019, we generated about $3.5 trillion in tax revenues. The CBO now states that 2019 was the last year we will have less than $1 trillion in annual deficits, ever again. That is to say fiscal deficits will be $1 trillion or more from now on. It will only get worse each year as the Baby Boomer generation ages and receives more entitlements like Social Security and Medicare.

This issue of unsustainable public debt didn't happen all at once. Measured changes of federal policy over a century have contributed to this large-scale problem. The Federal Reserve, the income tax, fractional reserve banking, and government borrowing all came into existence under the Federal Reserve Act of 1913. The Federal Open Market Committee from 1923 on made it worse by direct market intervention and by sterilizing gold. Congress had to change the Constitution to get the Federal Reserve Act implemented. Globalization, the Bretton Woods agreement in 1945, deficit spending, and the decoupling of the US currency from the gold standard in 1971 all exacerbated the situation.

A fiat currency is money decreed by a government but not necessarily backed by a commodity like gold. There is no example in history where a fiat currency has *not* gone to zero except for the most recent instances of each countries' sovereign currency. It happened in the American colonies with the "Continental" dollar and after the Civil War with the "Greenbacks." This time will be no different. Fiat currency failed during the time of the Greeks (2,600 years ago), the Romans (1,700 years ago), Holland (500 years ago), France (300 years ago), the Weimar Republic (80 years ago) and many, many developing countries in modern times (China, Zimbabwe, Iraq, and more).

DH: *The argument in favor of going back to the gold standard seems like a backward solution. The only argument about gold seems to be that it has historically been a thing of value. Do you think we're going back to a gold standard?*

JR: Gold has maintained its value because technology has never improved the cost of production over time. However, I don't believe we're going back to a gold standard. I believe we're going into a period of a multicurrency world. We're going from a period of aggregation into a period of fracture. There will be several competitors to the US dollar for a reserve currency. None may win completely on their own, but a few can take significant market share. Bitcoin and digital currencies have created a technological revolution. I suspect they will play a role in the future of the global monetary system.

The US Dollar as the Global Reserve Currency

To understand the current state of the problem and potential opportunities, we must first understand the current state of the global monetary system. It starts with the US dollar being the world's reserve currency. The dollar didn't start out this way. It took years and decades of a particular set of circumstances to get us here. The history of the modern global financial system started during World War II.[2]

As the war progressed, specifically when Germany annexed Austria in 1938, most countries in Europe were in the process of sending their gold to the US for safety. They were worried what about would happen if Germany invaded and what Hitler might do with their gold reserves. Moreover, due to the lack of proximity to the theaters of war, the United States was relatively untouched by World War II and its manufacturing sector had grown supplying Europe with weapons and armaments with most of that paid in gold. By 1938, it's estimated that more than two thirds of the world's monetary gold reserves were located in the United States.[3]

It's this fact coupled with a series of international agreements that set the US dollar on a course of being the world's reserve currency. If the dollar were still backed by gold, as it has been for most of US history, there might be not be a setup for a global catastrophic situation. But, alas, the dollar is no longer a commodity-backed currency as we explain. Later in this chapter we discuss how the dollar became a credit-backed currency, and later in the book we discuss the many differences between commodity-backed and credit-backed currencies.

The Bretton Woods Agreement

In 1944, 44 countries came together in Bretton Woods, New Hampshire, to establish a new international monetary system. The principal goal was to create an efficient foreign exchange system. One of the agreements set forth replaced the global gold standard with the US dollar as the global currency, then link the dollar to a fixed exchange rate to gold and peg all foreign currencies to the US dollar. The initial exchange rate was $35 per ounce of gold. This aimed to prevent competitive currency devaluation and promote global growth. It also established the International Bank of Reconstruction and the International Monetary Fund (IMF).

The new effect of this agreement established the United States as the dominant power in the world economy because all foreign central banks had to hold US dollars and America was the only country with the awesome power to print money. Other countries could exchange dollars for gold and gold for dollars at the US gold window. This also meant that when any country wanted to buy oil or gold or any global commodity, they must first convert their currency to US dollars and then transact in US dollars.

The Bretton Woods agreement solved many problems of its day. With the war-torn countries in Europe in ruins, they needed a global financial system to rebuild. This also simplified and reduced currency exchange risk around the world. Members of the Bretton Woods system also agreed to avoid any trade wars. They agreed to regulate their currency to support global trade and adjust their currency values to rebuild after the war.

However, there were two big problems that came out of the Bretton Woods agreement. First, there was no reserve ratio that set how many dollars could be created for each unit of gold. This allowed the United States to print dollars and run budget deficits. Second, there was a parallel gold market operating alongside the Bretton Woods gold market. The gold market set rates based on market supply and demand, yet the Bretton Woods agreement set a fixed price. As we see later, this caused problems.[4]

Currency Wars – Tensions Rise

In the 1960s, it starts to become clear that the US government is deficit spending. Expenses started to accumulate from the Korean War in the 1950s. Under a gold-backed monetary system, governments would always need to raise money from their citizens, either through taxes or war bonds. But under this new monetary regime, the US could print money without necessarily having the gold to back it up. This deficit spending continued throughout the 1960s and grew with the Vietnam War. The Vietnam War was the first large war where the American public didn't make financial support directly through war bonds or increased taxes.[5] This was the first deficit war in modern history.

Many suspected that the United States was printing and spending more dollars than it had backed by gold. In 1965 the president of France, Charles de Gaulle, started a silent currency war with America. He was using loopholes in the Bretton Woods system to attack the US dollar. De Gaulle was openly critical of US monetary policy and of the Bretton Woods agreement. In public, he would call for a return to the gold standard. His suspicion that the United States was spending more dollars than the gold it had in its vaults was confirmed when the Treasury Secretary made a public admission that US payment deficits were moving higher than expected in 1964. From then on, Charles de Gaulle continued his currency war with the United States by demanding an exchange of dollars for gold. France was converting about $150 million at the gold window every month. Events around the world increased the demand for gold. It was the market demand for gold at market prices coupled with the fixed price of the Bretton Woods agreement that were at odds. Finally, the United States could no longer keep its agreement for a free exchange of dollars to gold at the fixed price.

The Nixon Shock – Executive Order 11615

On August 14, 1971, President Nixon ordered the end of gold convertibility in Executive Order 11615. This was supposed to be a temporary measure. The goal was to provide stabilization for prices and wages because unemployment was at 6.1%[6] and the inflation rate was at 5.84%.[7] The United States was losing all its gold via convertibility of gold to dollars at the gold window.

This was quite an about-face for Nixon. Remember, he is a Republican. Price controls and supports are not in the GOP vocabulary. "We are all Keynesians now," Richard Nixon proclaimed early in 1972, acknowledging the bipartisan support his wage and price controls then commanded as an example of what the government could and should do to reduce unemployment and curb inflation.[8] Something large must be going on behind the scenes to have such a drastic measure taken in what was seen as "out of the blue."

Sovereign Currencies Are Now All Fiat Currency

Since that "temporary" move in 1971 by Nixon, all global currencies are now fiat currencies with nothing to back their value. Once the US dollar could no longer be converted to gold, and since all other currencies were tied to the US dollar, any international gold standard ceased. That day, we converted from commodity money to credit money and, as we see in later chapters, that's a huge transformation.

For comparison, let's look at the periods based on their monetary policies and the impact those policies have had on the market price of gold and the national debt.

In 1913 (The Gold Standard Act):

- Price of gold was $20.67 per ounce
- US national debt was about $2.9 billion

In 1933 (The Gold Exchange Act):

- Price of gold was $35.00 per ounce
- US national debt was about $22.5 billion

In 1971 (End of the Gold Standard):

- Price of gold was $42.00 per ounce
- US national debt was about $398 billion

In 2013 (Period of Quantitative Easing):

- Price of gold was about $1,300 per ounce
- US national debt was about $16.7 trillion

In 2020 (Period of Fed Balance Sheet Expansion):

- Price of gold was about $2,000 per ounce
- US national debt was estimated at $28 trillion

The Currency Looks the Same, but It's Not

If someone looks at the US currency from the 1960s and from the 2000s, the specimens look almost identical. However, their meanings in financial terms are quite different. The $100 bill in Figure 1.2 is a gold certificate. It could be exchanged for gold. It is an asset, though it does have counterparty risk, in that you have to trust the institution to honor the commitment to convert it to gold. This is commodity-based or gold-backed money.

The $100 bill in Figure 1.3 is a Federal Reserve note. It cannot be exchanged for gold. It is a liability of the Federal Reserve, a debt instrument. It looks the same as the currency in Figure 1.2, but it has wildly different rights. The note in Figure 1.3 is fiat currency and only has value declaration. It is credit-based money.

All currency these days, whether it's the Japanese yen or the euro, is credit-backed fiat currency. It isn't tied to any commodity and it's constrained by any scarcity. As we see later on, this can have profound effects on the global monetary and financial system and the global economy.

Figure 1.2 Gold Certificate

Figure 1.3 Federal Reserve Note

2

Understanding Economic Cycles

Money is a great servant, but a horrible master.
— Francis Bacon

As an investor, it's important to understand the various cycles that affect your investments. In this chapter, we're going to define one of the most important cycles – *the economic cycle*. The economic cycle influences most of the mechanics that affect investments, like inflation and interest rates. Once we understand the economic cycle, we can then learn to determine where we currently are in the cycle so that we can optimize our strategy for investment.

Terms and Definitions

A short list of terms and definitions is helpful before we launch into the explanation of the economic cycle. This list defines the major nouns and verbs we use to describe the process of the economic cycle. Using this tool, our goal is to describe a complex process in simple terms.

Transaction – The atomic unit of an economy where a buyer and seller come together to transfer money and/or credit for goods, services, or financial assets within a market.

Economy – The sum total of transactions in all markets.

Buyer – A purchaser of goods, services, or financial assets.

Seller – A provider of goods, services, or financial assets.

Money – A unit of a store of value.

Credit – An asset to a lender and a spendable unit to a buyer.

Debt – A liability to the borrower.

Goods and services – Consumption in an economy.

Financial assets – Anything that stores value or generates a financial return like stocks, bonds, or business interests.

Productivity – The expansion of output from increased labor or efficiency.

Leveraging – The increase of credit in a cycle.

Deleveraging – The decrease or removal of credit during a cycle.

Sound money policy – A gold standard–backed money system where savers are rewarded and intervention is minimized.

Unsound money policy – A credit-backed money system where savers are penalized with a central bank whose primary objective is to intervene.

The Economic Cycle

There are several great frameworks that explain the economic cycle from a wide array of economists. Though Ray Dalio is a not an economist, he is a well-known, prolific investor. He's the founder and manager of Bridgewater Associates, which is the largest hedge fund in the world. His firm oversees about $160B in assets under management (AUM). The firm was founded in 1975, and it continues to this day. One of its key strategies is to understand the economic cycle and how that will impact investments. Ray breaks down the economic cycle into three distinct parts: productivity growth, the short-term debt cycle, and the long-term debt cycle. Each part has its own set of mechanics.

Dalio starts by defining what makes up the economy. It's a set of all the transactions in the marketplace. A transaction is when a buyer uses money or credit to buy goods, services, or financial assets. The economy is the sum of all of those transactions. He distinguishes money and credit. Credit spends just like money. Money is a store of value and an asset that a buyer has in reserve. Credit comes in many forms, from bank loans such as car loans to revolving credit like what credit card companies provide. Both money and credit spend, but they are distinct in that credit has a counterpart where money does not, at least not at the consumer level. That said, though it may hold true at the consumer level, at higher levels of spending, money is created through credit issuance from our central bank to commercial banks.

Credit is made up of a liability to the borrower and an asset to the creditor. Once the liability is paid off, the credit is complete. If you add up all the money spent, and all the credit spent, you can calculate the total spending. The total amount of spending is what drives the economy. If we can understand the total transactions, we can understand the economy. Credit is an important factor, the most volatile aspect of the economy, and probably the least understood, as Dalio says. If total credit is increased, then the total amount available to spend is increased; therefore, the economy is increasing. It's this credit that creates cycles. If we didn't have credit, then we would have a more linear growth based solely on productivity. So, it's credit that we need to think about and understand the most.

The Government

The government consists of two important parts – the central government and the central bank. In the United States, the central bank is called the Federal Reserve (the Fed, for short). Collectively, the government is the biggest buyer and seller. The central government is the body that collects taxes and spends money. The central bank, which is different from other buyers and sellers because it controls the money supply, prints money and sets short-term interest rates. The money supply is the amount of money and credit in the system. Together, they affect the economy in various ways. The central bank affects the economy through monetary policy, and the central government affects the economy through fiscal policy.

Monetary policy is governed and controlled by the central bank. The two primary components of monetary policy are the setting of interest rates and the printing of money. (The more accurate definition would be the expansion of the Fed's balance sheet because they have more tools than just printing money, but for the purposes of this explanation, we'll keep it simpler.) The Fed is an important player in the flow of credit from the central bank to commercial banks. If the Fed wants to incentivize more economic activity, it will lower interest rates (see Figure 2.1) or print money or both. If the Fed wants to curb economic activity, it will raise interest rates or reduce the money supply, though reducing the money supply is rare.

Fiscal policy is set and managed by the central government through its legislative body, and here in the United States, Congress enacts laws to either increase or decrease spending. For the most part, Congress enacts laws to spend more money. It's rare that the government acts to reduce spending, though that can happen during specific times inside the long-term debt cycle. I'll talk more about that later.

Productivity Growth

If we had an economy with no credit, then productivity would be the only way to increase, or grow, the economy. Thinking about this at the individual or consumer level, if a person couldn't borrow, then the only way to increase personal spending would be to work more and be more efficient/productive. If productivity increased, then the economy would increase linearly, and vice versa. In times when productivity decreased, then the economy would shrink linearly.

Innovation, knowledge, learning, and technology play important roles in our ability to grow productivity. Productivity growth raises incomes for individuals and therefore improves living standards and spending. It's productivity growth that matters the most in the long run, but it's credit that matters the most in the short run. This is due to the fact that productivity growth doesn't change much so it doesn't drive economic swings. Credit is volatile and allows us to consume more than we produce, so it's really debt that swings in cycles and affects the short-term.

Short-term Debt Cycle

Credit contributes to total spending, which therefore expands the economy. In the first phase of the short-term debt cycle, that's exactly what we see, expansion. With credit and productivity, spending continues to increase, and prices start to rise. When the amount of spending and incomes grow faster than the production of goods, prices rise. We call this *inflation*.

The central bank is charged with the responsibility of keeping inflation in check. At a certain point, it will raise interest rates in an effort to curb inflation. Higher interest rates cause fewer people to be able to afford new lines of credit, so lending decreases. Moreover, the cost of existing debts rises. The higher cost of debt service means it takes more money directed toward debt repayment, which in turn decreases spending. When people spend less, it causes prices to fall. We call this *deflation*. When economic activity decreases, we call it a *recession*.

When the central bank sees economic activity decreasing and prices falling, it will step in to lower interest rates. When it lowers interest rates, more people are able to borrow, and the cost of debt service falls. Borrowing and spending pick up. This helps create an economic expansion again. This is the short-term debt cycle at a high level.

We can see that it is the process of borrowing that creates cycles. Spending is constrained only by the lenders' and borrowers' willingness to provide and receive credit. If the cycle goes up, then eventually it will need to come down. When credit is easily available, there's economic expansion and vice versa. When credit isn't easily available, there's a recession. We can see that it's the central bank that is primarily driving the short-term debt cycle.

Long-term Debt Cycle

Over long periods of time, debts rise faster than incomes. This creates a long-term debt cycle. Even though borrowers have more debt, lenders are willing to extend more credit because usually there is an economic expansion going on, and everything looks like it's going great. Incomes are rising and asset prices are going up. Typically, the stock market is doing very well. Again, things look great. In the beginning of the long-term debt cycle, it pays to buy goods, services, and financial assets with borrowed money because interest rates are low.

At some point, when everyone is buying and exhibiting the same unrestrained behavior, a bubble ensues. This drives debt to increase. For a while, incomes are increasing in alignment with debt, so there is no problem. Over decades, the debts continue to rise. At some point, the cycle hits its long-term debt peak, which is the maximum amount of debt issued during the long-term debt cycle. Eventually, debt repayments start to grow faster than incomes. People are forced to cut back

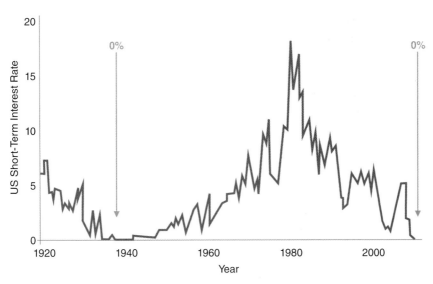

Figure 2.1 US Short-term Interest Rates
Source: "How the Economic Machine Works," video by Ray Dalio.

on spending. Since one person's spending is another person's income, incomes eventually start to go down. As incomes decrease, borrowers' creditworthiness decreases. The cycle starts to reverse itself. Debt burdens have become too big. Historically, in the United States this has happened twice, in 1929 and in 2008. When it gets really bad, we call this a *depression*. To address a depression, the process of deleveraging commences, which is the only way to deal with the long-term debt cycle.

In a deleveraging process, incomes drop, spending drops, credit disappears, asset prices drop, banks get squeezed, and the stock market drops. The entire process is a vicious cycle. As incomes fall and debt repayments rise, borrowers get squeezed. They are no longer creditworthy. They can no longer use credit to service debt. Borrowers are forced to sell assets to make debt payments. When everyone does this at the same time, it creates market crashes. Stock markets, real estate markets, and banks all get into trouble. Typically, in a deleveraging, interest rates set by the central bank are already at 0% (see Figure 2.1). Deleveraging is similar to a recession except for the fact that lowering interest rates will not solve the problem since they are already at 0%.

Deleveraging – Understanding a Debt Crisis

The process of deleveraging can be done well, or it can be done poorly. During the Great Depression, this was done poorly. The US government implemented austerity policies, then raised, not lowered, rates and decreased, not increased, the money supply. These were all the wrong moves done at all the wrong moments. It can be argued that the deleveraging from 2008 is being done well up to now, but there is still a long way to go in this deleveraging process.

There are four ways you can deleverage:

1. Cut spending – Austerity
2. Reduce debt – Debt restructuring
3. Redistribute wealth – Tax the wealthy; tensions rise between haves/ have-nots and debtor/creditor nations
4. Print money – QE, non-QE QE, balance sheet expansion

The central bank has injected inflation at times and managed/lowered interest rates at other times to match the deflationary pressures of the deleveraging process. However, it's important to note that we aren't finished with this deleveraging process, and there is still a lot more to go. This deleveraging process has been lengthened due to newly invented ways for central banks to respond to crises. Most notably, the quantitative easing (QE) and negative interest rate policies (NIRP) that began in the last decade are examples.

Where Are We in the Long-term Debt Cycle?

Now that we understand the structure of the long-term debt cycle, it begs the question: Where are we now in that cycle? To answer this question, we need to plot a few points on the proverbial map to see if we can find our location. The first thing I would look at is the first year that we hit 0% interest rate here in United States. For us, the most recent round was in 2008 when the Federal Reserve dropped interest rates to 0%. At that point, we started a deleveraging process, and we continue in that process similar to the events of the 1930s deleveraging process that began after the 1929 crash. The second point to help us locate ourselves in the cycle is to determine when the Federal Reserve started to print money. The Fed has doubled their balance sheet by 2020 since the Great Recession of 2008 so the printing press is been on. This we know. We go into greater detail in Chapter 6 about what the Federal Reserve is doing with its policies.

Where we are currently in the cycle is that the Fed is aiming for 0% in short-term interest rates. The central bank is at the floor in terms of the interest rate lever, and no longer has that tool in their toolbelt. With standard options no longer available, the Fed will turn to more exotic monetary policy. I suspect we will see credit continuing to rise, then cut. That will start to create the vicious cycle we discussed earlier. The stock market will crash, and economic activity will decrease, which will force the Fed to drop interest rates to 0% and implement far more exotic monetary policies like the purchase of US bonds and other non-sovereign debt and, potentially, US equities, like Japan. That is the point when we'll know that we're starting another deleveraging process and potentially encountering another depression like the 1930s.

What's Outside the Economic Cycle Definition

Ray Dalio's explanation of the economic cycle is very helpful to understand the basics of what happens in an economic cycle. However, it is simplistic, and it's important to point out a few things for context. For one thing, this cycle explains how markets work during periods of unsound monetary policy when central banks are managing the money supply. It's important to note that while this has been the case for the past 100 years or so, most of human history has not had a central banking authority managing a money supply. There have been other periods of unsound money policy throughout history, but it's not the norm. Most of human history has occurred during a period of sound money policy when the money supply was built on commodity-based currency, like gold, versus the credit-backed fiat currency of the modern day.

As stated earlier in this explanation of market cycles, it's the issuance of credit that creates the boom-and-bust cycles of the economy. Without credit, these cycles would not exist. That is not to say I'm promoting a scenario where economies should exist without credit. Not at all. Credit plays an important role. You cannot have capitalism without credit. It exists within the market's borrowers and lenders for the business cycle. Excess credit, however, is a major problem, along with the use of credit within the monetary system. What needs to be examined is this: Should credit play a role within the base system of money? That fundamental query is a topic we pursue in greater detail throughout the book.

Ray Dalio's economic model described here also doesn't describe or take into account the case where the central bank has printed so much money that markets cease to function due to a sovereign debt crisis. This has happened several times in history. In fact, it's happened every time a government has converted from a commodity-backed currency to a credit-backed currency. At some point, as we've seen time and time again in history from the French Revolution to the Weimar Republic to the New Republic in America, governments print money to such a degree that they fundamentally destroy the currency and the only final option is to default on the currency itself and start over.

When governments are forced to start over, they inevitably must start with a sound money paradigm where the money supply is constrained by being commodity-backed. This is the only way to start building trust again. They must start fresh with that new long, long cycle of sound commodity money and restrained government. The long, long cycle may begin again when a government starts regulating gold in some form to ultimately create a credit-backed currency again, allowing for an unrestrained government spending and a new cycle encapsulating the earlier-described economic cycle within.

The crisis is potentially much worse if the sovereign debt crisis is happening with the world's reserve currency. That has never happened before. We've had reserve currencies that have had to devalue at the same time, but we've never had a fiat world reserve currency. A sovereign debt crisis with a fiat world reserve currency is an investor's ultimate global macro risk.

Current Cycle Comparison to Past Cycles

This current business cycle is different from past cycles. The difference started with how the Fed, then other global central banks, chose to deal with the crisis of 2008. The process of quantitative easing expanded the Fed's balance sheet enormously, more than any other time in history. Right after the 2008 crisis, the Fed printed $2 trillion in new money and allocated it to commercial banks throughout the country. It forced banks to take the money to help mask which banks might be in financial trouble and which were not. However, it wasn't that first injection of capital, through a program called TARP (Troubled Asset Relief Program), that was the sole culprit; it was the continued QE and continued manipulation of the yield curve. All over the world, central banks issued negative yield sovereign debt. Today they are still finding new and creative ways to expand their sovereign balance sheets. Collectively, the global central banks are putting off the inevitable, but in so doing, they are making the problem much, much worse.

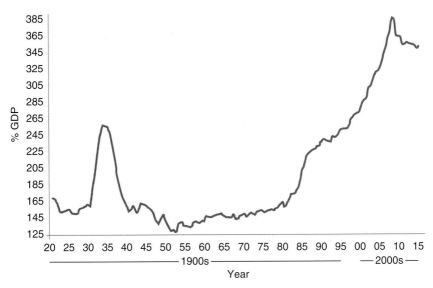

Figure 2.2 Total US Credit Market Debt to GDP
Source: Board of Governors of the Federal Reserve System.

In 2016, the total debt outstanding, both public and private, was roughly 350% of gross domestic product (GDP). As you can see from Figure 2.2, we experienced this cycle's debt peak in 2008 at roughly 385% total debt to GDP, and we've been deleveraging for the past decade. Still, we're not even down to the levels of the Great Depression, which peaked at 255% total debt to GDP. That's how large the problem is that lies ahead of us. Each time the global central banks intervene to attempt to help the current short-term predicament, they push off the inevitable and make the long-term problem of debt much worse.

Central banks are trying to fight fire with fire. It doesn't pass the commonsense test that the solution to high debt is more debt, right? Debt is addictive. Saifedean Ammous said it best in Chapter 7 of his book, *The Bitcoin Standard*, when he compares the similar behavior of a government managing the money supply to that of a drug addict:

> It functions like a highly addictive drug, such as crystal meth or sugar: it causes a beautiful high at the beginning, fooling its victims into feeling invincible, but as soon as the effect subsides, the come-down is devastating and has the victim begging for more. This is when the hard choice needs to be made: either suffer the withdrawal effects of ceasing the addiction, or take another hit, delay the reckoning by a day, and sustain severe long-term damage.[1]

In looking at history, we will be lucky to have only a "lost decade" here in the United States. We haven't begun the healing process yet. We continue to take on more and more debt personally, privately, and publicly. At some point, we will be facing truly disastrous consequences. That final leg of deleveraging is going to be felt worldwide. For the fact is, the US dollar is the global reserve currency, and when there is a problem in the US monetary system, it will be felt the world over.

3

The Long-wave Economic Cycle

Audaces fortuna iuvat.

—Virgil

You've heard the phrase "Fortune favors the bold"? It also favors the prepared. Cycles are valuable informational frameworks because they help provide a reference point for what's happening and what's about to happen. Cycles provide the first layer of constraining an investment universe. Combined with other layers, they can give a prepared investor vital information that most may not be factoring into their investment decision making. This provides an investor an edge.

An investor needs to know where the markets are headed based on a variety of factors that impact them. Between the short-term debt cycle, which is about 5–10 years, and the long-term debt cycle, which is about 75–100 years, there is the long-wave economic cycle. This was invented by Russian economist Nicolai Kondratiev in the 1920s and further improved upon by Joseph Schumpeter in the 1930s and later by Carlota Perez at the turn of the millennium.

Kondratiev found the long-wave structure and explained it had four phases to it. Then Schumpeter improved upon it by saying that the long-wave cycle is driven by entrepreneurship and innovation. He also showed how this long-wave cycle fit in with several other cycles.

Finally, Perez expanded upon it further by showing that the long-wave cycle was driven specifically by technological revolution and illustrated five cycles in the past 200 years. She describes more detailed structures for what happens within the cycle. We go into more of Perez's book in Part II.

The Kondratieff Cycle

In this chapter we break down this long-wave cycle, 50 to 60 years, and its original for phases/seasons: Spring, Summer, Autumn, Winter. The Kondratiev cycle, or K-wave, is made up of those four parts (Figure 3.1). Each phase has difference characteristics for preconditions for entering the new season, market structure, investor sentiment, inflation/deflation trend, the issuance of credit, and interest rates, as well as which asset classes will perform the best for that season. Each season also has an indication for the season change.

Spring – The Start of Inflation

A new cycle begins with Spring. There are still reminiscent concerns from the past cycle's Winter season. The cycle begins with an indication that a stock market bottom has occurred. There is still fear of a return to the past depression and confidence is fragile, but optimism starts with small green shoots. There is a gradual increase in business activity and employment. As the Spring continues, inflation starts mildly increasing. Banks begin to supply credit to businesses and individuals. Interest rates on that credit start at low levels. The Federal Reserve or other central banks begin with low interest rates to commercial banks. Consumers start to feel more confidence that there's growth in the economy. The market cycle feels new, like something has finally changed. Investors start to see the stock market rise and other investments start to produce consistent returns. The best asset classes for Spring are stocks and real estate. This continues for years, typically between 10 and 15 years. Spring ends when there is a bull market peak in the equity markets.

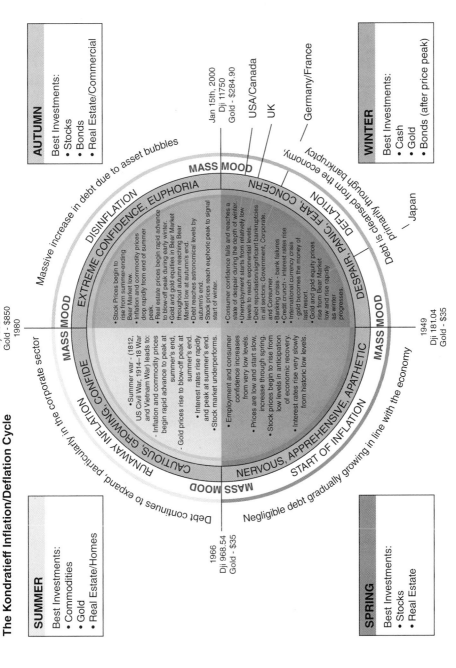

Figure 3.1 The Kondratieff Cycle
Source: Longwave Group.

The Kondratieff Inflation/Deflation Cycle

The following text appears around the cycle diagram:

SUMMER
Best Investments:
- Commodities
- Gold
- Real Estate/Homes

AUTUMN
Best Investments:
- Stocks
- Bonds
- Real Estate/Commercial

WINTER
Best Investments:
- Cash
- Gold
- Bonds (after price peak)

SPRING
Best Investments:
- Stocks
- Real Estate

Massive increase in debt due to asset bubbles

Debt continues to expand, particularly in the corporate sector

Debt is cleansed from the economy, primarily through bankruptcy

Negligible debt gradually growing in line with the economy

Dji 838.74
Gold - $850
1980

Jan 15th, 2000
Dji 11750
Gold - $284.90

USA/Canada
UK
Germany/France
Japan

1949
Dji 181.04
Gold - $35

1966
Dji 968.54
Gold - $35

MASS MOOD

DISINFLATION
EXTREME CONFIDENCE, EUPHORIA

DEFLATION
PANIC, FEAR, CONCERN
DESPAIR

RUNAWAY INFLATION
CAUTIOUS, GROWING, CONFIDE

NERVOUS, APPREHENSIVE, APATHETIC
START OF INFLATION

• Stock Prices begin to rise from summer-ending Bear Market low.
• Inflation and commodity prices drop rapidly from end of summer peak.
• Real estate prices begin rapid advance to blow-off peak during early winter.
• Gold and gold equities in Bear Market throughout autumn reaching Bear Market low at autumn's end.
• Debt reaches astronomical levels by autumn's end.
• Stock prices reach euphoric peak to signal start of winter.

• Summer war - (1812, US Civil War, 1914–18 War and Vietnam War) leads to:
• Inflation and commodity prices begin rapid advance to peak at summer's end.
• Gold prices rise to blow-off peak at summer's end.
• Interest rates rise rapidly and peak at summer's end.
• Stock market underperforms.

• Consumer confidence falls and reaches a state of despair during the depth of winter.
• Unemployment starts from relatively low levels to reach exponential levels.
• Debt repudiation/significant bankruptcies in all sectors, Government, Corporate, and Consumer.
• Banking crisis - bank failures
• Credit crunch - interest rates rise
• International currency crisis - gold becomes the money of last resort.
• Gold and gold equity prices rise from Bear Market low and rise rapidly as winter progresses.

• Employment and consumer confidence increases from very low levels.
• Prices are low and start slow, increase through spring.
• Stock prices begin to rise from low levels in anticipation of economic recovery.
• Interest rates rise very slowly from historic low levels.

Summer – Runaway Inflation

Summer begins from an indication that the stock market has peaked. What is counterintuitive about Summer is that market participants, investors, and the general public have a growing confidence in the market and the economy. Inflation is rising at a faster rate of change. In fact, at the end of Summer inflation rates will peak. There is a growing increase of credit, but mainly to businesses, not necessarily individuals. As inflation increases, the Federal Reserve responds and interest rates increase all-around. Credit is much more expensive in Summer than Spring and at some point will threaten to slow the economy. With inflation increasing, gold and commodity prices start to rise. The stock markets begin to feel the pressure and begin to falter. Summer ends with a bear market low in the stock market. The best asset classes for investment during Summer are commodities, precious metals, and real estate.

Autumn – Disinflation

Autumn begins with the stock market bottoming, interest rates peaking, inflation price peaking, and typically a recession. In Autumn, confidence is high. I repeat, confidence is high. There is an increasing, almost extreme confidence coupled with a euphoria in the markets. Inflation is typically falling throughout the Autumn season. There is a massive increase in credit with banks extending large amounts of credit, typically to individuals and consumers, not businesses. Interest rates fall with inflation falling throughout the season. With falling interest rates, bond prices start to outperform. The best asset classes to own in Autumn are stocks, bonds, and real estate and staying away from commodities and precious metals. Autumn can typically last longer than other seasons with its duration being 15–20 years. The end of Autumn is typically marked by a bull market peak in the stock markets.

Winter – Deflation

The beginning of Winter is marked by the bull market peak. The stock market begins to crash, leading to concern, fear, and panic. Confidence is falling fast. The rate of change of inflation rates increases to downright deflation. With massive amounts of debts already extended to business and individuals, banks feel a credit crunch and there is virtually no credit available for anyone. Interest rates fall, then rise throughout Winter as the credit crunch ensues. Then interest rates fall to 0% toward the end of Winter. A major bear market breaks out in the stock market with all asset prices falling as everyone looks to sell assets. The best asset classes to own during this season are cash, gold, and then bonds, but only after the credit crunch is complete. This season can take a long time as banks and corporations deleverage and work through the credit crunch. Asset prices fall lower than could ever be expected. Winter marks the end of the cycle.

Technological Revolutions – Building on the Long-wave Cycle

Dr. Carlota Perez, who wrote *Technological Revolutions and Financial Capital*,[1] improved this idea of the long-wave economic cycles and defined her own framework. Her theory is grounded in why these long-wave cycles occur. She explains that these waves arise when clusters of basic innovations are bunched together, which allow improvements to arise by applying each of these innovations to one another. This cluster of innovation ultimately gives rise to a technological revolution that leads the business cycle into a major transformation. Furthermore, she outlines a case that these cycles have patterns with specific markers, attributes, and events. In her book, she walks through five technological revolutions of the past 200 years with the last being the Age of Information and Telecommunications.

Perez describes each of these cycles as a surge. Each surge has two periods that are very different in nature: the Installation Period and the Deployment Period. Generally speaking, each surge lasts 40–60 years and each period within the surge lasts 20–30 years.

Each period has two phases within it. The Installation period has the Irruption phase and the Frenzy phase. The Deployment period has the Synergy phase and the Maturity phase. The Installation and Deployment periods are separated by a key milestone, something Perez calls the Turning Point. Among other things, this is where "the crash" happens.

The Past Longwave Cycle – The Age of the Internet

In Perez's book,[2] she walks through five technological revolutions of the past 200 years with the last being the Age of Information and Telecommunications. This was the Age of the Internet.

If we went through the full long-wave cycle for the Age of the Internet, Perez started the cycle in 1971 with the advent of the microprocessor chip. It experienced its first phase (Spring) or irruption phase from the 1970s into the 1980s. Here's where inflation began and where technological revolution started to gain momentum with the cluster of innovation.

The next phase of the cycle was the Summer phase for the Frenzy phase, which began in 1990s. During the 1990s there was great fever and a great movement in investment toward the Internet. We saw production capital and financial capital being deployed in massive rates toward many technologies related to the Internet and telecommunications. This is where we saw a decoupling of financial capital and production capital. We started to see a bubble or a mania in public stocks that were Internet stocks or dot-com stocks throughout the 1990s. Price and value were decoupling. This continued until 2000 when the dot-com bubble popped. This event marked the beginning of what she calls the Turning Point for this market cycle – when there is a breakdown of the market.

Most people would say 2000 was the beginning of the Turning Point, and that it continued until roughly 2008 when we had the financial collapse and Great Recession. The Turning Point phase can have many booms and busts and last for a period of time. We saw new laws enacted to address the new innovations of the Internet – laws that forced taxes to be paid by e-commerce companies, laws signed like the Consumer Financial Protection Bureau being created, the FCC's Net Neutrality (though it was under attack during the Trump administration), and many other legislative items to affect this innovative market. The final milestone that completed the Turning Point is the Institutional Recomposition where laws and governance are enacted to address past problems. Corporations and businesses reform, reorganize, and recapitalize. I would say most would estimate that the Turning Point was completed in 2010 or so, this technological revolution. Though, I would point out that Dr. Perez thinks we are still in the Turning Point of the Age of Information as of 2020.

The next phase of a surge is the Synergy phase where there's a recoupling of production capital and financial capital. Production capital is at the helm, leading with productive uses of financial capital. Growth is coherent. In the Age of the Internet surge, we've seen rapid growth with companies like software-as-a-service (SaaS) companies, disruptors like Airbnb, Uber, and Lyft, as well as the core Internet companies like Facebook, Google, Amazon, and Netflix (also called the FANG stocks, see Figure 3.2).

Many believe we entered the Golden Age for the Age of Information in 2009. For the next decade, we were in productive times for this long-wave economic cycle where production capital has recoupled with financial capital. Large gains were made within the cycle and the technological revolution made broad and rapid enhancements to the global community. Internet technology is ubiquitous. Global communications are both fast and cheap. An entire sector of the economy and telecommunications has been disintermediated as we no longer pay huge long-distance telephone call expenses.

The Age of Information has entered its fourth phase, the Maturing phase of the Deployment period, the end of which will complete the full long-wave cycle. During this phase, most of the user adoption has happened as we are in the later stage of the technology adoption cycle. Capital deployment in that later stage and maturity has taken over the final decades of this technological revolution.

The Golden Age was confirmed in part by the performance of the FANG stocks (Facebook, Amazon, Netflix, and Google) from 2012 to 2020, which outperformed the rest of the S&P 500 by more than two times. Combined, these four stocks represent a total market capitalization of more than $4 trillion. Apple, which wasn't even in the original four FANG stocks, had a market capitalization of $2 trillion in mid-2020 and was the world's most valuable company.

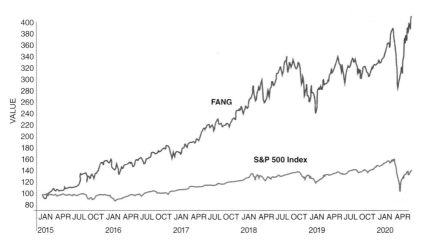

Figure 3.2 FANG Stocks versus the S&P 500
Source: S&P Dow Jones Indices.

Moving in Cycles

Markets and economies move in cycles. They oscillate like waves. This is due in part to the fact that they are driven by human behavior. As investors and market participants, we react, which affects the market, which reacts, and it all continues in a volatile but predictable way. Nothing about the financial markets fits into a simple equation. What's important to understand as an investor is where you're at in a particular cycle. The understanding of cycles is a tool. As an investor, knowing your location and position within a cycle can be your compass to guide you in developing your investment plan.

4

Safe Is the New Risky

There is no safety. Only varying states of risk and failure.
— Lois McMaster Bujold

If you are of Generation X, then you learned about money from a Baby Boomer, and your grandparents were most likely from the Greatest Generation. This, as likely as not, puts you in perilous circumstances because of what you were taught about money. It's not that the knowledge they were passing down was bad or wrong, it's the change in the world that's happened over the past three or four decades that creates the risk. The fact is that your parents learned about money when money was under a sound money policy. This means they learned about money prior to 1971 when the currency was backed by gold. If you learned about money during a sound money period but then had to operate with money during an unsound money period, *you are at risk.*

As we discuss in subsequent chapters of this book, there are big differences in money during a sound money period, which is commodity-backed money versus money during an unsound money period, which is credit-backed money. It's almost like Bizarro world, from the Superman series, where money goes from an asset to a liability. Suffice it to say that knowledge gained from one period could do you harm in another period.

The Problem – Historical Truth, Contemporary Fallacy

These six statements used to be true:

1. A job is safer than starting a business.
2. Pensions and retirement plans will be there in retirement.
3. Investing in government bonds is a risk-free investment.
4. Saving in a savings account is safe.
5. Most investments are assets.
6. The news is news.

Today it's different. Having a job doesn't imply your income is safe. The average worker changes their employer every three years. Full-time employment is a mess. Salaries have not kept up with inflation. Over the past decade, the average salary of a new college graduate has fallen. An average salary can no longer provide an average lifestyle.

If you invest mainly in bond funds, you are set up exactly the wrong way for the big tidal wave that's coming. Since bond prices and their interest rates are inversely related, all bond prices will decline as rates rise. The end of the 35-year bull market in bonds is here. After the Great Recession of 2009, the Federal Reserve took short-term interest rates to zero. That means interest rates have nowhere to go but up in the long-term. That change is going to have huge implications across the investment landscape.

Inflation eats away at the purchasing power of savings accounts' dollars. Does a dollar from 1995 buy the same amount of goods today? Not even close! Our parents had pensions; we have to save for retirement ourselves. The main retirement investment vehicle is a 401(k), but it's fraught with tremendous fees and hidden expenses. We need to tackle the problem differently from eras past.

Counterparty risk is everywhere in our current financial markets. Because traditional commercial transactions require a trusted third party to settle financial trades and transactions, it's fraught with counterparty risk. On average and for most of the long periods of functional markets, this risk is minimal, if not nonexistent. However, when markets and cycles break down, that is the time when counterparty risk really matters. Look no farther than 2008 and the fall of Lehman Brothers. There are many aspects of finance that were historically true, but now are false.

US Treasuries Are a "Risk-free" Asset

I still watch CNBC and Bloomberg and listen to portfolio managers who come on the shows referencing the "risk-free rate." The last time I can think of this term being mentioned, I was watching Bloomberg and a portfolio manager opined that the high-yield junk bond sector would outperform the risk-free bond sector. How on earth can we still reference US Treasuries as "risk-free"?

On August 5, 2011, several credit ratings agencies around the world, including Standard & Poor's, downgraded the US federal government's rating from AAA to AA+. This was the first time in history there was a downgrade to US sovereign debt by a nationally recognized statistical rating organization (NRSRO), which is a credit rating agency (CRA) approved by the US Securities and Exchange Commission (SEC). The two other main agencies in the United States, Fitch and Moody's, both left the US rating at AAA, but did announce a negative outlook on the US credit rating later in 2011. And although not a part of the Big Three ratings agencies, Egan-Jones downgraded the US credit rating to AA− in 2012.[1] If ratings agencies downgrade the sovereign debt, how can it be risk-free?

None of those ratings agencies have upgraded the rating of US sovereign debt. Back in 2011, the total federal debt was at $13.7 trillion, and the debt-to-GDP ratio was 67.7%.[2] In mid-2020, the total federal debt is $25.1 trillion, and the debt-to-GDP ratio is 106.7%.[3] The financial picture has deteriorated, not improved, in the past nine years. What happens when there is another credit rating downgrade?

The US Treasury is not a risk-free asset. I will concede the Alan Greenspan quote, "The United States can pay any debt it has because we can always print money to do that. So, there is zero probability of default." But this begs the question as to what is more important to the Treasury investor (lender), to be paid back in the correct units of currency from when you lent the money or to be paid back the same amount of purchasing power as when you lent the money plus interest?

US Treasuries have gone from risk-free interest to interest-free risk. The US government is playing a game of semantics and with the Federal Reserve's money printing of 2020, it's clear to anyone watching that US Treasuries are not risk-free and that at some point in time, lenders to the US government are going to be paid back in dollars that have far less in purchasing power than when they lent the money. Look no further than any 10-year period to see how much erosion occurs in purchasing power. The question becomes whether the interest rate covers the erosion of purchasing power from inflation.

Owning a Stock Was Always Owning an Asset

If you have parents from the Boomer generation and grandparents from the Greatest Generation, many things in finance were different when they learned about them. When they bought stocks, they probably received stock certificates and those stocks were assets as fractional ownership of public companies. Those stock certificates were bearer instruments and as such they had no counterparty risk. I think most people today believe that having a brokerage account with stocks is the same thing as holding stock certificates. It is not.

If you're holding stocks inside a brokerage account, those assets are the assets of the brokerage and are an IOU to you. If anything goes wrong with the brokerage firm, for example, if it was trading on leverage and lost all of its capital, that would include assets in your account that you thought you "owned." Holding stocks in a brokerage account carries counterparty risk. Granted, you may have a strong claim on the leftovers in bankruptcy court, but you are not legally bound to get 100% of your assets back. There are government programs and departments, like FDIC and SIPC, that provide some insurance, but if you're over those amounts, those are your losses.

I bet all the investors and account holders at MF Global thought they directly owned the assets in their account, too. MF Global traced its roots back to a sugar trading company in England in 1783. While they were a derivatives and commodities brokerage firm, the risk was the same as a stock brokerage firm. In 2010, the firm reported total assets at $42.4 billion. On October 31, 2011, MF Global declared bankruptcy. Through the restructuring process, the account holders got most of their money back, but it was a harrowing ordeal, and I'm sure they never thought their own accounts were at risk. Holding assets in a brokerage account creates counterparty risk and, by extension, default loss risk.

There Is No Counterparty Risk to Owning Gold

When your parents or grandparents owned gold, they owned physical gold. They stored it in a safe at home or in a safe deposit box at a bank.

That gold was physical gold and it had no counterparty risk. However, these days most investors are getting exposure to gold through paper assets, either through an ETF like $GLD or, worse, through a closed-end fund like $PHYS. These paper assets representing a claim to gold do have the gold to back them. However, an investor is still taking on counterparty risk. How our grandmothers owned gold and how most people are owning gold today are not the same. The new way is more convenient but carries more risk. The more you know. . .

Savings Accounts Are Safe

It used to be that a saver could put their money in an FDIC-insured savings account and generate interest returns far in excess of what the inflation rate might be. Savings accounts always had a net positive real rate of return. That is sadly no longer the case. Most savings accounts generate no interest rate yield, or, if they do, it's a fraction of a percent. With no real interest, savings accounts are exposed to inflation risk. Even if the inflation rate is 1–2%, a saver is losing money every year by holding their wealth in a savings account.

That loss is also worse than it may seem if you're only looking at the CPI to gauge inflation. There's a lot more inflation in the world than just consumer inflation. One type of inflation we've experienced since the Great Recession of 2008 is asset price inflation, which has occurred because of the Fed's quantitative easing (QE) program(s). As the reserve ratio for US Treasuries decreases, and as public companies are able to borrow at very low rates and increase their stock buyback programs, the whole investment community has experienced cheap money being invested in a variety of asset classes. In 2019, gold, stocks, real estate, and bonds were all up for the year, and that's only possible from all the money printing. One area where this really affects the consumer is in rents or mortgage payments. As asset price inflation continues, the price of homes increases so more investors park their money in inflation-protected real estate. Higher home prices mean higher mortgage payments and rents. For those who have not locked in a long-term mortgage, they've really experienced an increase in how much they have to pay for their shelter. This type of inflation affects money saved in a savings account because it's contributing to the decrease in purchasing power of that money.

The News Is News

Back in the day, news channels actually delivered news. Whether it was Walter Cronkite or Katie Couric, there was a news anchor delivering the who, what, when, where, why, and how of the news of the day. That is no longer the case. We should no longer call these "news" channels because they're nothing but propaganda. If you learned about news channels back when they really were reporting news, then you may be struggling with your relationship to the news, confusing that with propaganda. We should call the old news channels something different. We already have comedy channels, so I vote we call them tragedy channels.

Okay, Boomer

In 2020, there was a huge meme that started on the Internet – "Okay, Boomer." It was especially bantered on Crypto Twitter. At first, it seemed like every other meme, but then I started to think about it more and what people were trying to express when saying "Okay, Boomer." The two-word meme expresses the way generations think differently about subjects such as the state of the world.

First, here's what the meme means. Generation Z and Millennials believe their parents, specifically, Baby Boomers, have not been responsible in spending, saving, or how they've funded all the entitlement programs like Social Security, Medicare, Medicaid, and the pension system. They think boomers are irresponsible, clueless, and, worse, they are hypocritical.

I'd say Generation X is on the sidelines of this one with popcorn in hand. The younger generations believe the older has been irresponsible with how they have voted and governed. Boomers voted for entitlements they are now getting, but the Millennials and Gen Z are going to have to pay for them and, most likely, will not benefit from them. They are using the entitlement programs for themselves, but there won't be enough for the next generation. Millennials and Gen Z see the deficit spending that's gone on for decades and they know they'll have to pay for it. Moreover, Boomers haven't saved enough for retirement, and now Millennials and Gen Z are going to have to pay for it.

The meme also captures the idea that Boomers say they want to leave the world a better place for their children but none of their actions are in alignment with that commitment. This gets to the hypocrisy. For the first time in modern history, Boomers left the world for their children worse off than when they were children. Boomers voted against several pieces of legislation for climate change, and in doing so Boomers are leaving the physical world in a much worse off position for Millennials and Gen Z. Boomers voted for, both Democrats and Republicans, the deregulation of the financial industry that led to the greatest recession since the Great Depression. And, they voted for the War on Terror that cost more than $6 trillion and killed more than half a million people.[4]

The meme also gets down to fundamentals like respect and wisdom. The Millennials and Gen Z believe that respect still needs to be earned and none of the Boomers' "wise" actions have been wise, and they therefore haven't earned respect from their decisions or their actions. They think Boomers are clueless. For example, Millennials think Boomers don't know what a "Karen" is, they've never tweeted, and they probably haven't interacted with the police in three decades. Without some of this basic knowledge, how can they understand the social tensions of the day? Millennials and Gen Z have access to so much information now through the Internet that they don't need Boomers' "wisdom." The young, like the Millennials and Gen Z, no longer equate age with wisdom. They think Boomers are selfish, self-centered hypocrites who never think about the community or the group.

The meme shares the different ideas about money and how to transact business. They believe it's wrong and not sustainable or viable that Boomers are willing to do business in harmful ways that end up being at the expense of another group of people. For example, if producing a particular type of furniture product destroys the rain forest, Boomer executives look at that as an "externality," while Gen Z and Millennials disagree with that business practice and express their opinion that it's time for business practices to be sustainable and holistic.

I think the final notion conveyed in the "Okay, Boomer" is, in its brevity, saying, "Boomers don't get it and are so clueless that, as a Millennial or Gen Z, I can't even waste my time explaining it to them."

This meme captures the rage and frustration of the younger generations about what they see as the irresponsible spending and policy making of the Baby Boomers. In 2017, before the meme even existed, Bruce Gibney wrote a book, *A Generation of Sociopaths: How Baby Boomers Betrayed America*.[5] In his controversial book, he lays out the case for how Baby Boomers' reckless selfishness destroyed American prosperity through terrible policies. The author argues that Millennials and the younger generations have a limited window to hold the Baby Boomers accountable and to fix what they broke.

Most of the younger generation knows that it's going to be up to them to transform their own future. The critique of the younger generations is that they are going to have to learn the difference between knowledge and wisdom. However, as it relates to money – Millennials and Gen Z are digital-native, with them growing up with the Internet, and it's going to be an easy transition for them to understand digital assets and things like crypto asset investing. They are going to get the value of bearer instruments, securing their own assets, and the pitfalls of counterparty risk. It will be on the Boomers to get with and understand the real value of securing scarcity through cryptography and to understand the value of digital assets overall.

I believe this generational frustration is not Baby Boomer specific but is systemic from our current time. The Boomer generation was the first generation to continue deficit spending because of the removal of financial restrictions by taking the dollar off the gold standard. Additionally, the older generations have never had a need to relearn and unlearn in times of exponential technology. Today and in the future, this will be an ever-important skill.

The hypocrisy stems from the fact that concepts have actually shifted from underneath. News is now propaganda. Money is no longer an asset but a liability. Savings accounts are no longer storing value or producing income. Government bonds used to deliver a risk-free return; now they deliver return-free risk. Those who are able to unlearn and relearn concepts will be able to apply their agility in the future and adapt to the changing conditions. Those who don't will suffer the consequences.

Conclusion

As I've outlined, safe is the new risky. Whether you're a Boomer or in the Millennial or Gen X or Z generations, you have more risk to consider when thinking about what assets are safe and what risks exist even with safe assets. Much of the risk comes in the form of changes that have occurred over decades and the fact that we may have not updated our understanding of these assets or products.

Most of the progress made over the past few decades has improved convenience, not safety. Many ideas about money or investing look the same as in the past, but in reality they are quite different. I think most people have incurred more risk than they realize, so when they are comparing a new asset class, they are not factoring in all the risk of their current situation.

5

Credit and Commodity Currencies

Money is certainly too dangerous an instrument to leave to the fortuitous expediency of politicians.

— F. A. Hayek

Today, 100% of the world's currency, which is all of our currency, is fiat currency. Fiat by definition means "by declaration." That means there is nothing backing any of the global reserve currencies whether that's the US dollar, the Japanese yen, the Chinese yuan, or the European euro. As I previously discussed, the US dollar is the world's reserve currency. It started out as commodity money with currency notes that could be exchanged for gold or silver. That backing was removed in 1971, and the US dollar was converted to credit money with Nixon closing the gold exchange window. Since all the world's major currencies were pegged to the US dollar, they too converted from commodity money to credit money. In this chapter, I talk about the differences of each type of money with some of their history, but first, let's start with the original function of money.

The Purpose of Money

I think it's important we step back a bit and set the whole context of this topic by discussing the purpose of money. The purpose of money is to allow for delayed purchasing (storing future purchasing power), solving the "double coincidence of wants" problem of inefficiency and establishing a market pricing mechanism for all goods and services which creates continuous improvement. We know from economist Carl Menger that economic value is subjective.[1] Let's continue this with a recap of Adam Smith, who is considered to be the father of modern economics. His idea of a market economy, basically, was that a division and specialization of labor would lead to economic growth through economies of scale.[2]

This process started with the division of labor. Let's use an example in the Middle Ages, where perhaps you would have seen blacksmiths starting to form guilds, dividing their labor from the iron miners and beginning to specialize in their skill of designing and building armor, swords, and iron tools. In a similar fashion, you may have seen the stone masons start to divide their labor from the quarry miners' and form guilds to then specialize their skill in cutting stone and designing and building stone structures. It's this specialization of labor that allows focus on one task or set of tasks, instead of multiple tasks or multiple sets of types of tasks, which allows a worker to improve and perfect. Specialization leads to continuous improvement, which leads to a decrease in time and money in the production process. This division of labor and specialization of skill ultimately allows for economies of scale.

Economies of scale provide every participant in the economy with a cost advantage because each participant in the labor pool is continuously improving in their specialization, and that drives out inefficiency. This in turn increases production and lowers costs because a producer is able to spread the fixed cost over a larger number of goods. Reducing unit cost is the main advantage of economies of scale, and everyone benefits from it. It's these economies of scale that drive industrialization and economic growth.

Now, without money, everyone would still be bartering for goods and services. Bartering is literally the trading of one product or service for another. It's wildly inefficient because the entire economy has to continuously coordinate the double coincidence of wants. That is, the market has to coordinate the trade of each particular want in a synchronous fashion. If someone has a cow and needs chickens, they have to go find someone who has chickens and wants a cow. Moreover, they have to agree on an exchange rate each time. Money provides an abstraction, a middle layer. The function of money is to provide a store of value, a medium of exchange, and a unit of account. It allows for a middle layer where the owner of the cow can exchange it for money, and the owner of the chickens, too, can exchange them for money because it's a medium of exchange. Then, everyone can purchase what they want or need without having to find another producer that has what they want, too, at the same time. The extreme inefficiency gets removed from the economy, and that is of benefit to everyone. Money is also a store of value because it allows for producers to exchange their product or service for money, and they can simply hold the money for a future time when they need something. And finally, it is a unit of account because a market quickly finds and agrees on a unit of account – the market quickly agrees that a cow is worth so much, and a chicken is worth so much, and the whole community can benefit from not having to repeatedly rehash the value of each product or service.

Anything that takes away from this cycle of continuous improvement in the function and purpose of money creates inefficiency, increases cost, and causes a breakdown in an economy. Any activity that takes away money's ability to be a store of value falls into this category. Herein lies the opportunity.

Commodity Money (Sound Money)

Currencies backed by commodities, whether they're seashells or gold, have been around for at least five millennia. This is called *sound money*, because it is backed by a commodity where the free market determined its value.[3] Most of history has used commodity money, and economists like Hayek and Mises call these sound money periods. The British Empire from the fourteenth century to the early nineteenth century had a long period of sound money policy where their currency's purchasing power was not deflated away through debasement of the metal as in other periods in history. Going into much detail is beyond the scope of this book, but if you want a more detailed account of sound money and unsound money periods, I recommend you read *The Bitcoin Standard* by Saifedean Ammous.[4]

Sound money creates monetary value from six required characteristics of good money – portability, divisibility, scarcity, acceptability, durability, and uniformity. Commodities that incorporate these six things well can create monetary value. This is why commodities like seashells and precious metals have been used as money. There were times when other commodities were used for money. For a time, cows were used as money. However, over time it became clear that cows didn't live forever (i.e. were not durable) and couldn't be cut into pieces to be used for payment (i.e. not easily divisible). Over the centuries, it was gold that provided the most monetary value because it was the best at embodying the six characteristics of good money. Fiat money currently serves the monetary function, but does it qualify as good money? Fiat money is portable, divisible, durable, and uniform. However, it is not scarce. For now, fiat money is accepted, but for how long?

Gold was great commodity money throughout history because it represented all the six characteristics of good money. Moreover, its production rate over a long period of time stayed constant as roughly the rate of global economic growth of around 2%. Technology did not improve efficiency in the total cost of production over time, so the cost of production stayed relatively stable, in terms of resources and human labor. Additionally, its stock-to-flow ratio was the highest of the precious metals, which meant that it held its value the best. We discuss stock-to-flow more in later chapters of this book. These properties of gold made it the ideal commodity for good money, and it was the commodity used most by far for sound money over millennia.

Periods of Sound Money Policy

There have been many periods of sound money – we oscillate between those periods and periods of unsound money policy. We can see that there have been many consequences along with many lessons learned if we go back and really look at what happened during periods of sound and unsound money throughout history.

Money, in the form of metallic coins, started in Lydia around 600 BCE, though some historians have noted the use of metal as currency going back to 5,000 BCE. We know the Lydians minted coins in electrum, which is a naturally occurring alloy of gold and silver.[5]

The first currency was decentralized. It required no third party to transact business. Trust was formed by the minter's mark, so we'll say it was a trust-minimized, not trustless, form of commerce. We know that money started under a sound money period because it was commodity-backed and did not require a state or a bank, credit or the evaluation of creditworthiness, and did not have counterparty risk.

Many periods in history, and typically the most prosperous periods, began under a sound money period. We saw it with the Egyptians, the Greeks, the Romans, the Chinese, and the Europeans during the Renaissance and the Industrial Revolution. The world saw the greatest growth and economic expansion during periods of sound money policy. Then, every time the same thing happened. The state took over the management of the money supply and implemented unsound money policies that always ended in disaster.

Bi-metal Periods

Most of the time that the world was using commodity money, it was using some version of metallic alloy coins for currency. The most common metals used were gold and silver, but many alloys and other metals were used also, including electrum, bronze, and copper.

In early 2020, I got into a Twitter spat with Murad Mahmudov about the reality of gold as a medium of exchange. (He is an avid advocate of Bitcoin and a Bitcoin Maximalist.) Murad piped into one of my Twitter discussions to let me know that gold has been used as a medium of exchange for thousands of years. His point was that gold was used as a single currency for both a store of value and a medium of exchange. I countered his position with the fact that, though gold was sometimes used as a medium of exchange, it wasn't used very often as that. Silver was in fact the commodity money that was used more in everyday purchases, and it was silver that transacted 90% of commercial trades both in ancient and Medieval times.

I think the notion that one currency will optimize for all three properties (medium of exchange, store of value, and unit of account) needs to be rethought. A currency should prioritize these properties. A currency that is a great store of value can be a good medium of exchange, and, conversely, a currency that is a great medium of exchange can be a good, if not great, store of value. We see evidence of this in history with gold and silver. Gold is a great store of value, but its scarcity is a hindrance to its acceptability/usability. Great stores of value are hoarded. Historically, when gold was used as a currency, not enough existed to fully support an economy. Furthermore, no one wanted a tiny, tiny gold coin. While still scarce, silver was much more common and much more available, and therefore most commercial transactions happened in silver. Silver can support an economy because more of it can be minted (i.e. its inflation rate is higher than gold's). Gold can be a great store of value over longer periods of time because less of it is minted (i.e. its inflation rate is lower; therefore, it's harder money; therefore, it holds its value over time). I think we need to reexamine the idea that the hardest money is the only good money and whether one currency fits both the need for economic growth and the need for store of value. It may be that two currencies provide the best economic model – one global currency as a store of value and one local currency as a medium of exchange and unit of account that adjusts with local economic growth and demand.

Credit Money (Unsound Money)

Unlike commodity money, credit money is backed by no asset; it is backed by fiat or by declaration of a government. In credit money, every unit of currency is borrowed into existence. As such, it requires a central authority. It's a counterintuitive concept because if money is borrowed into existence and must be paid backed with interest, how does a borrower pay the interest? The only way is to have an ever-increasing money supply.

As outlined, there are many periods in history where the money starts out as sound money but gets converted to unsound money policy. These periods happen in stages, and the powers that be aimed to make the new credit money look, feel, and act like the old commodity-backed money, but nothing could be further from the truth.

Time and time again, the state has taken over the management of the money supply and gradually converted from sound money policy with commodity money to an unsound money policy with credit money. The process happens slowly. First, the state must convince its citizens to accept paper currency, or notes, which can be converted to the commodity that used to back the money, typically gold or silver. These currency notes are claims on the real money stored in the central banks. Once the citizens are used to using the paper fiat currency, the government starts to print more money and starts to spend more money through fractional-reserve banking. Now that the money is credit and not commodity, money is created by extending more and more credit. It starts with the central bank extending credit to commercial banks, and commercial banks extending credit to businesses and individuals. It is actually the process of credit creation that also increases the money supply. As credit gets increased, so, too, does the money supply. Conversely, as credit is either paid off or defaulted on, the money supply is decreased. It is credit that brings money into existence, not valuable commodities like gold or silver locked in a central bank vault.

After this happens for a while, the downfall starts to happen. Since the money is managed by government, it is managed by politicians. It never fails that when pressed to raise taxes to cover additional spending or to print more money, political expediency and ease always win the day. It's too tempting when the cost of money production is effectively zero. Governments start spending more than they take in. They start to issue bonds. They continue deficit spending. They end up building a large debt, many times through war as war is the most expensive human endeavor. The debt gets to a point where it no longer can be paid, and the currency is now in jeopardy.

The last time this happened in a developed country was in the United States in 1971, as I discussed in Chapter 1. When Nixon took us off the gold standard "temporarily," the United States converted from credit money to credit money. The United States has been deficit spending ever since. In 1971, the Federal Reserve balance sheet was under $200 billion.[6] In 2020, the Fed's estimated balance sheet by the end of the year is $8 trillion! As a civilization, we have repeated this cycle many times before.

Problems with Credit Money

The problems with unsound money are always the same. When state and money are collapsed, it's the political process that ultimately governs the monetary policy, regardless of attempts at independency. In the end, it's always easier to print more money than it is to reduce spending or raise taxes. But, therein lies the opportunity. What if there exists an option that separates money and state?

War and Political Promises

There have been 775 paper currencies studied and three quarters of them are now gone.[7] There are roughly 100 left, each for a modern country's current money. Gold is the only currency that's been around more than 2,500 years, and more likely has been used for 5,000 years. Every time the demise has come down to government's deficit spending on war and/or political promises. In the end, it's always easier to print.

From DinarDirham.com:

According to a study of 775 fiat currencies by DollarDaze.org, there is no historical precedence for a fiat currency that has succeeded in holding its value. Twenty percent failed through hyperinflation, 21% were destroyed by war, 12% were destroyed by independence, 24% were monetarily reformed, and 23% are still in circulation, approaching one of the other outcomes.

The average life expectancy for a fiat currency is 27 years, with the shortest lifespan being one month. Founded in 1694, the British pound sterling is the oldest fiat currency in existence. At a ripe old age of 317 years it must be considered a highly successful fiat currency. However, success is relative. The British pound was defined as 12 ounces of silver, so it's worth less than 1/200 or 0.5% of its original value. In other words, the most successful longstanding currency in existence has lost 99.5% of its value.[8]

Periods of Unsound Money Policy

Prosperity breeds experimentation. That's all fine and good unless it's the state that's experimenting with monetary policy to try and solve their deficit spending. They say history doesn't repeat, but it sure does rhyme. That is certainly true when it comes to every experiment in history where the state has gone from a sound money policy to an unsound money policy. Here are just a few of those experiments.

Greece

As we all know, ancient Greece was the first democracy of the world. They had credit currency – the drachma – which was a coin made of silver. It was one of the world's earliest coins. Greece back then was comprised of several city-states, one of which was Athens, which minted the most common drachma at the time. As Mises discusses in his book *The Theory of Money and Credit*,[9] Greece and its predecessor Lydia, which minted the first commodity-backed currency, thrived economically as long as they retained a sound money currency.

The Hellenistic empire expanded under Alexander the Great, who had come from Athens in the fourth century BCE. Athens was thriving and, as such, it kept its drachma pure, whereas other ancient Greek states did not. Other states started to add copper to their drachma, which was the first currency debasement to occur in a political democracy.

Mises notes that the state, under political pressure to solve fiscal problems, had to choose between debasing their currency or raising taxes. (The former is much easier from a political perspective and is often the path chosen.) The Greek city-states made that choice, too, and many started to debase their currency. There was even an ancient Greek idea called "Gresham's Law," which stated, "Bad money drives out the good." This meant where two forms of legal money were in circulation, people would prefer to save higher value coins and spend the lower value coins.[10]

Rome

At its height, the Roman Empire was 130 million people strong and covered a vast territory that spanned over 1.5 million square miles. The Roman Empire had conquered much of the world, building all kinds of leading-edge infrastructure like roads, aqueducts, city plumbing, and planning. Much of the work we can still see today, 2,000 years later.

With the conquering of territory came the profitable activity of trade. They imported a wide variety of goods from all over, including dyes, silk, olive oil, marble, silver, timber, and wine. Over time, however, the administration of the empire became quite expensive. Adding to administration expense, the Romans also invented welfare. At one point, the government was giving wheat to almost 20% of its citizens. During a particularly bad economic period, the government hired thousands of new soldiers and funded many new public works projects. Military costs, social costs, and logistical costs were ballooning, and the empire started looking for novel and creative ways to pay for their deficit spending. They implemented the first state-run monetary policy – the debasement of their currency.

The first currency debasement started in Rome around 60 AD.[11] Roman emperor Nero initiated the reduction of the silver content of their currency; by 210 AD, the silver content was reduced by 50%. By 265 AD, the silver in their currency was down to 0.5%. Like I said earlier, wars are expensive. By the time the denarius was only 0.5% silver, price inflation had skyrocketed 1,000% across the Roman Empire. Foreigners began to only accept gold.

You might think, "That doesn't sound so bad," but it got worse for the Roman empire. Starting in 301 AD, a pound of gold was worth 50,000 denari. Fifty years later, it was worth 2.12 billion denari. The denari had lost 42,400 times its value relative to gold.[12]

Ultimately, the world's first documented period of hyperinflation – the cost of administration, heavy taxation, and the high cost of war – brought down this empire.[13] The entire region reverted to a barter system.

England

With the fall of Rome came the Dark Ages, and it was quite a long time before currency debasement was tried again. England was next to step up to the currency debasement plate in 1544 with what was known as the Great Debasement.[14] Under Henry VIII, the crown ordered a currency debasement policy to be introduced. The order debased both gold and silver coins minted by the crown and used instead copper and other base metals. In some cases, the entire coin was replaced by these base metals and no precious metals remained. The need for this debasement came from the overspending of Henry VIII in order to pay for his lavish lifestyle and to fund wars with Scotland and France.

During the debasement period, where they went from a sound money period to an unsound money period, England replaced their fully gold-backed currency with slow debasement. Their gold coins started out as 23 carat and went as low as 20 carat and their silver coins were reduced from 92.5% silver to just 25%. This debased currency was ultimately removed from circulation by Elizabeth I in 1560. However, the damage had been done. Confidence in the monarchy was completely lost by the country's trading partners.[15] Foreign merchants ended up refusing to be paid with the debased coinage.

France

We could learn a lot from mistakes made in the eighteenth century as well. In September 1715, Louis XIV, the king of France, died. With his death he left a handful of problems, including a terrible economy, a treasury on the verge of bankruptcy, and a citizenry violently opposed to any type of entitlement reform. Phillipe, the Duke of Orleans, appointed regent after the king's death, was left to deal with these problems.

In comes John Law, a Scotsman on the run who has fled to France after being arrested for murder in London in 1694.[16] Law travels to

London from Edinburgh and learns about money and banking from the English financial revolution in the 1690s. Out of coincidence, or just plain bad luck for Phillipe, Law appears before the regent who has earlier met him while gambling. You see, around the same time as he is meeting the Duke, he publishes a paper on the benefits of paper currency. He pitches an idea to Phillipe to solve his economic problems and Phillipe wastes no time taking Law's ideas and putting them into practice.[17] His proposition of a solution all started with paper money.

In 1716, Law creates the Banque Générale, which prints France's first paper money. This becomes the first central bank in history, as this bank has the right to print legal paper currency. The next year Law creates the Company of the West, which is France's first corporation. Later on, these two entities together would be known as "The System" and, boy, would they find out how much damage the System could do.

As we've learned in history, it always starts out as a seeming benefit. The paper currency is backed by gold and silver and can be redeemed at the bank. As the people start using the paper currency, the bank starts increasing the currency supply but initially at a mild pace. This is how it started with Law and his bank. The increased money supply started to bring the economy back, and Law was seen as a genius. Seeing his economic problems getting better, the Duke rewarded Law with the sole trading rights from France's Louisiana Territory in the New World.[18]

Everyone at the time believed the Territory was packed with gold, and people wanted in on the action. With Law retaining exclusive trading rights and owning the Company of the West, he began issuing shares in the company to would-be investors. Initially, he issued 200,000 shares. Shortly after that initial offering, share prices rose 30 times.

Seeing more benefit to France, the Duke, now King Regent, rewarded Law again. He received more exclusive rights to trade in new goods and in new territories. Everything seemed to be going great for John Law and for France. Paris was booming because of all the currency being printed and was in the middle of a stock mania with John Law selling so many shares to multiple companies that owned exclusive trading rights.

It was only a matter of time before problems arose. Due to massive inflation, prices spiked, and the currency's purchasing power decreased by the week. It wasn't long before real estate prices and rents increased 20-fold! Soon it was clear the bank could not meet its obligations to exchange all the paper money for gold and silver, and a bank run ensued. In 1720, the bank had to "temporarily" close the redemption window and could no longer exchange gold and silver for the paper currency.

A few months later, the financial crisis came to a head, the banks were closed, and John Law was excused from the government ministry. That summer, bank notes were devalued by 50% and the exchange window was reopened. Soon, the bank's gold ran out, then its silver, and then its copper. Everyone came to exchange their bank notes for sound money. The boom was over and the damage was done.[19] It dropped France, and much of Europe, into a depression that lasted for decades.

First Continental Congress

In North America there is a currency that has gone defunct. In 1775, the continental was printed by the Continental Congress to help fund the American Revolutionary War. It had a lot of problems, including the British counterfeiting the currency and the cost of war destroying the trust in the currency because it wasn't backed by tangible assets.[20]

The continental did have an impact, though, because the Forefathers of the United States explicitly did not want a central bank or paper currency and wrote it so in the Constitution. The writers of the Constitution wanted gold and silver to be the only legal tender of the United States, and this they included in the gold and silver clause. They knew their history.

Weimar Republic

The history of the Weimar Republic is probably the most known currency debasement case of all time. They, too, started out with sound money and ended up in disaster by way of unsound money. There's little need for me to go into the specifics of hyperinflation from the Weimar Republic as this is common knowledge. If you want the best book on the matter, I recommend *When Money Dies: The Nightmare of Deficit Spending, Devaluation and Hyperinflation in Weimar Germany* by Adam Fergusson.[21]

Modern Developing Countries

Modern history has its fair share of examples of unsound money policies as well. I will simply mention them by country and year (Figure 5.1). The full table is provided in the Appendix.

LOCATION	START DATE	END DATE	MONTH WITH HIGHEST INFLATION RATE	HIGHEST MONTHLY INFLATION RATE	EQUIVALENT DAILY INFLATION RATE	TIME REQUIRED FOR PRICES TO DOUBLE	CURRENCY	TYPE OF PRICE INDEX
Georgia[26]	Mar. 1992	Apr. 1992	Mar. 1992	198%	3.70%	19.3 days	Russian Ruble	Consumer
Argentina[77]	May 1989	Mar. 1990	Jul. 1989	197%	3.69%	19.4 days	Austral	Consumer
Bolivia[28]	Apr. 1984	Sep. 1985	Feb. 1985	183%	3.53%	20.3 days	Boliviano	Consumer
Belarus††[29]	Jan. 1992	Feb. 1992	Jan. 1992	159%	3.22%	22.2 days	Russian Ruble	Consumer
Kyrgyzstan††[30]	Jan. 1992	Jan. 1992	Jan. 1992	157%	3.20%	22.3 days	Russian Ruble	Consumer
Kazakhstan††[31]	Jan. 1992	Jan. 1992	Jan. 1992	141%	2.97%	24.0 days	Russian Ruble	Consumer
Austria[32]	Oct. 1921	Sep. 1922	Aug. 1922	129%	2.80%	25.5 days	Crown	Consumer
Bulgaria[33]	Feb. 1991	Mar. 1991	Feb. 1991	123%	2.71%	26.3 days	Lev	Consumer
Uzbekistan††[34]	Jan. 1992	Feb. 1992	Jan. 1992	118%	2.64%	27.0 days	Russian Ruble	Consumer
Azerbaijan[35]	Jan. 1992	Dec. 1994	Jan. 1992	118%	2.63%	27.0 days	Russian Ruble	Consumer
Congo (Zaire)[36]	Oct. 1991	Sep. 1992	Nov. 1991	114%	2.57%	27.7 days	Zaire	Consumer
Peru[37]	Sep. 1988	Sep. 1988	Sep. 1988	114%	2.57%	27.7 days	Inti	Consumer
Taiwan[38]	Oct. 1948	May 1949	Oct. 1948	108%	2.46%	28.9 days	Taipi	Wholesale for Taipei
Hungary[39]	Mar. 1923	Feb. 1924	Jul. 1923	97.9%	2.30%	30.9 days	Crown	Consumer
Chile[40]	Oct. 1973	Oct. 1973	Oct. 1973	87.6%	2.12%	33.5 days	Escudo	Consumer
Estonia††[41]	Jan. 1992	Feb. 1992	Jan. 1992	87.2%	2.11%	33.6 days	Russian Ruble	Consumer
Angola[42]	Dec. 1994	Jan. 1997	May 1996	84.1%	2.06%	34.5 days	Kwanza	Consumer
Brazil[43]	Dec. 1989	Mar. 1990	Mar. 1990	82.4%	2.02%	35.1 days	Cruzado & Cruzeiro	Consumer
Democratic Republic of Congo[44]	Aug. 1998	Aug. 1998	Aug. 1998	78.5%	1.95%	36.4 days	Franc	Consumer
Poland[45]	Oct. 1989	Jan. 1990	Jan. 1990	77.3%	1.93%	36.8 days	Zloty	Consumer
Armenia††[46]	Jan. 1992	Feb. 1992	Jan. 1992	73.1%	1.85%	38.4 days	Russian Ruble	Wholesale
Tajikistan[47]	Oct. 1995	Nov. 1995	Nov. 1995	65.2%	1.69%	42.0 days	Ruble	Wholesale
Latvia[48]	Jan. 1992	Jan. 1992	Jan. 1992	64.4%	1.67%	42.4 days	Russian Ruble	Consumer
Turkmenistan††[49]	Nov. 1995	Jan. 1996	Jan. 1996	62.5%	1.63%	43.4 days	Manat	Consumer
Philippines[50]	Jan. 1944	Dec. 1944	Jan. 1944	60.0%	1.58%	44.9 days	Japanese War Notes	Consumer
Yugoslavia[51]	Sep. 1989	Dec. 1989	Dec. 1989	59.7%	1.57%	45.1 days	Dinar	Consumer
Germany[52]	Jan. 1920	Jan. 1920	Jan. 1920	56.9%	1.51%	46.8 days	Papiermark	Wholesale
Kazakhstan[53]	Nov. 1993	Nov. 1993	Nov. 1993	55.5%	1.48%	47.9 days	Tenge & Russian	Consumer

Figure 5.1 The Hanke-Krus Hyperinflation Table

Data source: Randall E. Parker and Robert Whaples (eds.), *Routledge Handbook of Major Events in Economic History*. New York: Routledge, 2013, amended 2020.

6

The Fall of Credit Money and the Rise of Multicurrencies

How did you go bankrupt? Two ways. Gradually and then suddenly.
— Ernest Hemingway

The Fall of Credit-based Currencies

The thing that I've found the most disturbing is that the government had rigged the most important price in the world. We learned in economics that price controls don't work. Yet we decided to put price controls on the most important price in the world, which was the price of long-term interest rates, the price of money.
— Stan Druckenmiller (top 100 investor of all time)

I think Stan captures it all in his quote above. The global central banks are manipulating and distorting the price of money and that has huge ramifications to the global financial system. As I discussed in the previous chapter, the key benefit of money is it allows us to set prices in an efficient manner through markets. It's not that money printing directly leads to inflation. It's that money printing distorts the pricing mechanism for risk that is used in all of capitalism, which then distorts the economy, which then distorts all market participants' behavior.[1] If you can no longer trust a market pricing mechanism to set the price of a good or service, then you lose the ability to efficiently allocate resources. It is akin to price controls and, as we've seen throughout history, price control, in the form of price floors and price ceilings, destroys a market and leads to rationing and black markets. What we've seen from global central banks is a form of socialism where enterprises are encouraged to take risks and where the enterprise privatizes the profits and socializes the losses. It's socialism for rich people. Let's explore more how we got here.

The Ever-Increasing Size of Bubbles

Usually when the word "modern" is used, it means post–World War II. Modern art . . . yup, post–World War II. However, in the context of modern monetary policy, we're going to start at the change of the millennium with the first modern asset bubble: the dot-com bubble of 2000. This is when we start to see a change from the central banks' playbook and the amount of money they start to pump into the system. Over time, it appears the Fed starts to move away from its dual mandate of price stability and maximum employment toward asset price stabilization, and in doing so, starts to really increase the size of the bubbles in the markets.

The Dot-com Bubble of 2000

The Federal Reserve has been printing money and creating ever-larger asset bubbles that eventually pop. This first started in the 1990s with the dot-com bubble. Speculators, largely in the United States, were following the latest technological revolution and were speculating in tech and dot-com stocks like Dell, Microsoft, Cisco, Oracle, Qualcomm, and others like Buy.com and Pets.com. It was a bubble because it was a technological revolution in its Frenzy phase as described by Perez.[2] The bubble eventually burst in 2000 and we saw the NASDAQ fall from 117 on March 20, 2000, to 20.35 on September 30, 2002, using today's NASDAQ index numbers. From peak to trough, that was a drop of 78% in roughly 30 months. It took the NASDAQ 16 years before it returned to its 2000 peak.

This was the first bubble initiated in modern history by a technological revolution. It was the government's response to this that fueled the next two asset bubbles. Each bubble would become bigger than the next.

The Great Recession of 2008 – A Consumer Debt Bubble

The next bubble was the real estate bubble of 2008. This wasn't caused by the Federal Reserve or any central bank, at least initially. It started with the change in legislation brought about by the repeal of the Glass-Steagall Act in 1999. Investment banks and commercial banks no longer had to be broken out and kept separate. Now, protections and restrictions were chipped away, and the banking and securities industries could commingle. This allowed new leverage for commercial banks, which used to be required to keep loan leverage under a 10:1 ratio. Moreover, they could create new financial instruments that could package old mortgage loans into securities that could be sold as such to investors.

Over time, these legislative changes allowed participants to push boundaries way past what was healthy for the financial system. Some banks were leveraged up to 30:1 in some areas of banking and lending. Small changes in the value of underlying assets could drive them to insolvency and because of some of the new financial instruments like CDOs and CMOs, which weren't thoroughly understood, financial institutions had more risk on their books than was manageable. Ultimately, those dominos started to fall in 2008 with the bankruptcy of Lehman Brothers.

This is when the Federal Reserve started to step in to change the course of history. This was the beginning of the end when everything changed. The Federal Reserve, under Ben Bernanke, was about to create the biggest asset bubble in history and one we're still dealing with today. From a cyclical perspective, this began the inflating and then ultimately the deflationary cycle we've been dealing with after the Great Recession.

The Coming Sovereign Debt Bubble

It's not quite here yet, but it's coming. We are about to experience the mother of all bubbles – the public debt bubble of the twenty-first century. As the Fed, and other central banks around the world, continue to pump money into the system, we're seeing public debt explode. Everyone's heard the old adage "a billion here, a billion there, and pretty soon we're talking about real money." That was funny because at the time, $1 billion was a lot of money. One billion dollars is no longer a large amount of money. We will have to update the adage to "a trillion here, a trillion there, and pretty soon we're talking about big money."

In 2016, the US public debt was $16 trillion. At the end of the first term of President Trump, it is estimated that the US will have $28 trillion in national public debt. That's not a political statement – it's pointing to the fact that public debt could increase 100% in a single term of a president; that is frightening, and there's no end in sight.

Public debt is accelerating. In 2000, the national debt was $5.8 trillion. In 2010, right after the crisis of 2008, the national debt was $11.4 trillion. The national debt doubled in 10 years. At the end of 2019, the national debt was $21 trillion. The Congressional Budget Office (CBO) came out with a statistic that said after 2020 the annual deficit will never be under $1 trillion again. That means every year we will add at least $1 trillion to the national debt. This CBO estimate came out before the pandemic. It is estimated that at the end of 2020 we will add $7 trillion to the national debt, in one year. That means from 2010 to 2020, the national debt has almost tripled. At the end of 2020, the national debt level is estimated at 131% of debt to GDP, which is higher than it was after World War II. There is no end in sight, which points to a sovereign debt crisis. At the end of all of this, I wouldn't be surprised to see the US national debt at $100 trillion. Check https://www.usdebtclock.org/ for the latest.

The Federal Reserve's Modern Policies and Positions

The Federal Reserve's modern policies created the risk we're having to deal with today. They continue to outweigh current market stability for increasing tail risk. In simple terms, tail risk is a financial risk that is highly improbable, but whose impact is extremely damaging. You can only do that for so long before the tail risk comes to your front door. It's going to have to be dealt with someday.

Now, I'm not saying all of the world's financial problems are the central bankers' fault per se. There was no way for politicians to draft fiscal policy that would address the issues in time. Moreover, due to the makeup of the legislative branch at the time, there was plenty of doubt that any meaningful fiscal policy could make it through the process. Just about the only tool left in the government's toolbox was monetary policy and it was used to some beneficial effect to stem the crisis that began in 2008. However, it also started us on the slippery slope of monetary intervention.

Balance Sheet Expansion: QE 1, QE2, Operation Twist, QE3, Non-QE QE, QE to Infinity

The Federal Reserve began its monetary intervention in November 2008. Its initial round of quantitative easing (QE) was called QE but it's now referred to as QE1 because of all the subsequent intervention. This initial QE monetary intervention was distinct from the Troubled Asset Relief Program (TARP), which was initiated and managed by the US Treasury. Under QE1, the Fed proposed to buy $100 billion of agency debt and $500 billion of mortgage-backed securities. It was extended, and the Fed ultimately purchased an additional $850 billion in mortgage-backed securities and began purchasing longer-dated treasuries.[3] The program started as a "temporary" purchase of assets.

The next round of monetary intervention occurred in 2011 and was called QE2. The program purchased $600 billion of longer-dated treasuries that completed in the summer of 2011. Then came Operation Twist. This program looked to add longer-dated treasuries and lengthen the duration of bonds in the portfolio. The Fed purchased $400 billion worth of treasuries under this program. Then finally in this initial period of monetary easing, the Fed initiated QE3 from 2012 to 2014. Under this program, the Fed purchased $40 billion per month in mortgage-backed securities. The Federal Open Market Committee (FOMC) maintained the size of the balance sheet until late 2017.[4]

Before 2008, the Fed's balance sheet was about $800 billion. After all the QE programs, the Fed's balance sheet ballooned almost six times, to $4.5 trillion. It took 98 years to grow the Fed's balance sheet to $800 billion and then just five years to grow from $800 billion to $4.5 trillion. Everything appeared fine; there were seemingly no long-term ill effects from all this monetary easing.

Most say the Fed's QE program was a success. There was even an article in *Forbes* to that effect in 2015.[5] It staved off the next great depression that was bound to happen had they not intervened. That may be true, but time will tell if it really was a success or just the next domino falling. The Fed cannot undo their easing and they are going to have to keep going down this path to keep the status quo. Every time they prioritize currency stability, they increase the tail risk – the risk of damage that's going to be done when this ultimately gets unwound, that is, the risk of currency collapse.

We began to see hints of such a possibility when the Fed began the mildest of quantitative tightening (QT). Without getting into the details of runoff and balance sheet normalization, the Fed began a program, known as QT, to reduce the size of its balance sheet. QT is the opposite of QE. Instead of monetary easing, QT is monetary tightening. This was the first and only time the Fed initiated QT. All they did was reduce the purchasing on bonds from $30 billion per month to $15 billion per month and all hell broke loose. The repo market, which is the overnight lending market between commercial banks, seized up. The stock market fell 18%. Ultimately, the Fed stopped QT just a few months later. It became clear that it was going to be difficult to unwind all of this monetary easing.

In 2020, the Fed came out with a barrage of programs, designed to address the pandemic, that dramatically increased the size of its balance sheet yet again. Some of the recent programs included "Non-QE QE" in late 2019. Then in March the Fed announced, "QE to infinity," which essentially meant as much monetary stimulus as required, with no limit. The Fed's balance sheet expanded more than 75%, from $4.5 trillion to almost $8 trillion, in less than one year! All of this monetary intervention ballooned the Fed's balance sheet to unimaginable levels (Figure 6.1). The famous billionaire investor Howard Marks asked, "Will the Fed spend trillions of dollars, every year, forever to support the market? Is that its role? It's not its role."

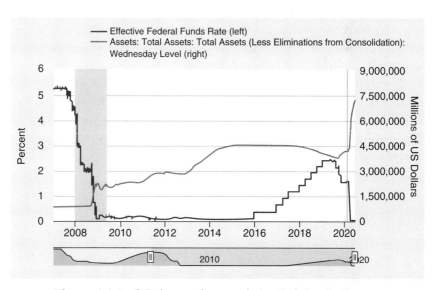

Figure 6.1 Fed Balance Sheet and the Fed Funds Rate
Source: Board of Governors, New York Fed.

International Balance Sheet Expansion: Japan QE, Japan Buys Equities, ZIRP, NIRP

It didn't take long for other global central banks to catch up with the Federal Reserve and initiate their own QE programs. Japan had experienced a deflationary spiral since the 1990s and it has continued its efforts of quantitative easing. The Bank of Japan went so far as to start buying their own sovereign bonds and even buying Japanese equities via Japanese ETFs. In 2020, the Bank of Japan owns more than 80% of all Japanese equity ETFs.

Both Japan and Europe have experimented with zero interest rate policies (ZIRP) and negative interest rate policies (NIRP). All of this experimentation is an effort to boost economic activity by manipulating the interest rates lower. However, none of these efforts have led to long-term economic growth.

Unintended Consequences

All that monetary intervention has a consequence. As we've seen, trying to maintain stability and the status quo has a price. Where the real liability lies is in the breadth of unintended consequences. We have several pendulums swinging to their most extreme points, including debt levels, aggregation, and the importance we put on capital over labor. As of mid-2020, the richest 10% of Americans now own 84% of all stocks.[6] Capital gains tax rates are at record lows at 20% – much lower than the highest bracket of tax rates on labor. With NIRP and ZIRP, corporations are being punished for holding cash, so central banks are, in essence, forcing them to deploy capital. As a response, of course, companies buy back their shares as a way to improve capital efficiency, but that in turn leads them into a position where they are in no way prepared for downdraft in the economy, especially something like a global pandemic. When governments make policy changes, there are always unintended consequences.

Cantillon Effect

The Cantillon Effect refers to the change in relative prices resulting from a change in the money supply. When money gets created and deployed, it enters at specific points within and through the economy. People and organizations in closer proximity to the entry point get to benefit the most from the money. People farther away from the money centers benefit the least because by the time the money gets to them, inflation or price changes dilute the benefit. This makes the centralization of money and central banks' monetary intervention have the unintended consequence of benefiting one group of people (those that are close) to the detriment of others (those that are distant).

Public Trust in Governments Near Historic Lows

It should come as no surprise that all of this monetary intervention has led to global distrust (see Figure 6.2). The public trust in governments is at historic lows. Financial systems are built on trust. When trust erodes the financial system erodes. The best analogy for this is the temperature of water. When water goes from 160° to 180°, we don't see any difference from that incremental increase. However, when water goes from 200° to 210°, we start to see bubbling. There's no difference between 210° and 211°. However, when water hits 212° it starts to boil. The incremental temperature increases cause incremental changes to the state of the water until it hits a breaking point. Trust works in a similar fashion. It continues to stay in one phase until it hits a point of phase shift and then it's something completely different.

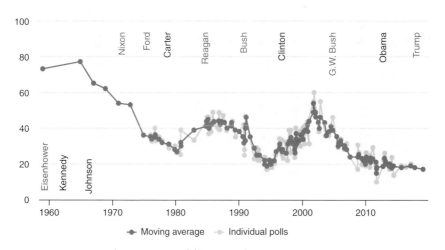

Figure 6.2 Public Trust in Governments
Source: "Public trust in government near historic lows." Pew Research Center, September 24, 2019. pewresearch.org/chart/public-trust-in-government-near-historic-lows/.

The Pension Crisis

There is a real pension crisis in America. The average pension in the United States aims to generate 7% per year. That estimate and forecast is based first on a risk-free return of 3½% from US treasuries. With all US treasuries yielding under 1%, except for the 30-year bond, right now pensions have to take more and more risk to try to generate a return. Most pensions are underfunded and not hitting their annual performance goals.

This is compounded by the shifting demographics that have fewer workers contributing to pensions in the workforce, lower birthrates, and retirees living much longer after retirement. Most companies have shifted retirement risk off the corporation and onto the individual following the ERISA laws in the 1970s and have converted from a defined-benefit plan, like a pension, to a defined-contribution plan, like a 401(k). This means fewer workers are contributing to pensions.

This is not going to end well. It is estimated that by 2025 the Pension Benefit Guarantee Corporation (PBGC), which is a federally chartered corporation to help ensure pension benefits, will have insufficient funds to meet pension obligations for defaulted and insolvent plans.[7] The problem is only getting worse with the continued manipulation of the bond market and the treasury rates.

The Housing Crisis

I don't know about you, but I've seen a lot of homeless people in the past five years. In Los Angeles and in Austin I have personally seen a huge increase. I know San Francisco has a terrible homelessness problem. This can partially be tied directly to the actions of the Federal Reserve.

The Fed's QE programs have created another asset bubble. The Bernanke asset bubble started in 2010 and has been continuing for a decade. It is now the Powell asset bubble, named after Fed Chair Jay Powell. When the Federal Reserve prints money, most of it goes into asset purchases. We saw that from 2010 to 2020, with corporations implementing tons of stock buyback programs. That is one of the core reasons we've seen the longest bull market in stocks. We've seen it with all asset prices increasing. In 2019, we saw bonds, real estate, gold, and stocks all go up together. That's not typical. The only way all asset classes can go up at the same time is when there's monetary expansion.

This has also affected home mortgages and rents. Real estate prices have increased. Rents, too, have increased along with the home prices. Asset price inflation has caused homelessness. And the worst part is that we're seeing more and more of the same from our central government. I think we can expect more homelessness in the future.

Modern Global Monetary Policy – Money Printer Goes Brrrrr

There's another great Internet meme: "Money printer goes brrrrr. . .." It alludes to the unprecedented global central bank printing of fiat currency. Google it; it's fantastic. Global banks continue to print money while they have decades, if not centuries, of data showing that money printing does not lead to economic growth. One of the best articles that outlines this case is from *Zero Hedge*, "Here Is the Stunning Chart That Blows Up All of Modern Central Banking."[8] It shows in no uncertain terms that QE is deflationary, not inflationary. One of the article's main arguments is that lower rates force households to save more and savings represent monies not spent in the economy. Economist Dr. Lacy Hunt has been detailing a similar argument for a decade – that rates will continue to go lower until they reach the lower bound and that QE does not create inflation; rather, it suppresses growth due to the increased debt load and cost of debt service.[9] He was right, despite most of the investment community thinking the opposite for many years.

The Modern Currency War – The Race to the Bottom

All central banks have employed monetary expansion. They are all manipulating the price of money. Their goal is to devalue their currency so that exchange rates benefit their export trade in hopes of improving their economy. There is a race to the bottom in terms of interest rates. Countries are employing ZIRP and NIRP policies around the world.

As so eloquently stated in Investopedia, "The Bank of Japan (BOJ) keeps trying to print Japan back into economic prosperity and it is not letting 25 years of failed stimulus policy get in its way."[10] That continues today. The BOJ has added NIRP to their monetary policy arsenal so that a bank holding money does not produce a return, but rather an expense, to the account holder. In 2019, in an effort to create inflation, Japan set its short-term interest rates target to –0.1%. Japan has still not had real economic growth since the 1990s.

Europe isn't any better. The European Central Bank (ECB) has had its own QE programs for a while. The ECB launched its first QE program in March 2015. It ended its bond-buying in December of 2018,[11] but that didn't last. The ECB announced in November 2019 it would begin a second QE bond-buying program. They expanded the program in 2020 due to the pandemic. Central banks continue to manipulate the price of money in an effort to induce inflation, but it hasn't worked in 25 years for Japan, for more than a decade in the United States, or for five years in Europe.

The Eurodollar Crisis

Since in a credit-backed money regime currency is brought into existence through loan creation, international commercial banks outside the US can basically "print" US dollars. All they have to do is create a loan that is denominated in US dollars. These are Eurodollar loans and they are created all throughout the world outside the United States. They came about through demand because investors didn't want currency risk in their bond portfolios, so bond offerings created US dollar–denominated debt. The one thing about Eurodollars is that they are outside the purview of the Federal Reserve.

Since creating more debt, by definition, creates more leverage in the system, there are times when the global financial system is more leveraged and is short dollars. They need more dollars for the system to effectively work. In certain pathological cases, the entire world is short of dollars and a crisis ensues. The global economy needs more dollars for the economy to continue to function properly. In crisis times, there is a huge demand for US dollars. If the crisis is created in the Eurodollar market, we call it the Eurodollar Crisis or more generally the Dollar Shortage Crisis.

This has been a problem with the Eurodollar market over the past few decades but really at crisis levels several times from 2015 to 2020. It flared up in September 2019 as well as in January and March 2020. When there's a Eurodollar shortage, this forces people to sell US dollar–denominated assets to get US dollars. We've seen massive global market turmoil when this happens. There is much more to this problem, but it's outside the scope of this book. Suffice it to say there's a crisis and there's no monetary governing body in charge to address it. The system is getting much more complex and in doing so, it's becoming much more fragile.

Modern Monetary Theory – This Time It's Different

There is a new economic theory brewing called modern monetary theory (MMT). It states that the state should print as much money as it needs to govern. Kids, and I mean that pejoratively, have witnessed all this money-printing from 2008 on with no looming disaster occurring, as predicted. They want to take the experiment one step further and just print all the money we need. This idea is championed by Stephanie Kelton but Pavlina Tcherneva developed the first mathematical model of MMT. Bill Mitchell, professor of economics at the University of Newcastle, coined the term.

MMT goes about constructing a monetary regime from an entirely new perspective. The MMT monetary theory builds upon the idea that the state should print as much money as it needs to function. There are no deficits in MMT. There is no need of monitoring the national debt under MMT. It takes the present state of deficit spending to the pathological case. Those who support MMT believe that tax cash flows are not what give the money system its power, but only the declaration and need of the state that does.

From Wikipedia, citing three Bloomberg articles with economists like Stephanie Kelton and Paul Krugman, MMT's main tenets are that a government monopoly on money issues its own fiat currency:

- Can pay for goods, services, and financial assets without a need to collect money in the form of taxes;
- Cannot be forced to default on debt denominated in its own currency;
- Is only limited in its money creation and purchases by inflation, which accelerates once the real resources (labor, capital, and natural resources) of the economy are utilized at full employment;
- Can control demand–pull inflation by taxation and bond issuance, which remove excess money from circulation (although the political will to do so may not always exist);
- Does not need to compete with the private sector for scarce savings by issuing bonds.

Modern monetary theory is controversial and dare I say dangerous. While the framework does a better job of explaining how modern central banks actually operate, it lacks historical context. It will allow the next wave of spending of government money like we've never seen. It won't matter if the Democrats or Republicans are in charge. If the Democrats are in charge, we'll get free health care for all, free college for all, college debt forgiveness for all, and infrastructure spending. If the Republicans are in charge, we'll get stronger national policy toward isolationism, stronger military spending, potentially more tax cuts and credits, and infrastructure spending. It's all this government spending that will finally bring inflation, and inflation at a level that will help destroy the US dollar regime. It will fail like all historical government schemes because it requires force (of the government's monopoly on money) and trust (of the government.)

I would argue against MMT using the simplest of common sense. We need our system of money to represent our actual physical and economic world. Since our current physical and economic world is limited and resource-constrained, so, too, must be our money system. Since scarcity exists in our economic reality, it must exist in our money system. The day the world has infinite resources is the day we could implement MMT. That day is not today.

The Decline of the US Dollar as the World's Reserve Currency

The United States' largest export is none other than its dollar. Just less than 80% of all the world's transactions are done in US dollars. This number has nowhere to go but down. As we discussed, international banks create more dollars by creating dollar-denominated debt outside the United States. They do so to avoid currency risk for the investors. What happens when investors see the risk of holding dollars is higher and no longer want dollar-denominated debt? Starting in the late 1970s, we established the Petrodollar with Saudi Arabia. This locked in huge demand for US dollars. Russia and China are already settling oil contracts outside of US dollars. What happens when all of OPEC-plus does? The world has seen behind the curtain. They've seen that the United States is acting only in self-interest and is not managing the world's reserve currency for the benefit of everyone. Plans are already in motion to reduce US dollar dependence all over the world. What happens when those plans are fully realized? What happens when there's no longer much demand for the US dollar?

My favorite word is *entropy*. I like it for its definition. Not the one you're used to from thermodynamics but its second definition: *the slow and inevitable degradation of a system.* The global fiat monetary system is in entropy. Central banks cannot unwind this. The Fed tried a little unwind in the form of QT, as discussed, and the markets couldn't handle it, so Fed Chairman Jay Powell quickly reversed course. We won't see QT again. There is only one direction, and that's continued and ever-increasing money expansion until the system ultimately collapses. No one knows the timeline. It's probably a decade out. A sovereign debt collapse is coming – we are past the event horizon. There will be an end to the US dollar as the world's reserve currency.

The World's Intent to Reduce Dependence on the US Dollar

China, Russia, Iran, and many other countries are trying to remove the US dollar as the requirement for international trade. Prior to a few years ago, all oil required use of the US dollar to settle trades. In 2013, Russia started trying to reduce the number of transactions in US dollars for both foreign and domestic trade. In 2015, Russia and China agreed to trade oil using Chinese renminbi. Both countries have different reasons. Russia wants to operate outside of the sanctions from the United States while China sees US monetary hegemony impeding their path to becoming the next world superpower. It's estimated that the Chinese market will be the largest market, outpacing the United States, by 2025. The United States has the largest military and military budget for physical conflict, but it uses its monetary power of being the world's reserve currency every day to influence global activity. Some say the largest weapon the United States has isn't its military but the world reserve status of the US dollar, which allows the United States to influence and control so much of what goes on the world over. China wants to end that.

The End of a Sovereign Debt Cycle

All cycles come to an end and it is no different with the sovereign debt cycle. The US has a large outstanding public debt and it's getting bigger. There is nothing to indicate that this is going to get fixed. There is no plan from the government to address the public debt problem. At some point, we have to consider that we're coming to the end of a sovereign debt cycle.

It's happening. The currency is going to need restructuring or it's going to collapse. It's going to happen just as clear as the *Titanic* was going to sink after four of its hull compartments were compromised. The iceberg has hit and torn through the ship just as the public debt is tearing through our economy. This ship is going down. You have two options. You can either gently and confidently step onto a life raft to save yourself, or you can drivel to your lover about the life that she's going to have as you hang off the ass end of the ship as it's about to sink to the bottom of the ocean. The movie *Titanic* was good, but don't be Jack Dawson.

A Checklist for the End of a Sovereign Debt Cycle

Ironically, the last sovereign debt bubble was in the same year as the last global pandemic: 1918, about 100 years ago, when six of the major global reserve currencies had to devalue. That was due to World War I and started when countries began to borrow in 1914 to fund it. The Paris Peace Conference ended the war, but countries were unable to come to agreement to solve their debt problems.

This next asset bubble will be much larger than the tech bubble of 2000 or the mortgage and real estate bubble of 2008. The coming public debt bubble is going to be huge and this bubble is global since it resides inside the world's reserve currency.

Signs that we're at the end of a sovereign debt bubble are:

✓ Trade wars (to address the balance of payments problem)

✓ Beginning of currency wars

✓ Decoupling price for physical and paper gold (e.g. gold ETFs or units in trusts)

✓ Sovereign gold repatriation

✓ Global central banks buying assets other than sovereign debt: buying corporate bonds, then equities, and then eventually gold

✓ Central bank interest rates reduced to 0%

✓ Central banks expanding their balance sheets with no limits

✓ Central banks reentering a long period of gold purchasing

✓ Financial repression – negative real rates less than real rates

✓ "Temporary" restrictions of rights by government

✓ Central banks changing the rules on those they're supposed to regulate

✓ Sharp rise in CDS price (insurance) on US sovereign debt

✓ Bailouts to corporations because in a highly leveraged system

✓ Social unrest

The final end to the cycle is when:

- Gold price rises in large price spurts, that is, periods of sharp increases in the price of gold
- Capital controls – disallowing capital flight from a country
- Currency conversion controls
- Then, a sovereign debt crisis ends in one of three ways:

    1. The central banks buy all asset classes, including equities, to prop up the financial system in a continuing deflationary spiral.
    2. Interest rates rise, potentially out of the control of the central bank, into high inflation or hyperinflation.
    3. The central bank capitulates and goes back to sound money policy, creating painful austerity and balanced budget policy that is politically unpalatable, and a re-pricing event occurs.

Deflation

The status quo would be to continue in a slightly deflationary economy with anemic growth becoming the best possible outcome. If we continue to implement some of the same monetary policy as Japan, we may end up like Japan in a deflationary period that lasts two to three decades. It's still happening in Japan. Economists like Dr. Lacy Hunt believe QE and the Fed's monetary policy have a consequence. He's been almost on his own forecasting lower interest rates throughout the 2010s and he was right. Most believe that the consequence of QE is inflation, but Hunt believes that it is muted growth. Hunt lays out a case of decreasing interest rates to the 0% lower bound and slow growth as a function of those low rates and high debts. Some believe the West, and more specifically the United States, will be in low-growth-rate economies for decades to come until we deal with deficit spending and the debt problem.

Inflation

There are four factors, in general, that produce inflation. It should be stated that whether inflation occurs cannot easily be calculated by some equation. It involves the mechanics of the money supply along with factors like human psychology. The Federal Reserve plays a part – the Fed is required but is not sufficient to create inflation. We saw this from 2008 on, where the Fed increased the money supply, but we saw no inflation. The other factors that are needed to create inflation have to do with: increased economic activity that increases the velocity of money, spending by the US Treasury through fiscal policy, which needs to be involved because it manages government spending; a change in the equilibrium of production/consumption, where production on balance decreases relative to consumption or vice versa, where consumption increases on balance; or, a change in human psychology, which alters group spending to drastically increase spending based on fear or other human emotions.

Many are concerned about inflation with the Fed's balance sheet expansion in 2020. If we start to see more government spending, that would increase the chance of inflation. Moreover, if the public continues with restrictions on movement or employment, that will create inflation in consumer staples because production relative to consumption is decreased. It takes employees and labor to produce things and if we're all at home, production is decreasing. We saw this with the first shelter-in-place order of 2020. Toilet paper and bleach were hard to find in grocery stores. I can't find my favorite pickle, because I suspect they weren't able to produce their product when all the workers stayed at home. If you check prices on paper towels or bleach, you'll notice they are higher. Most experts believe inflation is coming but that it won't happen until 2022 or beyond.

Hyperinflation – Inflation, but Worse

Hyperinflation seems to be the economic fear *du jour*. However, a lot of things have to go wrong for a country to go into hyperinflation. The book *When Money Dies: The Nightmare of Deficit Spending, Devaluation, and Hyperinflation in Weimar Germany*[12] is out of print, but it's really interesting. It was written by Adam Fergusson, who is a historian, not an economist. It chronicles the death of the German mark during the Weimar Republic and what happens to a nation's currency that depreciates beyond recovery. So many people run to the idea of "hyperinflation" as if it's easy to get there. It's not.

If you're interested, read this book. It's basically the feeling of despair in prose form. The thing to get is that the people of Germany and Austria really didn't know what was going on and they kept thinking, "Well, it can't get any worse." But it did. It kept getting worse and worse and worse. You can't run from your debts, especially as a country that deficit-spends and prints money to pay for it. Someone's got to pay.

The End – A New World Reserve Currency

Everyone except the United States is clamoring for a new world reserve currency to overtake the US dollar. The Federal Reserve will fight as long as it can, perhaps a decade or two, to hold onto US monetary hegemony. With China's economy estimated to overtake that of the United States in the mid-2020s (see Figure 6.3) and with the entire world looking for a replacement, chances are slim that the United States will hold onto its dominance. There may not be a clear winner until a new world war establishes a new world order, but what was once aggregated can certainly become fractured. The world is looking for a new reserve currency and I suspect a few candidates may come onto the world stage in the years to come.

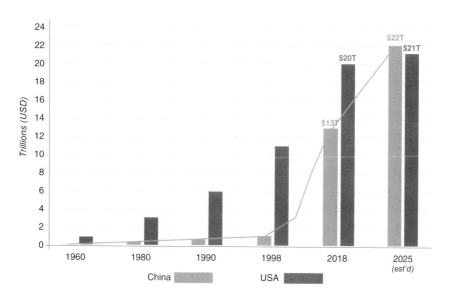

Figure 6.3 US versus China GDP
Source: "The Rise of China," S1:E3 of Netflix series *History 101.*

The Future – A Multicurrency World

I assert that we're about to enter a multicurrency world where many currencies become world reserve currencies. We are about to enter a time where there is no clear winner, perhaps only a loser – the US dollar. Right now, the US dollar is the most accepted global money and therefore has strong network effects. The US dollar is probably America's greatest export. However, as trust erodes from the United States mismanaging and misusing the world's reserve currency, everyone will be looking for options. As the US dollar is used less and less to settle global trade and as less and less debt is denominated in the US dollar, it will start to break US monetary hegemony. As the trust of the homogeneous global financial system slowly fractures, so, too, will the building blocks of capitalism. Loans collateralized with US Treasuries will be at the front and center as the strong collateral turns to weak collateral – banks, nations, and other lenders will make their margin calls.

Right now, there is no other option that could replace the US dollar as a world reserve currency. It's the biggest, most liquid, and most trusted, and it was how the world was set up after Bretton Woods. The Japanese yen couldn't take over due to Japan's demographics and other economic issues. The euro couldn't take over with the current NIRP policies and all the problems they are having right now at the currency level and at the economic level. The Chinese yuan lacks trust and is currently informally pegged to the US dollar via a host of measures that aim to keep it devalued relative to the US dollar. So, there is no fiat currency out there that could take over.

There is no one currency that could take over, but there are several that could share the job of reserve currency. One currency that global central banks are adding to the balance sheets is gold. Most countries in the East are adding a lot of gold to their central banks. That includes Russia, China, Poland, India, UAE, Qatar, and others. The only central banks that aren't adding gold are in the West, including United States, the UK, France, and Italy. Gold has been a store of value for millennia and when confidence is shaken, central banks will add more gold. However, I don't think we would ever go back to an international gold standard because it's incompatible with central banking – I don't see central banks relinquishing their control.[13] Gold is a reserve currency that will play a role in a multicurrency future. Here are a few more to be considered and developed.

Terra – A Commodity-based Currency

One idea that was considered was the idea of a new commodity-backed currency, called the Terra. It would be based on a basket of commodities and therefore inflation-resistant by definition. This idea was proposed in 2001 by Bernard Lietaer, but not much has happened since.[14]

The SDR – Special Drawing Rights, A Foreign Exchange Reserve Asset

Special drawing rights are foreign exchange reserve assets managed by the International Monetary Fund (IMF). They have existed since the late 1960s, but were another idea proposed after the Great Recession by the IMF to help solve the financial crisis. This would be a nonsovereign monetary instrument that can be used as a reserve asset that is not tied to a specific country and therefore not maintained or affected by one specific country's economy or central bank action. In its current modern form, an SDR would be based on a basket of fiat currencies. While this instrument would address some of the problems present in today's global monetary system, it still wouldn't address all the problems that come with fiat currency.

The Bancor – A Supranational Fiat Currency

The bancor is a conceptualized supranational currency thought up by John Maynard Keynes. The idea was a global fiat currency – a currency that would be a world reserve currency used for international trade settlement. The benefit of this fiat currency is that it would be a reserve currency that was not connected or governed by any one particular sovereign nation and therefore not influenced or affected by one nation's fiscal and monetary policy. It was proposed at Bretton Woods by the United Kingdom but not accepted. While it does not exist today, it wouldn't surprise me if its concept made a comeback.

The Central Bank Digital Currency (CBDC)

Central bank digital currencies are digital assets that are minted and maintained by a government. CBDCs are sovereign digital currencies and are managed by a central bank. They are different from cryptocurrencies because they do not rely on cryptography to secure scarcity and they are not aiming to eliminate a third party to allow for peer-to-peer transactions. Central banks will still be the trusted third party that manages these CBDCs.

Now that the entire world has seen behind the curtain and gotten confirmation that the United States will act only in its own self-interest, every other country will be designing and deploying their own central bank digital currency in an effort to minimize the impact of US policy. The entire world, but especially Russia and China, are sick of paying, through exports inflation, for all the things the US deficit allows the United States to buy. They know they will not be paid back with principal that maintains purchasing power parity. All governments are actively reducing their US dollar-dependence and the effect of US policy on their local economies. They want more effective monetary and fiscal policies for themselves. Those who have large negative trade account balances with the United States will want to impact trade policies and control their own payments. Finally, all countries want more autonomy, surveillance capabilities, and control. They want their own data gathering capabilities and their own controls on payments and want to eliminate US monetary hegemony. CBDCs go a long way as a tool for giving countries what they want.[15]

China's DC/EP – Their Plan for Digital Currency

China has its own CBDC called the DC/EP (digital currency/electronic payment). They want to build a digital asset, that may be partially backed by gold, that could become a world reserve currency. This would solve a lot of their problems with the US dollar as described above. It could be the case that the East uses one reserve currency and the West uses another. Countries are vying for position to provide a solution to the fall of the US dollar, and China is in the pole position.

Libra-like Currency – A Private Digital Currency

Facebook has created a group of corporations called Calibra, which initially created a digital currency called Libra. This was to be a digital asset backed by a basket of fiat currencies. Calibra and Facebook ran into strong headwinds in the form of government regulators who pushed back hard on the release of the Libra token. They have now moved to the idea of a wallet, called Novi, which will hold sovereign stablecoins,

CBDCs, or other. It's not impossible for another Silicon Valley startup or big tech company to come in and create their own version of a private digital currency.

Bitcoin – A Digital Commodity Currency

There is another option, which is a nonsovereign, decentralized, capped-supply, sound money asset: Bitcoin. This currency aims to separate money and state. We explore this option next in Part II.

Cryptocurrency – A Future Option

There is a final option, which is some future cryptocurrency that is nonsovereign, scarce, decentralized, and cryptographically secure. However, as you'll read in the following section, I think this has a very rare chance of happening. The way Bitcoin came into existence and the fact that no one particular group owns or controls it, coupled with the fact that it's scarce and the most accepted cryptocurrency with the greatest network effects, makes it extremely difficult for another cryptocurrency to come in and take its place.

An Analysis of Odds – Which Has What Chance

With an understanding of what creates monetary value, and therefore what is a reliable instrument of good money, let us analyze these options for the coming multicurrency world. The framework to analyze these currency candidates are the six characteristics of good money. Since all the candidates have portability, divisibility, durability, and uniformity, there's no need to analyze these attributes. The focus is digging deeper into scarcity and acceptability. This also breaks down to supply and demand. If a currency can alter its supply, more than a supply schedule, then it's not really scarce. If it has a fixed supply schedule, then it follows the properties of scarcity. Additionally, if a currency is usable by more customers and vendors, has higher network effects, and has higher demand, then it has higher acceptability. Factors that comprise acceptability include: users' trust and confidence in the money system; the network effects of the total users of a money system (since money is a network good); and the market adoption as the rate of adoption of a money system. Let's use these two properties to analyze the long-term potential for success in a multicurrency world.

The terra is conceptual at present. Since it's commodity-based, it would have scarcity; however, it has no acceptability, no one is using it, and consequently it has no network effects. The SDR has some limited use, and therefore some acceptability, but it's based on a basket of fiat currencies and therefore has no real scarcity. The bancor too is conceptual; it's based on fiat currencies and therefore has no scarcity. It could be better than the US dollar in that it's not managed by a single country, but it is unlikely to reach the network effects of the US dollar faster than the fall of the US dollar due to its lack of scarcity. CBDCs have yet to come into form and their success will largely depend on their implementation. If countries continue having central banks, which is very likely the case, then they will most likely not implement sound money because of the constraints to spending. If CBDCs are implemented as their analog fiat currency counterparts, then they will suffer the same fate, long-term. CBDCs can co-opt the networks of the fiat currencies they replace or augment, so their acceptability may be high. Again, their failure comes from their lack of scarcity and lack of being sound money. The long-term success of China's DC/EP depends on whether they want to back the digital currency with digital or precious metal commodities. Private digital currencies can gain acceptability quite rapidly. Just think – if Facebook did implement Libra, it wouldn't take very long to get its two billion users to use the currency. The question of long-term success comes down to scarcity. For a private digital currency to gain long-term viability, it would need to have a fixed supply schedule.

The US dollar could go back to a gold standard and increase its long-term chance for success, but the pain that would have to be endured to get the country back into fiscal discipline is practically impossible, politically speaking. Bitcoin is the only candidate, other than gold, that addresses the issue of scarcity. With its fixed supply schedule, Bitcoin is sound money. The outstanding question remains, how fast can it build adoption and network effects? Other cryptocurrencies may have a chance in the future, but I doubt they will overtake Bitcoin because of how Bitcoin came into existence, which we discuss in Chapter 7.

The most probable outcome of this multicurrency world is that central banks continue to exist with the fiat money they govern, used locally within each of their sovereign boundaries, and a new global digital market grows on the backbone of digital sound money (Bitcoin and stablecoins, discussed in Part II). With all the market and political forces stirring around the globe, and with all the complexity of the global markets as we know them, adding an additional layer of digital capital markets makes the most pragmatic sense – that is, until the underlying global central banking model breaks. The race is on.

PART II
THE RISE OF BLOCKCHAIN
AND THE AGE
OF AUTONOMY

Nothing is stronger than an idea whose time has come!
— Victor Hugo

Knowing where you are in a variety of cycles is critical when plotting a financial course of action. Locating where you are in the cycle and then coupling that with what you see coming improves anyone's investing and risk management skill. Analysis of the past and the future, coupled together, is what creates a compelling investment strategy.

Technology and innovation play essential roles in the progress of an economic cycle. A savvy investor can glean a lot from analyzing the long-wave economic cycle combined with the long-wave debt cycle. Throughout the 2020s, we are going to continue in a deleveraging process, though I expect it to be volatile. Unfortunately, long-term public debt is ballooning. The amount of monetary expansion in the first two quarters of 2020 is more than all the QE used to battle the Great Recession of 2008. Central banks are trying to solve a debt problem with more debt. Common sense tells us that won't work. One cannot fight fire with fire. At this point in the cycle, central banks are the problem, not the solution.

The sovereign debt crisis is going to accelerate because governments are about to add fiscal policy to the already-existing monetary policy that is contributing to public debt exploding. Governments around the world are now looking to increase deficit spending. As commercial banks start to fuse together with their central banks, and as central banks start to fuse together with government treasury departments, the rules of the game will change. The #1 debate in finance and investing is whether we are all going to experience inflation or deflation. The answer to this question will drive global investment strategies in the years to come. It's important, as an intelligent investor, that you have a plan for both.

The survellience state is here. Survellience capitalism is here. As global citizens, we are at a crossroads. Either we stand up for our privacy or we don't. The solution is the proper application of technology. This will become more and more important as citizens' lives and potential opportunities get filtered by algorithms evaluating not the citizen themselves, but their digital twin. We all have a digital twin on the Internet. It's the set of profiles and information from us and about us all over the web. Over time, AI algorithms that we never see or directly interact with will determine what options get presented to people throughout their lives – from insurance rates to job offers to what schools your kids can go to. We have a chance to take back individual control and individual privacy. It will take a fundamental reevaluation of what is important – privacy or free services and convenience.

A new decentralized digital economy is being built where sound money is required but not sufficient. New forms of capital and capital systems are being built in this new long-wave economic cycle – with it come new means of production.

In Part II, I outline what the next long-wave economic cycle looks like, what is driving it, and how one can take advantage of it. A new cluster of technological innovations are hitting the main stage. These technologies are transforming what's possible in the financial system. An economy using the US dollar is built on trust. An economy built on blockchain may not require it. Bitcoin doesn't require trust; it's got math underpinning it. A new digital financial system is being built where anyone can access money and financial services like lending, trading, insurance, and borrowing without the need of permission or a trusted third party to settle the transaction. The incumbent often falls due to a failure of imagination. We've seen it many times in the past in the innovation of communications, transportation, and electrification. This time around the wheel may be no different – this time the innovation is within the financial system. As we discuss through Part II of the book, this fundamental axiom, along with a cluster of new technologies, will drive the next wave of the economic cycle.

7

A Digital Commodity: Bitcoin as Digital Gold

Why do you stay in prison when the door is so wide open?

— Rumi

Bitcoin is a new form of money. What makes it so transformational is that it is a bearer asset with no counterparty risk that can be transacted peer-to-peer (P2P) without an intermediary either creating the money or requiring a transaction settlement. Bitcoin is thought of as digital gold,[1] but said better it's digitally based money, and as such it's the reserve asset for the next digital financial revolution.

The innovation of Bitcoin isn't at odds with the status quo. The current sovereign fiat monetary system is not going away anytime soon, nor does this book aim to forecast a future where bitcoin becomes the world reserve currency. On the flipside, I'm not excluding that as a possibility, either. Bitcoin provides a free-market alternative for a store of value and a reserve asset, and that is its power. It provides a "check and balance," so to speak, from the constant manipulation of money supply by central banks via monetary policy. As people start to lose increments of faith that their fiat currency du jour is unable to maintain its purchasing power, they are going to look for alternatives, especially when their currency's bonds do not produce income.

Bitcoin is a digital commodity. A commodity is defined as "a useful or valuable thing." It's a digital commodity because it's produced and used in the digital world. Just like gold miners need to expend work by labor, equipment, and energy to produce gold, bitcoin miners need to expend work by labor, equipment, and energy to produce bitcoin. Bitcoin is not just a string of characters – verifiable work needs to be completed in order for bitcoin to be minted. There is a cost of production, just like with gold or any other precious metal; and unlike fiat currency, bitcoin is not an attempt to create value out of thin air. Production costs exist at market prices at the time each bitcoin is minted, whereas with central banks, there is no actual cost of production for fiat currency. Central banks print money out of thin air. This is a key distinction – bitcoin has a real cost of production. And, if you think the optimal cryptocurrency would be a cryptocurrency backed by gold in the future, then I recommend you reread this paragraph.

In 1984, Nobel prize winner and famous Austrian economist F. A. Hayek said, "I don't believe we shall ever have a good money again before we take the thing out of the hands of government, that is, we can't take it violently out of the hands of government, all we can do is by some sly roundabout way introduce something that they can't stop."[2] Bitcoin is that sly roundabout way.

A Primer on Bitcoin

The first time I heard the word "bitcoin" was in 2012, on the TV series *The Good Wife*. In the show, they talked about a cryptocurrency. I had to look it up for myself. I was fascinated by it, along with The Onion Router (TOR) browser and the idea of the dark net. Could we really have an anonymous Web? My background is in computer science and specifically in using artificial intelligence for anomaly detection identification on a computer network, so I was curious whether the TOR browser and Bitcoin were truly anonymous. What I found was that the TOR browser is basically anonymous; however, Bitcoin is pseudonymous, not anonymous. Bitcoin, with a capitalized "B," is used for the blockchain network and entire system while bitcoin, with a lowercase "b," is used for the cryptocurrency (abbreviated BTC). Any way you slice it, I saw that the technology was improving and there was innovation happening for sure.

I kept an eye on bitcoin the whole time it charged up to $800 the first time back in 2013. It then dropped something like 90%, and

I put it away as a thought experiment for 3½ years. In 2016, though, bitcoin came back on my radar. It had survived a few events I assumed would kill it. In 2014, I had read a book by Nassim Nicolas Taleb called *Antifragile: Things That Gain from Disorder.*[3] The book was very thought-provoking to me. In the book Taleb defines a new distinction: antifragile. It's the opposite of fragile, and I don't mean resilient or robust. In the first chapter of the book, Taleb gives an example of someone shipping wine glasses to Central Siberia. One would write "fragile" on the side of the package because the contents are easily breakable, they are fragile. Then he poses a question to the reader: What is the exact opposite of "fragile"?

Upon further examination, resilient, robust items neither break nor improve, so in the shipping package example, you would not need to write "robust" on the package. In our language, we have yet to distinguish a definition of the opposite of fragile and Taleb creates such a concept, antifragile. Antifragile is the idea of a characteristic of something that gains from disorder. In the shipping package example, it would be an item that improves if mishandled. An antifragile package would have "please handle carelessly" written on its side.

Taleb gives a good analogy for how to think about the triad of the concepts of fragile, robust, and antifragile. One example is to think about Greek mythology. An example of fragile in this context would be the Sword of Damocles and the Rock of Tantalus. An example of robust would be the Phoenix and an example of antifragile in Greek mythology would be the Hydra: when you cut one head off, two grow back in its place.

So, how would such a concept apply to investment? Well, an antifragile asset would be one that gains from disorder and from chaos. Economies and markets are getting more and more complex, and with the complexity comes fragility.[4] In some ways, gold is antifragile, though it's not the *asset* of gold, but rather the *perception* of gold, that improves with disorder. The same is true of bitcoin. As the economy and the markets, with their increasingly complex investment instruments like derivatives and CDOs (collateralized debt obligations), CLOs (collateralized loan obligations), CDSs (credit default swaps), and the alphabet soup of acronyms for invented financial instruments, continue to add complexity, they continue to add fragility. This makes investment options like gold and bitcoin more and more appealing.

Bitcoin has anecdotal proof that it is antifragile. It takes a licking and keeps on ticking. It's survived many catastrophes and market crashes over its 11-year existence. Bitcoin has survived four full cycles of bull and bear markets, where the bear markets saw the price of bitcoin drop over

70% each time. It's also survived many exchanges being hacked, with the early and major hack of Mt. Gox, which was the largest exchange in the early days, back in 2014. When it started as an exchange in 2011, Mt. Gox was the only real exchange where bitcoin holders could trade their bitcoin. In 2013 and 2014, it handled 70% of all bitcoin transactions. It was hacked in 2014 and there was a significant loss: 850,000 bitcoin were stolen. At the time, it was unclear whether bitcoin itself could survive such a scandal. But it did. Bitcoin survived the March correction of 2020 quite well, too. In the pandemic chaos of 2020, bitcoin has outperformed all other asset classes, including stocks, bonds, oil, real estate, and gold, at the timing of this book.

Primitives of Bitcoin

There are a lot of characteristics of bitcoin that make it an interesting technology to implement and an interesting asset to own.

Pseudonymous, not Anonymous

The Bitcoin network is pseudonymous but not anonymous. This is different from what we have to go through currently in the normal course of a financial transaction using a credit card. Customer data such as name, address, and other personal information are attached to everyday financial transactions in the current system. This allows surveillance capitalism to continue and to grow. That's not so with Bitcoin. Personal information is not required to complete a transaction.

Just to be clear, it's not completely private, either. Anyone can see the entire ledger with addresses and amounts. Any user of the Bitcoin blockchain can see transactions moving amounts from address to address. Through antimoney laundering (AML) and Know Your Customer (KYC) processes, plus Internet meta-data, one can tie a user to a Bitcoin address. Companies out there like Chainalysis do this as their primary service.

Decentralized Ledger

An open, decentralized ledger is a balanced design feature that allows transactions to happen in a trust-minimized environment without the need of personal information but allows anyone see the ledger to verify all account balances to verify reconciliation. The open ledger is copied to a network of decentralized nodes running the bitcoin software. All the nodes manage their own copy of the data. It's global.

No one owns or controls the Bitcoin blockchain network. There are an estimated 100,000 miners running the software who are helping to secure the Bitcoin network. There is no corporation or government that owns or controls Bitcoin. There are developers who can upgrade the software but only after bringing three large groups of users to consensus. Bitcoin, as a network, is decentralized. This is highly advantageous when compared to centralized currencies, especially those that can be manipulated by a central authority.

Proof of Work (PoW)

A proof of work is a function that is meant to be difficult to produce (costly, time-consuming) but easily verified by others. Bitcoin uses the Hashcash[5] proof-of-work system.[6] This proof-of-work consensus mechanism is used in Bitcoin for block generation where the first miner who solves the proof gets to produce the new block of confirmed transactions and receives a mining reward (newly minted bitcoin) for the service of securing the network. This is novel because it provides built-in incentives for miners to compete against each other to secure the network and also solves the double-spend problem (discussed in Chapter 8), which is the potential of the same single coin being spent more than once. Solving the double-spend problem is what creates actual digital scarcity, which has never been achieved prior to Bitcoin.

Provable Scarcity

Prior to Bitcoin, if you sent a digital file, it was still only a copy of the file. Companies made improvements on digital rights management, but that required a centralized authority to create and manage those rights. There was no way to have verifiable uniqueness in the digital world without some sort of third-party intermediary verification process. Bitcoin has created a provable digital scarcity intrinsically, without the need for third-party verification/validation, and that's transformational.

There will only ever be 21 million bitcoin. As of mid-2020, about 18.5 million have already been mined. This makes bitcoin more scarce than gold in that the inflation rate of bitcoin gets cut in half every four years while gold stays roughly the same or reacts to price elasticity. There has never been a harder, more scarce money than bitcoin.

Unspent Transaction Outputs (UTXOs)

A UTXO is a construct in a specific type of blockchain. It's an output of a blockchain transaction that has not been spent, that is, used as an input in a new transaction. It's the change left over to the owner after a transaction is complete and may be used for future transactions by the wallet owner. UTXOs are a critical function in how the accounting system of the ledger works, and they can be analyzed in order to understand the current state of the blockchain network. They are one of the mechanisms that provide the capability of triple-entry accounting, which I discuss later in this chapter. A simple example might be if a person holds three bitcoin in their wallet and spends 2.5 BTC. The 2.5 BTC get sent to the vendor and 0.5 BTC is the unspent amount left over in the wallet – the UTXO.

Multisig Feature

One of the key features of Bitcoin, as a protocol, is *multisig*, which refers to the requirement of more than one signature to sign off on a transaction. It allows for one Bitcoin address to divvy up roles and responsibilities. You can think of a business check that requires the signature of the CEO and the CFO on amounts over $10,000. Multisig also provides the feature of removing a single point of failure – if one key signature gets hacked, you won't get all your bitcoin stolen. Additionally, if you had a single-signature wallet and you lost the keys, there's really nothing you can do to regain control of that Bitcoin address. There are ways to set up the multsig feature to allow for redundancy. This is a critical feature as Bitcoin increases in value and establishes itself as a reserve asset.

Digital and Internet-based

That Bitcoin is digital helps advance one of the six characteristics of good money. Good money needs to be portable, divisible, scarce, acceptable, durable, and uniform.[7] Because Bitcoin is digital, it's easily transferable over the Internet, which makes it portable. It's divisible down to eight decimal places, so that makes it divisible and uniform. It's probably more accurate to just say digital- and not Internet-based because a user can sign and send a bitcoin transaction over a shortwave radio[8] without using the Internet at all.

Nonsovereign Money

That bitcoin is nonsovereign gives it an incredibly valuable characteristic over sovereign money. As a reminder, sovereign money is currency
managed and controlled by a government. It's true that sovereign money
is protected by a country's army. However, nonsovereign money means
that it is not involved in a state's political system. It is free from being
manipulated. If something is politically expedient, it's almost guaranteed
to be a bad idea. The separation of money and state is a hugely valuable
characteristic of Bitcoin. As most people familiar with the situation will
tell you, the current world reserve currency, the US dollar, is causing
massive problems as outlined in Part I of this book. The next world
reserve currency will most likely be a nonsovereign money system.

Peer-to-Peer (P2P)

Bitcoin is P2P and does not require permission or a third party. This is
unlike the way money works today. All money in the traditional capital
system requires a third-party intermediary, whether it's a central bank to
issue the money or a commercial bank to settle a transaction. This layer is
not required with bitcoin and removes the friction (cost) and counterparty
risk. It also does not require permission or trust to complete a transaction.
This is transformational and will reduce the cost of financing transactions
as well as allow for many more people to use this new digital financial
system. Being P2P and permissionless makes it more acceptable than any
other money in existence. It is transacted around the world. As of 2020
it can be traded for 180 fiat currency pairs.[9] As previously stated, Bitcoin
does not require permission to be transacted as no trusted third party is
required to settle transactions. This means neither party needs an account
with a bank or to sign up for a credit account to be able to use bitcoin.

Seizure Resistant

Bitcoin is a bearer asset, which means if you hold the private keys, you
fully own and control the asset. This makes it seizure-resistant. It's the
combination of being decentralized, permissionless, and secure that creates its seizure-resistance. That's important to a lot of investors even today.
It's certainly one of the appeals of a Swiss bank account. It's away and
out of the control of the US government. Bitcoin is almost a Swiss bank

account 2.0. If you hold the private keys privately, you can own millions of dollars' worth of an asset and move across any international boundaries, knowing your assets can't easily be seized.

What's Unique About Bitcoin

While there may be more than 5,000 crypto assets, there is only one bitcoin. It was the first, and there are many characteristics of this crypto asset that make it special and unique. It's *the* asset where an investor is looking for a store of value. This has been proven over the past decade in many ways.

First Hard-Capped Digital Currency with Known Supply Schedule

Bitcoin is the first digital currency to exist with a P2P architecture, a hard-capped and known supply of 21 million bitcoin, and a known disinflationary supply schedule. Every 210,000 blocks that get produced, which happens about every four years, the block reward decreases by half (see Figure 7.1). This means, too, that the inflation rate decreases by half because the only way for bitcoin to get minted into the system is through the block reward to miners. More about the miners and mining in subsequent sections of this book.

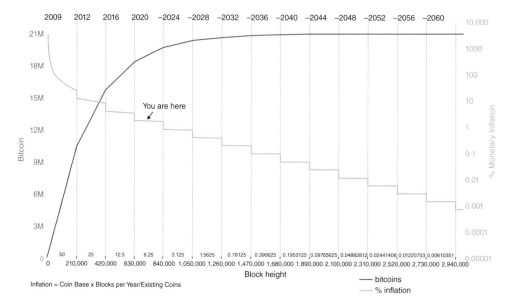

Figure 7.1 Bitcoin Monetary Inflation
Source: Bashco.

Prior to the first such halving, dubbed "the Halvening" or "Halvening Event," the mining reward was 50 bitcoin. After the first Halvening event, it was 25 bitcoin, and after the second Halvening event it was 12.5. After the third Halvening event in 2020, the mining reward was set at 6.25 bitcoin. A block reward is delivered when a block is produced, which on average is every 10 minutes. If the competition for solving a block reward is high with a lot of computing power or a high "hash rate" focused on solving the complicated mathematical puzzle, the blocks of transactions will start to be produced faster than every 10 minutes and the difficulty-adjustment of the bitcoin software will make it harder to solve, requiring even more computing power to produce a block. If less competition happens, it will take longer for a block to be produced and the difficulty will decrease. This tension is built into the system from competition and sets how much hash power it takes for the proof-of-work consensus mechanism to get the mining reward. This is the incentive for miners to invest in their operations, which increases the security of the Bitcoin blockchain. More detail of this topic is covered in Chapter 8.

Bitcoin's Immaculate Conception

Satoshi Nakamoto invented Bitcoin. It was released conceptually via a whitepaper titled *Bitcoin: A Peer-to-Peer Electronic Cash System*.[10] However, Satoshi is a pseudonym. No one knows whether Satoshi is a he, she, or they (group, not individual pronoun, though I guess we could ask them their pronoun too if we ever figured out who they were). There is no corporation behind bitcoin; it is truly decentralized. This makes it unique, or at least very rare, in the crypto asset universe. The first time I heard the phrase "immaculate conception" applied to Bitcoin was with Nic Carter as a guest on Peter McCormack's *What Bitcoin Did* podcast,[11] but the term most likely was initially used on the Bitcointalk forum[12] years before that. I think the term is appropriate and descriptive about Bitcoin. It refers to the fact that Bitcoin had one creator that is unknown to this day, that there is no figurehead or corporation backing it, and therefore no entity that a government could go after; it came about in a truly decentralized way and most other cryptocurrencies cannot declare that fact; and finally, it's the first time all of these revolutionary technologies are used in one application that is truly transformational.

Bitcoin had no initial coin offering (ICO). It had no premine where it set aside some allocation of the crypto asset for its inventor's use before anyone else could mine it. Bitcoin started running and anyone who ran the blockchain node and miner's software had a chance at receiving the miner reward. There are few crypto assets that can make this claim. Crypto assets that are tokens don't count because they aren't mined. Any crypto asset that had a premine doesn't count, either. This leaves a handful of crypto assets that have followed under this classification, and I think it's an important classification to consider as an investor. All of these characteristics and events helped mold the completely unique crypto asset that is bitcoin.

Triple-Entry Accounting

One of the significant advancements of blockchain technology that is not heralded enough, in my opinion, is the popularization of what is known as triple-entry accounting. In order to understand this, let's first look at the origins of accounting and ledgers.

A ledger is a book or a collection in which accounts are recorded. Ledgers aren't new. In fact, they were first used more than 7,000 years ago in ancient Mesopotamia and were used to track transactions and goods. That was the origin of single-entry accounting. Management is simple – it's like a checkbook. Every transaction gets written down for each account. Every company, entity, or organization in the world that is doing any business must have some kind of ledger to track its fiscal state of being, inventory, and/or items of value.

Single-entry accounting evolved into double-entry accounting, which simply means that each and every transaction is recorded in two accounts. One account is always debited, and another is always credited. As an example, let's say a company owes a vendor $100, and the company wants to pay that vendor in full. When paid, the vendor account is credited with $100, showing that there is no additional balance owed. Simultaneously, the company's cash account is debited, showing a reduction in cash by the $100. The concept of double-entry accounting is that one is always able to see where funds come from, where they go, and the complete fiscal picture at any given time. The advent of double-entry accounting has been attributed to Friar Luca Pacioli, who published the first book on double-entry accounting in 1494, and this has been the standard for the past 500 years.

This is all well and good; however, there is one missing piece. As evidenced by Al Capone, just because there is a set of books does not mean that it is accurate. So how do we trust that the books are not "cooked"? Today in the world of traditional finance this is addressed via complex audits – third-party verifications – combined with a healthy dose of trust, as the auditors themselves must be trusted. Even then, there is no guarantee that an audited set of books is the real, correct, or, indeed, only set. A great example of this was the Enron scandal in 2001, where even though books were kept and audited, there were still multiple sets.

This brings us to triple-entry accounting. Triple-entry accounting was invented in 1989 by Yuri Ijiri to very little fanfare. Its real breakthrough is that it requires a third party to guarantee that double-entry transactions are in fact valid as they are written. In this way it is much like a real-time audit and formalization of each transaction that is known to an independent group or groups. This is important, as it is a way of agreeing on objective economic reality. (Had Capone been alive, he would not have been a fan.)

You've probably never heard of triple-entry accounting, as there was never a practical way to implement it until blockchain technology. Blockchains are public, decentralized ledgers. This is truly the ultimate verification and validation system, as anyone can find any transaction at any time, unchanged after written (immutable) and visible to all. Important to note is that the system does all of this without the need to trust an auditor. Had we lived in a world of triple-entry accounting back in the days of Enron, we would have had no Enron.

As another example of public interest, in May 2020 there was quite a fervor about some BTC that was moved from the very first wallet address to a different place on the network. Many speculated that this was Nakamoto moving his/her/their original coins, and it created much interest. The brilliance of this was that *everyone* could see that the move happened. Despite laws and regulations, especially regarding insider trading, we just don't see this kind of transparency in modern financial markets. On the Bitcoin network we did, and that was because we have (maybe for the first time in history) true transactional ledger transparency.

Bitcoin as a Hedge Against Global Monetary Policy

In 2020, bitcoin started in a rising trend with the price around $7,200 level – and it shows no sign of slowing down. This has a flurry of people wanting to know more about bitcoin and wondering if it's a good time to invest in crypto assets. However, it's important to understand exactly what bitcoin is first. It's not a stock or a traditional investment but is a currency in and of itself. It's classified as a commodity in the United States by the Commodity and Futures Trading Commission (CFTC). There will only ever be 21 million bitcoin and that fixed supply is part of the reason why it's so enticing.

Bitcoin is interesting because it's a hedge, or insurance policy, against governments manipulating and destroying the value or purchasing power of their currency. In times of financial distress or during a cycle of deleveraging, central banks will print money to stimulate the economy. They do so at the expense of savers. Bitcoin has a fixed supply, so holders of bitcoin can rest assured that no third party or intermediary is printing more, thus destroying its purchasing power. Bitcoin is a store of value during this period of unsound money policy.

As discussed, national debt is increasing at a higher rate than ever before due to the pandemic. Many people project that the total national debt will be between $27 trillion and $31 trillion by the end of the year. The Fed has announced QE infinity. By many estimates, there are well over $200 trillion in unfunded liabilities[13] in the form of Social Security and Medicare entitlements that are starting to be used *en masse* by the Baby Boomer generation. Interest rates are bottoming out; stocks are volatile with political turmoil rising in the United States and abroad. Fear surrounding the economy is building and people aren't sure where to put their money. A lot of people have heard of bitcoin but think it is way too risky and aren't sure how to purchase it or how its value compares to that of other currencies or commodities. However, there are plenty of reasons why bitcoin could be an interesting investment and a case can be made that it's far riskier *not to have* a little in a portfolio.

On the Rise

In early August 2020, the S&P 500 was trading in negative territory at roughly −0.3%. The SPDR Gold Shares ($GLD) were up +18.0%, the SPDR Total Bond Index ($BND) was up 6.9%, the iShares Emerging Market Stock Index ($EEM) was down −3.0%, and the Vanguard Real

Estate Investment Trust Index ($VNQ) was down −14.3%. Bitcoin, however, climbed to +65.0% just in the seven months of 2020. It's been rising for the past decade and it looks like it will only continue to do so. This is because the investment community sees its scarcity value and that it holds value relative to its fiat currency counterparts. As more and more governments continue to print more and more money, bitcoin's hard, scarce, digital, and decentralized nature looks more attractive. We're starting to see public companies incorporate bitcoin in the treasury management.[14]

Cashless Economies

Many countries, like Sweden[15] and Israel,[16] are looking to go cashless. As central banks around the globe continue to print money, paper money loses more and more value. Many people say they don't need cash around for anything anymore. It's becoming a liability, and even retailers and vendors prefer card- or phone payments. Consumers are interested in the privacy and autonomy of their money that they get with the store of value — and that is what bitcoin can provide. A lot of countries, like India, are even getting rid of their top denominations[17] in their currency in order to reduce corruption. Larry Summers, the former Treasury Secretary and director of the National Economic Council in the White House, also thinks it's time to scrap the $100 bill.[18] There's a linkage between high-denomination notes and crime, and he argues that shifting to cashless economies or other, safer forms of currency is going to be much better for investors and for society. Will that further the surveillance state?

Bitcoin has seen some volatility over time, but the metric on it continues trending downward. As it becomes more stable, bitcoin will be involved in more real-world transactions, making it a more legitimate currency not backed by any particular government. Instead, people will only have to rely on technical progression, which seems to have no problem garnering faith even in turbulent economic times.

The Chinese yuan has been devalued[19] many times and is now at its lowest rate against the US dollar since March 2011. The Chinese are also intervening in equities and have suspended trading in their markets on multiple occasions. Financial experts like George Soros[20] think we are on the brink of a collapse like the 2008 crisis all over again. These are the types of events that panic investors and make assets much riskier. Crypto assets like bitcoin can diversify and weather dislocations in global markets and can help keep money more secure, even in rocky years, over time.

Bitcoin as Sound Money

Bitcoin is sound money. It does not have counterparty risk and is not a liability on another party's balance sheet. Bitcoin is thought of as digital gold, as previously stated. When monetary systems were backed by real, commodity-backed money like gold, as we talked about in Part I of this book, economies entered into sound money periods. The money system provided its core functionality, which is to facilitate transactions and specialization within an economy. When fiat currency, or credit-backed money, is used, economies enter into unsound money periods. As we've seen time and time again in history, bad things happen during unsound money periods. If you haven't yet read *The Bitcoin Standard* by Saifedean Ammous,[21] I highly recommend it because he goes into great detail on this topic. Bitcoin, as sound money, gives us a chance to use an alternative money system and return ourselves to a period of sound money again. A new decentralized digital financial system can exist without requiring bitcoin to be the world's reserve currency.

The Bitcoin Halvening Event

The Bitcoin Halvening Event is built into the bitcoin software and controls the supply issuance of new bitcoin. The mining reward, which is how newly minted bitcoin enters the world, is cut in half every four years. This creates a transparent and reliable money supply issuance schedule that is disinflationary by reducing consistently over time.

The Bitcoin Halvening Event has happened three times in bitcoin's history. The first was in 2012, the second in 2016, and the third in 2020. For the first two events, this was a massively bullish time for bitcoin one to nine months after the event, with bitcoin increasing in value some 10 times, each time. We'll wait to see through 2021 how the third event turns out, but at the time of the writing of this book, most investors were quite bullish on the Halvening Event. Some of that enthusiasm came from an analysis published in 2020 that took a price model used for precious metals and applied it to bitcoin. In 2020, anyone who knew about bitcoin has probably heard of the stock-to-flow model.

Scarcity Value and the Stock-to-Flow Model

In early 2020, before the pandemic, I was a panelist at a couple of registered investment advisor (RIA) conferences in Florida. Ric Edelman, the famous RIA with his radio show and outreach, was putting on a series of events about digital assets in order to help educate the financial community about Bitcoin. Ric is doing a fantastic job educating the financial community on the benefits of portfolio diversification using bitcoin through the RIA Digital Assets Council (RIADAC). The goal was to continue the conversation about why bitcoin was a valuable asset to add to a total portfolio. Ric recommended to the audience an allocation of just 1% to bitcoin and showed several scenarios in which it would improve risk-adjusted returns. Ric had lined up several speakers and panelists from the crypto-investment community, of which I was one.

The first conference we did was the Inside ETFs conference. I was a panelist with two others on the digital assets track that had four or five panel discussions that day. I didn't feel I particularly read the audience well and I did not speak in a way they could receive or hear. I'm from the West Coast and I'm a technologist, so I wasn't familiar with the level of skepticism that the East Coast financial world has around digital assets. All the prior conferences where I had been a speaker were generally receptive and excited about the transformational nature of bitcoin.

The next panel came on and an executive from a very prominent investment firm from the crypto-community was onstage. An equity analyst in the crowd said she just didn't understand how bitcoin could be valued. It has no cashflows. It doesn't generate a return. "What is the basis of value?" she queried. The guy on stage had no satisfying answer. The room was tense. I thought anyone in the crypto-investment community should be able to hit this out of the park. The best answer he came up with that day was that price was set at what people were willing to pay for it. All in all, it was a bad answer.

The next conference was two days later, and it was the TDAmeritrade LINC conference. I was determined to do one thing, if just one thing, and that was to educate the financial community on how to value bitcoin. My particular panel began, and Ric Edelman was guiding our panel discussion. Finally, we got to how does an investor value bitcoin? I sat onstage with Ric Edelman and answered it like this:

> From an investment context, bitcoin is a currency and should be traded more like foreign currency (FX). Trying to compare bitcoin to a stock is like trying to compare apples and Volkswagens. You can't look at an apple and say, "Wow, this is a terrible Volkswagen. It doesn't have a steering wheel, it doesn't roll very fast, you can't put gas in it. This thing sucks." Bitcoin is an apple; it's not a Volkswagen and trying to evaluate it as such will leave you wanting.

Bitcoin is currency. You can lend it out and generate an interest rate. Moreover, in FX trading you are always long of one currency and short of another. Buying bitcoin, at least here in the United States, is you being long bitcoin and short the US dollar. Bitcoin, when compared to other currencies, stands up quite well. It's got a fixed supply. It has all the six characteristics of good money, which we'll talk about in more depth later, and there are several models for valuation.

One of the more interesting models is a price regression model called the stock-to-flow ratio (S2F). It's mentioned in Saifedean Ammous's book *The Bitcoin Standard*,[22] but it was really taken to the next level by a pseudonymous trader on Twitter called PlanB.

The S2F is a model that models scarcity value. Now, just because something is scarce doesn't mean it will hold value over time. Platinum is 30 times rarer than gold, but is it 30 times more expensive? No. It's not even as high as gold right now. Why? Something called the stock-to-flow ratio.

Conceptually, stock to flow is the relationship between how much of a scarce resource is mined and above ground being stored (stock) compared to how much can be mined in one year (flow). The reason platinum is not more expensive is that it is used in goods like phones and catalytic converters. When it gets used up, it's removed from the stock, so its stock-to-flow ratio goes down. Of the precious metals, gold has the best stock-to-flow ratio because there are literally tons of it stored, unused, and only so much of it can be pulled out of the ground each year. Over time, it's something technology has not been able to improve (the relative cost per ounce to mine). With gold, it takes a certain amount of human effort, whether literally it being a human mining it or a stored value of human effort in money that has to be expended to mine it out of the ground.

Bitcoin follows this S2F Model, too. There's a lot of it mined and only so much is released each year. On May 11, 2020, the amount to be released each year was cut in half, which means the flow is going to be cut in half. That will have a dramatic effect on price. Each time the Halvening has occurred, the price of bitcoin has eventually gone up in order of magnitude. If the model is correct, bitcoin is forecasted to hit $100,000 by the end of 2021 (see Figure 7.2).

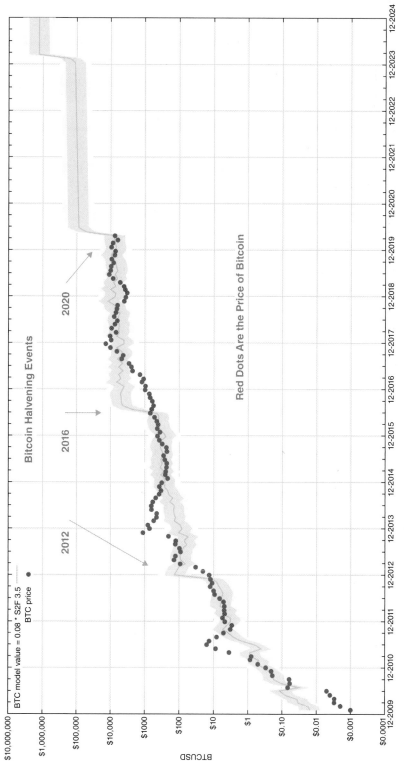

Figure 7.2 PlanB's Stock-to-Flow Model for Bitcoin, with Price

Other Ways to Value Bitcoin

When talking with anyone interested in trading bitcoin, the question inevitably asked is "How much is bitcoin worth?" It's a tough question to answer. Here are three ways to consider when evaluating what bitcoin is worth.

As an Asset/Commodity

If you want to take a stab at valuing bitcoin coming from the context that it's a commodity, one way might be to estimate it as a percentage of the total value of gold. The market cap of all the gold currently mined today is about $10 trillion.[23] Gold is a good commodity to use as a comparison because it's not consumable and is used mainly as a store of value. Today, everything is moving to digital, and bitcoin could be the store of value for future generations. If bitcoin garnered 10% of the total value of gold, then the market cap of bitcoin could rise to $1 trillion. To date, bitcoin has a market cap of over $200 billion.[24]

This is one way FundStrat Global Advisor co-founder Tom Lee is attempting to value bitcoin,[25] though he uses 5% of gold. That would still put the value of bitcoin at $500 billion, but I suspect it's much greater than that when you consider how many asset classes currently are used as a store of value where the wealthy park money for the long term. It is said that 30% of all real estate transactions in prime locations like Los Angeles and New York are unused and purchased solely as a long-term store of value. Moreover, how much fine art is purchased, stored in vaults never to be seen, but collected solely as a store of value?

As a Technology/Network

Lee also explains the network effect (its *acceptability*) and Metcalfe's Law.[26] Value is established in this way: the more engagement, the more value gets created. As more and more people use bitcoin, the higher the value will be because of the network effect. This focus on bitcoin as a technology or social network conveys the strong opportunity for nonlinear growth.

Seven Network Effects on Bitcoin

Bitcoin is a network good and, as such, has network effects. The Bitcoin blockchain has the biggest network of users, which is one reason it has the highest value. Both acceptability and scarcity play a role in its value. The bitcoin investor Trace Mayer has done a lot of work outlining the seven network effects bitcoin will eventually have on the financial market. They are:

1. **Speculation** – Every speculative dollar that trades in bitcoin increases the value.

2. **Merchant Adoption** – Every new merchant that accepts bitcoin increases the value of the network.

3. **Consumer Adoption** – Every time a new consumer can buy something with bitcoin the value increases.

4. **Security/Incentives** – As the speculators as well as merchant and consumer adoption raise the price, miners' and nodes' incentives are increased.

5. **Developer Mindshare** – As the moat around bitcoin increases, so does the value.

6. **Financialization** – As more financial products, like options on cryptocurrency and insurance, get created, there is more value added to the network.

7. **Adoption as a World Reserve Currency** – This one is off in the future, but as other fiat currencies collapse, the value of bitcoin increases. We're already seeing that from events in Venezuela and countries in Africa.

All of these "network effects" are working in concert, together creating more and more value for bitcoin. Tom Lee does great work showing that the price movement of bitcoin can be explained by one equation.[27] It's a nonlinear equation where the linear addition of users produces a nonlinear increase in value. That's the power of the network effect.

Metcalfe's Law

The value of a network is proportional to the square of the number of connected users of the system.

$$N^2$$

8

Blockchains

We can't solve problems by using the same kind of thinking we used when we created them.

— Albert Einstein

They say that necessity is the mother of invention. Bitcoin, the first implementation of blockchain technology, was born out of the 2008 financial crisis. With markets in disarray, and massive deflation and uncertainty on all financial fronts – to say there was a problem was an understatement. Providing alternatives for the future required a solution with a different kind of thinking.

Bitcoin, now in the limelight and the most well-known of all cryptocurrencies, is that solution. The underpinning technology that allows bitcoin (and all crypto assets) to function is blockchain technology, one of the great innovations of our time. In order to truly understand crypto assets, it's important that you understand this foundation.

Blockchains: The Basics

The use of the word *blockchain* over the past few years has become more and more ubiquitous. Spoken in Uber rides and dinner parties, boardrooms and classrooms, playgrounds and town halls, it has quickly become the word of the decade. Though used frequently, there are many who don't quite understand what it is, how it works, or why it is really relevant.

In this chapter, I break down the components of blockchain technology, as well as the purpose of each. When these individual components are combined, we have something innovative and formidable. This is an essential part of the foundation of the Age of Autonomy, which we explore in Chapter 9.

What Is a Blockchain?

Let's begin with a simple picture. A blockchain is a bunch of blocks linked together. Simple! That, however, begs the question, "blocks of what?" Now we have to dig a little deeper. According to Dictionary.com, "a blockchain is a type of decentralized database system based on linking together previous records in secure blocks of information."[1] This is a great example of something that really doesn't mean anything, so let's unpack that sentence so that it makes sense.

The first and most important word here is "decentralized." This means that there is no single (central) governing entity. It's hard to imagine this because most things in the world are centralized. Government is centralized, businesses are centralized, organizations are centralized, nonprofits are centralized, even families are centralized. Each of these constructs generally has a person (or persons) in charge and the entities themselves are often in charge of other entities. We're comfortable with this governance structure, which requires that there is always someone "on top" or "in control." Almost everywhere in the world people and businesses may seem to be operating autonomously, but really, it's at the pleasure of a central authority.

Let's continue with unpacking our definition, which goes on to say that it is *a decentralized database system*. We know databases hold data, so logically we can infer that a decentralized database holds data in many locations rather than one central location. What is interesting about this is that each location doesn't just have *some* of the data. Each location has a copy of *all* of the data. This is important, and we'll come back to the reason why later.

Finally, our definition finishes with *based on linking together previous records in secure blocks of information*. This is the "block and chain" of blockchain. It sounds more intimidating than it is. It means that every time there is new information it is appended to the information that came before it. Think of data being stacked upon data being stacked upon data.

This could be visualized as a stack of papers (blockchain). Each piece of paper in the stack holds information (transaction). Every time we have new information, we put it on a piece of paper (block). We fill up the piece of paper with information over a period of time (block interval). Once the paper is full, we make copies and give everyone in the network a copy. Every copy gets placed on top of the stack of paper that came before it. Information on paper, once written, is unchangeable (immutable) – since all peers in the network get a copy, everyone knows what the data is as well as its order. There is permanent recordkeeping that is visible to everyone, agreed upon, and unchangeable. In this example, each piece of paper is a block, and each block goes on top of the stack, which is an ever-growing chain – blockchain. Easy!

This is very hard to do and why blockchain technology is in and of itself such a breakthrough. Up until the creation of blockchain, we did not have the ability to have a group of peers working together in a way that ensured integrity and transparency. We could not have decentralized entities that worked with common governance.

Blockchain Properties

There are many individual components that allow this technology to work, so now let's dive into the properties and elements that empower blockchain protocols.

Immutable

Blockchains are immutable – unchangeable – a property that is both important and rare. In almost every other technology in use today, including financial instruments, transactions can be altered. They can be overwritten. In the financial world this can include bank balances, credit card charges, credit scores, loans, transactions, and so on. In the general transactional world, everything from deliveries to orders to health records can all be subject to tampering. This is in no small part due to the fact that most data are under the control of a central entity.

Blockchains do not work this way. In a blockchain, once a transaction is written into a block, it is there forever and may never be changed by anyone. Period. So, if Bob sends Sally one bitcoin (BTC), Sally has 1 BTC. That transaction is irrefutable. It's written on the blockchain, and, as we learned earlier, all players in the network validate it, and all have a record of the transaction. If Bob says it didn't happen, and even if Bob took Sally to court (that BTC may be worth $1 million someday!), we could look for the transaction on the chain and know the facts. It's unquestionable. Now, this does not mean that Sally will always have that 1 BTC. She may opt to spend a portion of it, but that's a different transaction entirely. There's no way for anyone ever to say that Bob did *not* give Sally 1 BTC. There are few places in the world where this kind of certainty exists, and it's especially important not only where currencies are concerned but, really, for transactions of any type.

Transparent

Blockchains share a fundamental property of being transparent. This means that everyone knows what everyone else is doing – and has done – forever. There is no opacity or obfuscation. There are some blockchains focused on privacy, but they are few in number. This transparency is unique to blockchains and is due to the fact that every node in the network (every miner) has a copy of every transaction ever done on the network. If ever there is a question about the information in any particular block, all one has to do is check other nodes (miners) in the blockchain to see what information they have stored in the block. If there is ever a disagreement, then all nodes on the network can be checked. Transparency is important as this is what impels everyone to "play by the rules."

Permissionless

Permissionless is just a fancy word for public; therefore, a permissionless blockchain is a public blockchain that does not require an account or permission to use. Public blockchains are akin to public infrastructure like the Internet. This means that anyone can participate in the blockchain without any prior approval. This is very different from a permissioned blockchain, which, as you have no doubt inferred by now, means a private blockchain.

Both types of blockchains have similarities. They are immutable, distributed ledgers that make use of consensus mechanisms to determine viability and finality of transactions. Permissioned blockchains, by their very nature, however, require the approval of some central or governing entity. If I have done my job so far, you are no doubt thinking "Wait! The whole *point* is to *not* have a central entity. . .," and you would be correct. A permissionless blockchain is the purest form, as Satoshi Nakamoto intended. It allows all to engage in the system with no single person in charge. Bitcoin and Ethereum are permissionless blockchains. Anyone can participate. Anyone can become a miner (though it is certainly more expensive to do now than it was 10 years ago). There is no central governance.

Hyperledger Fabric by IBM, in contrast, is a permissioned blockchain. It has an access control layer that grants or revokes user rights. For some situations there may be value in this. For example, not every corporation wants its corporate transactions available for everyone to see. In addition, speed is often greater as, by nature, permissioned blockchains have a smaller, more controlled footprint, and changes and management are often easier when one does not need to achieve consensus. The drawback of permissioned blockchains, however, is that we now have that single point of failure and dependency on a private, centralized, party.

In order for them to truly achieve their potential in widespread use, crypto should almost always be permissionless and managed on public blockchains.

Open-Source Software

One of the truly groundbreaking elements of permissionless blockchains is that they are public. Their code is "open-source." This means that anyone – and I mean anyone – can read it or copy it . . . or use it to create their own network via a "fork" (detailed later). In fact, this is exactly what happened with popular cryptocurrencies litecoin and bitcoin cash.

This is a huge breakthrough because it flies in the face of everything we've been taught about proprietary software, namely, that it must be kept secret, must be controlled, and if copied, legal and business consequences must follow. What we have seen, via open-source code, is that it actually delivers the opposite effect. Open-source software minimizes shenanigans and opacity in the software but also impels all miners (the ones who are running the network) to work together for the success of all.

In addition, anyone can audit the software. Any third party can look at the network at any time and determine whether it is operating as expected.

This is a huge change from the world of proprietary software, where third parties have no idea how a system is actually performing its tasks.

In many ways, this is the purest form of an open market. Let the best product win and let the consumers decide without any regulation. More importantly, it reduces risk since it requires all actors on the system to work for the benefit of all in the network and only allows survival if value is provided.

Trust-Minimized

Trust is an essential part of any transaction. In traditional systems, there is a central entity that validates that a transaction has happened. As discussed earlier, however, there is no central entity in blockchain solutions, so trust is established differently. In the blockchain world you might hear the word "trustless." Blockchains are often described as trustless, but this is really a misnomer and, at first glance, provides the impression that there is no trust at all. What it really means is that business can be conducted on the network without requiring the "trust" or validation of a central entity to keep things running smoothly.

I prefer the term "trust-minimized." Trust minimization is the concept that we can conduct business and do a transaction without needing to trust in a single third party who may have alternate motives and biases. This prevents deceit, abuse, and fraud.

In the blockchain world, because there is no one specific central entity, we have minimized the need to trust any specific organization or institution. Instead, we rely on the overall community to validate transactions. Obviously, we still need to trust the miner who validates the block; however, we can do so when we consider that their work is validated by thousands of other miners, and, because all of the code of the bitcoin network is open-source, all parties can see exactly how the network is running at all times and exactly how transactions are processed. Bad actors get flushed out, community prevails, and we can do business with a minimal amount of reliance on any single party. The need for trust is indeed minimized.

Forks (Hard and Soft)

A fork is the creation of a new blockchain based on an existing blockchain. Just like a fork in the road, a blockchain fork is a new path. This new path is based on the existing path but is different because of changes in some way that the "forked" chain now works as compared to the original blockchain. It could be in terms of processing, rewards, consensus, or any of the properties we've discussed.

Forks come in two kinds: hard forks or soft forks. A hard fork is when a complete copy of the blockchain is created, and then, going forward, changes are made that make it incompatible with prior versions of the chain. Since it is a full copy it becomes an entirely new network. Soft forks, on the other hand, are changes that exist going forward while still allowing backward compatibility with miners and previous nodes. Soft forks do not create new chains; they merely allow a change to take place in some of the network rules.

Generally, soft forks introduce new ideas, but do *not* require the network operators to implement them. For example, if you don't upgrade to the latest version of your computer's operating system, you can still use it (at least for a while), but you will miss out on new features that are offered in the new operating system. Likewise, all miners can continue to use the network with the original rules. Ultimately, however, once a majority adopts the new rules, then that will become the primary branch of the chain. Until then there may be versions of the same chain for a short period of time until one becomes the dominant, at which time the other will then die out.

Hard forks, on the other hand, result in a radical restructuring of the code and rules (like changing a computer OS from Mac to Linux). This can happen when someone wants to explore a new path and see if it gets traction. Forks can be friendly, such as Litecoin, or they can be contentious, such as Bitcoin Cash.

Litecoin, for example, started as a fork of Bitcoin. Charlie Lee, the founder of Litecoin, created a different approach to mining (among other things) that made Litecoin operate much faster than Bitcoin. Blocks could be written in seconds instead of minutes or, in the time of Bitcoin's infancy, hours or even days. This created an attractive solution for those who wanted to complete a transaction using a cryptocurrency because generally, when a transaction is complete, parties want to know that quickly. Litecoin fulfilled on that promise, and a new blockchain was born.

Hard forks can also be instantiated; however, when developer teams come to an impasse and cannot agree on a rule set going forward, multiple versions are created. For example, if one group of developers wants to follow a certain approach, policy, or plan, but another group of developers thinks there is a better approach, policy, or plan, they both go forward on different paths. Team A gets to have things the way they are, and Team B gets to make modifications. In such cases, a new blockchain based on the old blockchain is also born. This is what happened with Bitcoin Cash and Bitcoin SV. Both of these teams wanted to make fundamental changes to the Bitcoin network, but the three teams could not all agree, so the core original Bitcoin team remained, another group created the Bitcoin Cash fork, and a third created the Bitcoin SV fork. In each case, a full copy of the Bitcoin blockchain was created and then modified, ultimately becoming a new and distinct blockchain entity, and now all three currencies exist today.

Primitives of Blockchains

Now that we've gone through the fundamentals, I'd like to explore a few concepts that really allow blockchain technology to shine. These are only a few examples, and they only scratch the surface; an entire book could be dedicated to any one of these topics.

Smart/Autonomous Contracts

One of the ensuing big value propositions was conceptualized by Nick Szabo and popularized by Ethereum, and this is the notion of a "smart contract." A smart contract is exactly what it sounds like – it is self-executing code encapsulating a contract that has built-in rules. This code accepts inputs and, if those inputs satisfy a certain condition, then it generates a transaction on the blockchain automatically. They are called autonomous contracts because they can be self-executing and called by other smart autonomous contracts. Another way to think of these are as "programmable assets" that do something when something else happens.

Smart contracts have the ability to change the way business is done because they have automatic settlement, and the revolutionary part is that they are beyond reproach due to the properties of blockchain technology. Payment is not subject to interpretation and the need to be verifiable by all. A smart contract could be in the form of currency (a cryptocurrency transaction), a legal document (deed for property), or, indeed, any kind of two-party transaction. Use cases for this abound in almost every area of society. Imagine if the deed to your property was automatically granted to you once the note was paid. Or, if you were to get a commission on a project, that the commission was sent the day funds were remitted. No escrow companies, no chasing payments, and, importantly, no renegotiations. This will demand a higher level of integrity in business dealings, create transparency, drastically increase speed of payment, and, ultimately, create equality on both sides.

Miners and Mining

Miners are the blockchain network operators. Without them, we would have no operating chain. A blockchain miner is similar to a terrestrial miner of any earthly mineral, be it gold, silver, and so on, in the fact that they do some work and then get rewarded for successfully accomplishing that work. In the case of crypto, generally miners are awarded some amount of token/coin for validating network transactions. (Note that this is not payment by those using the network to send transactions – it's simple payment for operations.) The mining reward is actual new currency being "released" into the open marketplace.

In the case of bitcoin, there is a total established pool of only 21 million bitcoin. Of those 21 million, there are about 18.4 million currently in circulation today. Miners currently earn 6.25 BTC every time they write a block and, in doing so, introduce an additional 6.25 BTC into the world's supply of BTC. Blocks are written every 10 minutes or so, and only one miner at a time may write a block and earn the reward. Miners compete for the right to do these jobs as they are very lucrative. The rest of the mining community plays an important role as well, as they are essential to establishing consensus.

Consensus and Consensus Mechanisms

Consensus is a word you will hear often, and in its simplest terms it means "agreement of the majority for the benefit of all." When multiple parties agree on something, be it umpires in a ballgame, executives in a boardroom, or kids on a playground, one can say they have achieved consensus.

In the blockchain world, consensus is critical because a transaction can only be written into finality (remember all transactions committed to the blockchain are immutable) if the miners achieve consensus. When a transaction is proposed, one miner will earn the ability to approve the transaction, and once the majority of the other miners in the network agree, then the transaction will be confirmed and, ultimately, written on the chain. Consensus is what allows blockchains to work without having to answer to a central entity. From the network perspective, as long as everyone agrees, we're good.

How blockchains achieve consensus varies. From the earlier example, we see that one miner from the mining pool has to approve the transaction initially. That miner, by the way, is the one that generally gets paid for doing the initial "work," so this is a desirable role to play. The challenge then is establishing which miner gets the right to do that in a fair and egalitarian way. There are many solutions to this problem, but for the purpose of this section I'm just going to distinguish the two most popular mechanisms, proof of work (PoW) and proof of stake (PoS).

Proof of work is the consensus mechanism used by Bitcoin. Without going into too much detail, all miners in a PoW system are performing complex calculations to determine the next legitimate address on the blockchain (known as a hash). This is the work, and it requires a serious amount of number crunching. Whichever miner completes this work first gets to earn the mining reward, write the transaction, and be the one for whom all of the other miners provide validation. PoW requires all miners to compete with each other and whichever one solves the mathematical puzzle first wins the mining rewards. One of the fundamental drawbacks to this is that PoW algorithms require incredible amounts of energy to function if the blockchain becomes successful. They are resource-demanding and therefore expensive.

Proof of stake (PoS) is an entirely different way to solve this problem. In a PoS environment, miners hold some of the blockchain currency, and they lock some of it up, in a process called staking, which allows them the right to potentially mine the next token. The next miner who is given the right to validate a transaction is determined by a semi-random algorithm that is a combination of pure randomness with the amount that a miner has staked. This allows the next miner to write a block to establish consensus without requiring the huge amounts of computational power necessary for PoW. Importantly, it also minimizes fraud and bad actors, because if a miner does not act with good intent, they lose all of their "stake."

Oracles and the Oracle Problem

There is one final element that is required to make smart contracts viable. Smart contracts, by nature, exist on the blockchain in which they were created. In order to function, however, they require external data as an input. This data is provided by an "oracle," which is an external program, dataset, or input that provides information to the smart contract. Oracles can gather data from software, hardware, systems, or, really, anyplace. They are not bound and governed by the rules of the blockchain that is invoking their input; they simply exist to serve. This, however, does provide a challenge because execution of a smart contract is dependent on external data, and if that data is bad, then the smart contract may not execute properly or may execute even though it shouldn't have.

As the old computer science adage goes, garbage in; garbage out. The greatest threat to smart contracts, then, is that the inputs are inaccurate. This creates what is known as "the oracle problem." There are many solutions to this, which range from new blockchains, such as Chainlink, which are designed to be clear and transparent oracle delivery mechanisms, to sourcing proven sources, to inventing crowd-validated solutions. Ultimately, this is one of the key problems that must be solved in order for smart contracts to fully mature.

Vulnerabilities

With all of this overview of blockchain technology, you're probably wondering if there is any downside – if there is any risk of corruption. Nothing is ever perfect. Every technology has vulnerabilities. Blockchain technology, inherently, has very few; however, there are a few worth noting.

51% Attacks

The first, and perhaps main, vulnerability is the concept of a "51% attack." One of the fundamental tenets of blockchain networks is that they require consensus, which at the basic definition level means majority approval. If, on any chain, one interested party were to gain interest in more than 51% of the miners, then they could manipulate the blockchain because they could set the rules to be whatever they wanted them to be. They could control each block written and prevent the writing of blocks that they did not agree with.

Fortunately, there are safeguards to prevent this, the primary one being that the more valuable a coin is, the harder it is to control the network. This is because, generally, there are more interested parties when an asset is of value, and also it just plain costs way too much to truly gain control. Without showing my work here (that's another book), at a price of $10,000 per BTC, it would cost (approximately) $1.5 billion to control 50% of the network. At $20,000 per BTC, it would be $3 billion, and so on.

Of course, the converse is also true. If the value of a coin goes down, it costs much less to implement an attack, such as one that occurred in 2019 on the Ethereum Classic (ETC) chain. Costs had dropped so much that it was feasible for a small group of miners to gain control of the network. Fortunately, however, anyone can be a miner – another one of our safeguards. Realizing the attack, the rest of the ETC community stepped up, paid a little more to get into the game, and minimized this attack. This brings us to another safeguard, which is the transparency of the blockchain. It's not hard to see when an attack is happening, so the remaining players in the network (as in the ETC case) can easily move to thwart the attack. The requirement of transparency impels all players to be good actors and to self-regulate the network. It's in everyone's best interest to do what's best for the management of the blockchain.

The Double-Spend Problem

This leads us to another related vulnerability, which is the issue of double spending. This is when a coin is used in one place and then the same coin can be used in another; it is spent twice. As an example, if Mike has 0.01 BTC and he uses it to buy some tools, he should not be able to use the *same* BTC to buy dinner that night or to send to his good friend Jane. The prevention of double spending is managed through crypto-graphic security, but if a 51% attack occurred, blocks could be written again and again and again and double spending would be possible. This obviously would be to the detriment of the entire chain. There are safe-guards, as mentioned earlier, that enable other miners to thwart such an attack and regain network equilibrium.

Private Key Security

If a user loses her private key, it cannot be recovered. With a bearer asset like bitcoin or ether, that's a key risk (pardon the pun). Since there are no centralized institutions managing the blockchain, it's critical that each holder manage their private keys securely. Criminals are out there trying to steal in the digital world, just like in the physical world.

Use Cases

There are many different use cases for blockchain technology. A proper exploration would require much more than a book. This, then, is just a scratching of the surface. Some of these you are aware of, some may be an entirely new concept, and some may spark ideas of your own. The point is that blockchain technology allows us to create sovereign systems that minimize manipulation, maximize user independence and autonomy, and, most of all, level the playing field.

Money

Money is perhaps the most obvious use case for blockchain technology. Bitcoin and Litecoin (among many others) are implementations of money. Money created on the blockchain, if it's a traditional public blockchain, is self-sovereign, not subject to manipulation by governments, cannot be threatened by a counterparty and, ultimately, is the first digital implementation of a means of exchange that each individual user can truly "own." Notably, this money can be transmitted around the world, directly from person to person, for ridiculously low costs and with no red tape.

It is important to distinguish that the new Chinese digital yuan and upcoming American digital dollar are not blockchain implementations of money. They are digital representations of money that are ultimately controlled and backed by the issuing governments. Many will not understand this distinction, but it is fundamental because government-controlled money can still be manipulated, granted, and revoked. True implementations of money on a blockchain cannot.

Decentralized Businesses

We explored the concept of a decentralized franchise in the beginning of this chapter; now let's look at a new sector of business that's gaining popularity. Over the last few years we've seen a revolution in businesses that specialize in on-demand services. Popularized primarily by Uber and Lyft, which created on-demand rides, we now have iterations that include on-demand dry cleaning, on-demand car washing, even on-demand dog walking. Ultimately, however, these are all still centralized businesses. In each case there is a parent company that basically controls everything. Individuals then work as employees or contractors of that company. Imagine a different model empowered by blockchain technology – a decentralized on-demand business. In this model every provider follows agreed-upon rules, but they work for themselves, govern themselves (and each other), and, ultimately, get to realize much greater income for their efforts. Just as miners in a blockchain work within a public ruleset that allows transparent, immutable transactions in a decentralized network, so could almost any on-demand service.

Content Creators

Musicians, artists, authors, and even enterprise all create proprietary content. We now live in a world where distribution and access are a nonissue. Almost any song or book is readily available to a consumer at the touch of a button; however, this does not always mean that the content creator gets paid for this use. Through the use of smart contracts, there can now be a way to ensure proper transmission of royalty payments every single time a use occurs. Imagine, the moment a song is downloaded, a smart contract is triggered, and a crypto-payment is made to the owners, authors, and publisher of the song, all done in accordance with contract terms. This also happens immediately, with near-instantaneous settlement. This could apply to any type of content and not only put a serious dent in fraud and misuse but also ensure that individuals can benefit – and immediately – from consumers that gain value from their work.

Digital Assets

Just as we have never really been able to have true possession and control of digital money prior to blockchain technology, we have also never really been able to own digital assets. Any digital item we may have had has always been granted by a third party. Let's look at an example of a digital asset in a video game world. Perhaps you are playing a game and your character owns a pickaxe. That axe (generally) only exists inside that game world and cannot be taken out and held in some kind of storage that is distinct from that environment. This is now possible.

Of course, you are likely saying, "So what?" The "so what" is that we are moving into a world where our digital identities are as prevalent as our physical identities. We now have avatars on social media, electronic gaming sports tournaments that are as popular as their physical world counterparts, and digital representations of physical objects. Nike, for example, allows customers to create "CryptoKicks," or custom virtual shoes that customers own on a blockchain. It's a natural extension, and we're not too far from a place where digital avatars can wear these CryptoKicks. Just like we have favored brands in the "real" world, we'll be able to see our digital selves outfitted similarly. Just like your favorite brand of jacket, tie, dress, or shoe, blockchain technology allows true ownership of the digital goods and the ability to share among different environments.

Authentication of Physical Goods

Another variant of digital goods is that there can now be digital goods that are linked to physical counterparts. This opens up a world of opportunities, and one main use case is authentication, or rather, the prevention of counterfeiting. Counterfeit goods comprise an ever-growing marketplace that runs in the trillions of dollars annually. In many cases it's almost impossible to tell the difference between the original and the knockoff product. (Just ask Louis Vuitton.) Via blockchain technology, however, digital goods can be paired with physical goods to validate authenticity. This can be done with clothes, art, jewelry, sports equipment, medicine . . . the list is endless. When desiring to purchase an original product, customers would have the ability to validate authenticity by checking its one-of-a-kind digital counterpart. This digital counterpart would reside on a blockchain and be under the control of the owner of the item unless at some time that item transfers ownership.

This is especially relevant in the world of art where pieces are, quite literally, priceless and counterfeits are impeccable. How do I know that a Picasso is really a Picasso? Find its digital counterpart on a blockchain and use this to validate authenticity. In addition, a digital representation could contain a wealth of additional information, including history of previous owners (title history), details about prior transactions involving the piece, and additional information. All of this information can be verified and authenticated, and that would truly transform the art world.

Identity

Imagine that you want to buy a bottle of wine. Today, the vendor at the liquor store will ask you for your ID. When you show this ID, you are also showing the vendor your address, full name, and a host of other information that is not relevant. All that is needed is to know that you are of legal age. Companies are now racing to solve this identification issue by putting personal identity on a blockchain. Such an implementation would be owned by you, the blockchain would verify your identity via consensus mechanisms, and only the relevant portions for any given transaction would need to be shared. Moreover, this would also solve another key issue, that of proof of identity in case of a lost driver's license or ID card. A record available 24/7 on a blockchain, where control of who sees what is readily accessible, would resolve this. This would obviously extend to identity theft, and on-chain validation could greatly minimize such fraud as well.

Supply Chain Management

Perhaps the most important use case we'll consider is that of supply chain management. In today's world where everything is connected, the world is only as big as a plane ride, and goods from one corner of the globe are often spread to another, supply chain management is critical. The pathway of goods from origin into a consumer's hands is often complex, and rife with error, with many steps along the way. Let's say, for example, that you are an aficionado of fair-trade chocolate. In order for that to get into your hands, the beans must be sourced from a farm (where they are grown, harvested, collected, fermented, and dried), bagged, transported to a warehouse, placed on a transport, taken off a transport, sent to a wholesaler, sent to a manufacturer, and, finally, processed into a bar. Not counting the steps while on the farm, there are eight distinct steps before that chocolate can get to the shelf where you can purchase it. Each step is a potential point of contamination, interruption, or loss. How does one really know that the fair-trade bar of chocolate made from 100% small-farm, fair-trade Ghanaian beans is authentic, uncorrupted, and truly from an ethical source? The answer, of course, is blockchain implementation of supply chain management. Imagine that in each step of the process the beans are tracked, and at each hand-off the transfer is written on the blockchain. You would have an irrefutable way to confirm that the beans were actually from Ghana (just check the blockchain), from a farm that is fair-trade certified (check the blockchain), and that the beans you are expecting successfully made it to each point in the journey (check the blockchain).

While we used chocolate as an example, this could be used for any type of food or produce, hardware, parts – literally everything that has a source and a destination. From determining the point of contamination of bad lettuce to validating that the fender on your car is an OEM part, supply chain management on the blockchain is not only practical, but perhaps one of the best uses of this technology.

Solution to Surveillance Capitalism

Our current use of credit cards and electronic transactions here in the United States, and the current state of commerce in places like China, create opportunities for surveillance and abuse from third parties using our own personal data against us. Bitcoin and other blockchain technologies allow the facilitation of transactions without personal data leakage. Why not continue with the status quo – searching with Google, communicating with friends via Facebook/TikTok/Instagram, purchasing with Venmo/PayPal/WeChat/credit cards? Because at some point we will collectively realize the actual cost of giving up our privacy. As we all know, nothing in life is free. The problem with paying for products and services with our own data is that we don't realize how expensive the bill is until way after the services are consumed. Blockchain technology and public blockchain infrastructure will bring an entirely new paradigm for privacy and for monetizing our own data where we can benefit from our own self-soveriegn data.

Conclusion

These are just a few of the many examples available, but now you have a primer on the principles of blockchain. This is important as we are now in the Age of Autonomy, a new period where in the case of money and beyond, blockchain technologies will combine with others to transform our world. We explore this in the next chapter; however, I do ask you to take a quick pause so that you realize you are on the forefront of something amazing. Most people are not aware this is happening, so, given that you are reading this book, consider yourself an early adopter and a few steps ahead of most of the planet.

9

The Age of Autonomy

By 2005 or so, it will become clear that the Internet's impact on the economy has been no greater than the fax machine's.
— Paul Krugman statement in 1998; Nobel Prize winner in Economics

Let's think about where all of this innovation is heading. Innovation drives progress in an economic cycle. My thesis is based on 100 years of innovative economic theory. Short-wave economic cycles, the 5- to 10-year cycles, are driven by credit but the long-wave economic cycles, the 50- to 60-year cycles, are driven by technological revolution (TR). We've had five cycles over the past 200 years with the last wave being the Age of Information and Telecommunications (Age of Information).[1]

We've seen evidence that a new cycle has begun. Technological revolutions come by way of a cluster of new innovations. Around 2010 or so, we began to see AI, robotics, and IoT (sensors) delivering on automation. That's been powerful, but not transformational. It does not force businesses to fundamentally change how they do business. The last piece of the puzzle was cryptocurrency because it allows us to process and transfer economic value *without* human intervention. Soon there will be a global race to build autonomous operations. Businesses and organizations that do not have autonomous operations simply will not be able to compete with those that do. As we continue to get more data and knowledge at an ever-increasing rate, humans on their own will not be able to compete with autonomous operations, and they are just around the corner.

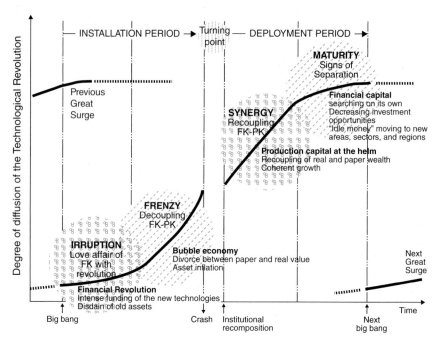

Figure 9.1 Recurring phases of each great surge in the core countries
Source: Perez, C. *Technological Revolutions and Financial Capital.*

In this chapter, I show why cryptocurrency is the mechanism that will unleash the wealth-building value of these technologies. It's cryptocurrency that allows for generating, processing, storing, and transferring value without the need for human intervention. It's competition that's a key driver to technology adoption. We saw this in the last cycle, the Age of Information. Offline businesses that didn't adapt could not compete with their digital competition (e.g. think Blockbuster or any print newspaper business). Once this technological revolution reaches a tipping point, companies around the world will push to reconstitute themselves once again just like they did during the last technological revolution in the Age of Information (aka the Internet Age).

It's innovation through technological revolutions that drives the long-wave economic cycles. We are early in this new long-wave cycle. We can see the new cluster of innovations that are driving this new technological revolution (see Figure 9.1). As with past technological revolutions, extraordinary value is created in the early and middle phases of the cycle.

The duration of a long-wave economic cycle is typically 50 to 60 years. The cycle is that long because of the amount of time it takes for innovations to get adopted and distributed globally. We are in a historical window for investment in this cycle. Looking at Figure 9.1, the best time to invest in a new technology is during the second and third phase (Frenzy Phase and Synergy Phase). The technology is proven in Irruption but adopted later in the cycle. I believe we're in the second phase of the cycle and about to see the Gilded Age where price decouples from value as we've seen in previous periods in the crypto markets. Since this is a global phenomenon, I'm expecting this wave to dwarf the market size of the whole dot-com bubble, which was mainly a US-centric event. That bubble created about $9 trillion in value before the bubble burst. I expect the crypto markets to surpass $20 trillion well before we're anywhere close to the Turning Point illustrated earlier, which will be the end of the Gilded Age and when the "bubble-bursting" begins.

Many people viewed Bitcoin as akin to tulipmania, a fad for techies and dark web lurkers, particularly in the period before the US government and the CFTC gave the green light to commodities exchanges to list bitcoin futures products. It is true that cryptocurrencies cycle through mania phases where the price is decoupled from productivity, but that does not tell the full story. Blockchain technology, and by extension cryptocurrency, is a technological revolution, and it follows the cycle of other technological revolutions like the Industrial Age and the Information Age. As Perez states, "Neither the Tulip mania of the 1630s nor the South Sea Bubble of 1720 qualifies in this sense as there were no technological revolutions driving the events. In fact, there are many psychological phenomena associated with speculative behavior, but not related to the assimilation of technological revolutions in a capitalist context."[2] It's easy to see there is nothing about cryptocurrency that relates to tulipmania or the South Sea bubble.

Many people have also written about the Age of Automation.[3] Just Google[4] the term. Automation focuses on artificial intelligence (AI), the Internet of Things (IoT), and robotics. There have been stories and documentaries aplenty on these topics the past couple of years. There are exchange-traded funds (ETFs) with investments focused on AI/robotics and automation, like $BOTZ and $ROBO. Automation is a significant trend, but it's not *the* critical trend. On their own, automation and robotics cannot bring about a technological revolution because it does not transform how business is conducted. The last required technology is blockchain and, within its architecture, the idea of decentralization. The important trend is *autonomization*. The Age of Autonomy forces organizations and businesses to adapt to a new environment – one where autonomous, permissionless software can optimize and make real-time decisions and move capital, 24/7.

Long-wave Economic Cycles – 100 Years of Economic Theory

Blockchain didn't drop out of the sky. The technology cycle was moving in this direction since the 1970s. Nikolai Kondratiev in the 1920s and later Joseph Schumpeter in the 1930s were among highly influential economists theorizing long-wave economic cycle theory during the twentieth century.[5] Kondratiev described the long-wave cycles and conceptualized the boom-and-bust phases of the cycles.[6] Schumpeter continued the work with his ideas around innovation-based economics and the term "creative destruction," which he coined. He named the long-wave cycle after his predecessor, Kondratiev (see Figure 9.2).

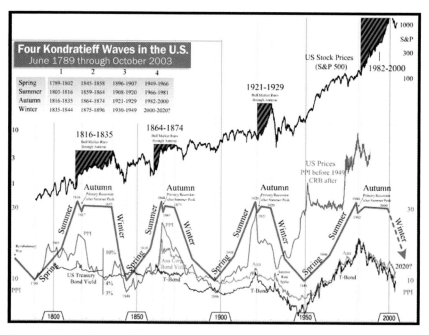

Figure 9.2 A Chart of the Kondratiev Cycle Showing Cycles over the Past 200 Years

Source: Chart courtesy of the longwaveanalyst.ca.

Technological revolution	Popular name for the period	Core country or countries	Big bang initiating the revolution	Year
FIRST	The "Industrial Revolution"	Britain	Arkwright's mill opens in Cramford	1771
SECOND	Age of Steam and Railways	Britain (spreading to Continent and USA)	Test of the "Rocket" steam engine for the Liverpool -Manchester railway	1829
THIRD	Age of Steel, Electricity, and Heavy Engineering	USA and Germany forging ahead and overtaking Britain	The Carnegie Bessemer steel plant opens in Pittsburgh, Pennsylvania	1875
FOURTH	Age of Oil, the Automobile, and Mass Production	USA (with Germany at first vying for world leadership), later spreading to Europe	First Model -T comes out of the Ford plant in Detroit, Michigan	1908
FIFTH	Age of Information and Telecommunications	USA (spreading to Europe and Asia)	The Intel microprocessor is announced in Santa Clara, California	1971

Figure 9.3 Five Successive Technological Revolutions, 1770s to 2000s
Source: Perez, *Technological Revolutions.*

Much of their work came to the venture capital community by way of leading venture capital (VC) firm Andreessen Horowitz and other top VCs touting Carlota Perez's book, *Technological Revolutions and Financial Capital: The Dynamics of Bubbles and Golden Ages.*[7] As previously discussed, Perez describes five technological revolutions of the past 200 years (see Figure 9.3). She continues building on the work of Kondratiev and Schumpeter by developing a relationship between technology and the economy. Kondratiev outlined the case for a long-wave cycle. Schumpeter built the case that it was innovation that drove the long-wave cycle. Perez improved upon their work by asserting that it was clusters of innovation that created technological revolution, and by outlining more detail to the model of the long-wave cycle.

Competition, the drive for efficiency, and continuous improvement ultimately push us toward the sixth revolution, the Age of Autonomy. If a business can operate without the need for human intervention, it will minimize its operational cost. If Uber can remove the expense of a driver with an autonomous vehicle, it will provide its service more cheaply than a competitor who can't. If an artificially intelligent trading company can search, find, and take advantage of some arbitrage opportunity, it can profit where its competitors cannot. A business that can analyze and execute in real time without needing to wait for a human to act is a business that will be able to take advantage of brief inefficiencies from other firms or markets. *Autonomy is the ultimate competitive advantage.*

Blockchain – The Last Piece of the Puzzle

Look at this another way. Technologies that advance automation, like AI or robotics, can easily fit within the current paradigm. Any company that invests in building these will reap the rewards of their investments. There is no paradigm shift and no change to the status quo.

Three innovations empower cryptocurrency to be the last pillar. The first is a new digital model for the global generation, transference, and store of value. The second is the ability of smart contracts to automate the rules-based transference of value. The third is decentralization, which allows us to cross organizational borders and break the constraints of a centralized organization or a central authority. Consider how using a blockchain can automate workflow as well as capital flow. Its ledger can provide record-keeping for the delivery of salmon caught fresh in Seattle and then transferred to Whole Foods trucks for delivery across the nation.

The paradigm shift is in the transformation of how we come together to produce work and how we govern relationships. The shift occurs through decentralized autonomous organizations (DAOs), smart contracts, and new governance models. The collective effects of these changes shift the power *and* the reward. The decentralized organization hands control back to the individual. All of these occur in the realm of cryptocurrency. Therefore, the last technology required to bring about a new age is cryptocurrency.

Just like in the last surge, the Internet was an essential component of the wave but not its core focus. It was an integral mechanism, but the revolution was about something more significant. It was the Age of Information. In the same way, this new surge is about autonomy. Cryptocurrency will be an integral component, but the revolution isn't just about cryptocurrency. It's the final pillar that will support a broader Age – *the Age of Autonomy*.

A Brief History

The new long-wave cycle had precursors with improvements in AI, IoT, and robotics starting around 2000. As described, the focus of that decade was on automation. Automation encompasses making systems and processes automatic, without the need for continuous intervention or input from an operator (a human). We saw companies focused on automating the supply chain and other aspects of business. We saw heavy investment in workflow automation for the knowledge worker as well. However, the "big bang" of Bitcoin started the new cycle in 2009. AI, IoT, and robotics made significant improvements as well in their respective areas. As of 2020, the clues tell us that we are at the end of the Irruption phase and beginning the Frenzy phase. This period highlights autonomy, which is like automation 2.0. Autonomy focuses on making an agent or system self-governing – on bringing real-time decision-making capability into the field and creating the ability to achieve an objective without human intervention.

The Age of Autonomy: What's Possible

This new age is going to bring about transformational change. It will alter every aspect of how a business or organization will go about producing goods and services. Throughout the globe, each industry, community, and government will begin building autonomous agents to create work, generate value, and then transfer and store value.

These actions will be created and enforced by software – agents and bots implementing smart contracts through cryptocurrency platform networks. Robotics will achieve all possible movement in the physical world. The IoT will provide sensors and networks to measure and communicate data. AI will provide the judgment, expertise, and evaluation within a closed system. Decentralized cryptocurrency platforms will provide movement across organizations via the smart contracts that govern and enforce the transfer and store of value.

This has the potential to restore balance between the individual and the group. Autonomous agents working in a decentralized world will allow people to invest and work on projects they're interested in and be paid or rewarded for their contribution. No longer will there be a rent-seeking intermediary like Facebook, Uber, Google, or any other to extract value from the whole. Central organizations will no longer accumulate all the benefits. The power will be restored to the individual because voting will occur within the "on-chain" governance systems. There will be no politics and no intermediary to circumvent the will of the collective individuals.

Even money itself is looking to become self-sovereign. Every time a government-backed currency has come off a commodity or gold standard, it fails, as discussed previously in Part I. We can look to Rome in the third century AD, where the value of silver depreciated 99.98% in a hundred years at the end of the Roman Empire. We can look to John Law and France's failure of its state finance in the early eighteenth century that, through a series of missteps, created crippling inflation of 13,000%.[8] We can look to the hyperinflationary period of the Weimar Republic in the 1920s,[9] which killed the German mark. Historically, fiat currencies fail as a store of value.[10] Always. Money gains its value by declaration and agreement, not by any intrinsic value. Money that can be secured can't be manipulated; money that can be stored and transferred without the need for human intervention could be the most valuable money created to date.

Bitcoin was the first "killer app" of blockchain technology. Bitcoin brought forth something innovative by creating a global system to transfer and store value digitally. Moreover, the next generation of cryptocurrencies brings forth the capability of smart contracts (i.e. programmable money). These capabilities are new, and they will spark an entire wave of technological improvement centered on how we globally generate, store, and transfer value.

Sometime around the year 2040 I estimate this long-wave cycle will begin a Golden Age where money, government, and ideas on labor within the social contract evolve – civilization will enjoy a more free, autonomous, and creative existence.

An Example of the Future Decentralized Autonomous Corporation

Let's paint a picture of where the world is headed in the *Age of Autonomy*. We'll use a co-op farmer in the Midwest. She's got a sophisticated farming corporation, and she knows where the world is headed. She has already bought and installed precision agriculture products that have sensors all over the farm, has robots tending to the crops, and has an IoT network so her robots, sensors, planting equipment, and irrigation can all communicate.

The farmer also purchases a few new AI agent software modules that will help the corporation turn all of the data they get from the crops' IoT and sensors into knowledge. They've purchased some precision irrigation software and some specific weed-management AI software for the robots.

She's now just set up a decentralized autonomous corporation (DAC). DACs are companies with board members, and decision-makers can help set goals, thresholds, and parameters for the growing season ahead. Based on the trend this year and their planting history, they are going to plant a specific allocation of their farm to corn, soybeans, beets, and wheat.

Under their new DAC, they set up a cryptocurrency account on a smart contracts platform like Ethereum or Tezos and build custom autonomous business contracts. If certain conditions or events are triggered, without the need of human intervention, the DAC writes some custom autonomous contracts that will act on behalf of the DAC. They are permissionless and run 24/7. The farmers have set their plans, goals, actions, and counteractions. They are ready for the season.

The preseason activities begin. One of the "buying contracts" notices a 4% better deal for soybean seeds from Brazil, so it purchases the seeds with its cryptocurrency account and sends the request to the seed company.

During the season, the weather AI agent notices a forecast that's going to produce serious flooding in the beets field, so the AI communicates with the irrigation equipment to stop watering the field until one of the soil sensors measures the correct water threshold. IoT sensors measure and communicate the entire picture of what's going on at the farm back to the autonomous contracts. The AI agents trigger an event on the autonomous-contracts platform. The DAC has a "risk management" autonomous contract that exists to help manage the grower's financial risk throughout the season. The autonomous contracts interact with an oracle that communicates vetted information from the physical world. If this flooding occurs, it will produce some serious financial risk to the farm, so it looks on the commodities futures exchange to see what price they could get if they sold some corn and beet futures. This will lock in a certain price for a percentage of the crops, which will help them mitigate financial risk. All of this is happening without the need of human intervention. This is what the world will look like in the *Age of Autonomy*.

The Knowledge Doubling Curve

It is hard to compete with autonomous operations if a team or operation is purely manually driven today. In the near future, that competition will become almost impossible. The Knowledge Doubling Curve was created by Buckminster Fuller. He was born in 1895 and was a theorist and futurist, probably most known for inventing the geodesic dome. In 1982 he came up with the idea of the Knowledge Doubling Curve (see Figure 9.4). It states that from 1400 to 1900, knowledge (or data) doubled every 400 years. By 1900, knowledge doubled every 50 years. Then by 1970, knowledge was doubling every 10 years.

He then predicted that knowledge in the year 2000 would double every eight years and by 2017, it would double every 13 months. IBM confirmed his hypothesis and added to his theory. In 2018, IBM predicted that by 2020 with IoT, sharing economies, and big data, knowledge (or data) will *double every 12 hours*. Think about that. Knowledge is increasing at an accelerating rate. How will humans compete with autonomous operations?

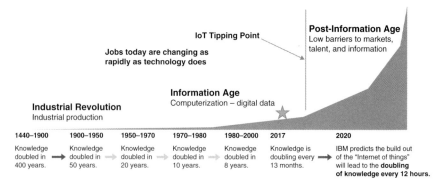

Figure 9.4 Knowledge Doubling Curve

Note: "IoT Tipping Point" refers to the anticipated acceleration of knowledge associated with widespread growth of the IoT.

Source: Presentation by Michael Richey, Boeing, at IBM Committee Meeting, September 14, 2017, slide 3.

The problem gets even more complex if you add the half-life of knowledge. As more and more knowledge comes at an ever-increasing rate, old knowledge becomes less and less useful. Alvin Toffler, author of the book *Future Shock*, comments that "the illiterate of the 21st century will not be those who cannot read and write, but those who cannot learn, unlearn, and relearn."[11] As such, those who are unable to learn and unlearn are going to be disproportionally affected. Software organizations have been building the concept of continuous improvement into their systems and processes for decades. Look no further than the CMMI,[12] the Capability Maturity Model, which looks to create systems and processes that are definable, repeatable, measurable, and therefore continuously improvable. Which entity is going to iterate and capitalize faster – man or machine, humanity or heuristics?

The Case Against a Continuation of the Old Technological Revolution

I'd like to lay out a case for why we're in a new long-wave cycle based on a new technological revolution and not in the Turning Point period of the last long cycle, the Age of Internet/Telecommunications. First, this technological revolution (TR) is about transforming financial operations and how that will impact business, whereas the Age of Information was about the transformation of communications. Second, there is an entirely new cluster of innovations around autonomy. Artificial intelligence, as an innovation, is bringing more pattern-matching, inductive logic, and decision-making into software and systems, helping to make more real-time, in-the-field decisions. The IoT is bringing sensors to everyday home appliances, new applications of autonomous driving, and everything in between. And, finally, robotics is starting to make huge advancements. Gone are the days where the only application humanity can envision from robotics is an autonomous vacuum cleaner. We're seeing robotics used in tons of applications, from the next-generation farms' harvests to drones of all types incorporating autonomous motion. The new cluster of innovations has nothing to do with the Age of Information, though it does build on that.

I want to draw a clear distinction between what happened in the Age of Information and what is happening with the Age of Autonomy. The Age of Information was about transitioning from analog communications to digital communications. What is taking place now is digitization; there is a distinction between that and digital communications. Digitization is the process of taking everything from the physical world and representing it in some digital form. This allows for new applications of AI, IoT, and robotics. Digitization is modeling the real world into digits that can be used, applied, and encapsulated inside a software system. Digitization allows us to build a representation of the world that an AI system can start to learn, understand, and act upon or allows a robotics system vision capability that it can then start to act upon. Digitization is the key to the Age of Autonomy, and it wasn't a part of what was transforming in the Age of Information. This is *Ready Player One*.

There are many signs that point to the fact that the Age of Information is in its Mature Phase. First, that would fit the initial model of a long-wave economic cycle being 50 to 60 years. If we were still in the Age of Information's Turning Point, then that would make the long-wave cycle much, much longer than the stated 50- to 60-year cycle. Per Perez's work, the Age of Information started in 1971, which would put us already almost 50 years into that cycle.[13] I think by applying Perez's model to the Age of Information, there is a case to be made that the Turning Point of that cycle started in 2000 and ended in 2009. There were multiple crashes. There was a lot of legislation that came out to address the new technological revolution, whether it was taxes for internet commerce companies or the Consumer Financial Protection Board (CFPB).

Production capital and financial capital recoupled starting in March 2009, and we've seen massive growth of mature companies focused on the Age of Information. Look no further than the FAANG stocks of Facebook, Apple, Amazon, Netflix, and Google, and the amount of profits these companies generate. They've outperformed the S&P 500 and these five stocks account for 20% of the S&P 500. Profit margins of these companies are huge because of their network effects and their defensible moats from their winner-take-all process during the Age of Information. Starting in 2009, the last decade was truly their Golden Age.

Other aspects of the framework that Perez outlines in her book detail a primary location from which the technological revolution sprang. As you saw in Figure 9.2, the first TR, the Industrial Age, started in Britain and the last TR, the Age of Information, started in the United States. When evaluating the location of the current TR, it is certainly not focused in the United States. The Age of Autonomy has the most adoption and the most effort focused in Asia. The United States is definitely a part of the innovation aspect of this TR, but it's clearly not focused in the United States. One of the primary reasons for this is the onerous regulatory bodies like the SEC and the CFTC. They have regulations that they must enforce, and those regulations are at odds with the latest innovations in finance.

All of these aspects point to the fact that the Age of Information is in its Mature Phase and that a new cycle has begun. This cycle is building on the past cycle, but its focus isn't just about information or telecommunications. Furthermore, new technological revolutions come when past technological revolutions reach their limits. That is in fact the case now. The Age of Information was focused on enabling humans by digitizing once analog information, but humans are now the limiting factor. Moreover, we are at a period of the sovereign debt cycle where we can no longer have economic growth under the status quo. A change in the structure of money is required. The Age of Autonomy is removing the limiting human factor through the application of the revolutionary technologies – AI, IoT, robotics, and blockchain. The economics of this change will be transformational. This new long-wave cycle is about the intersection of technology and finance, how that will redefine money, and what it means to move from automation to autonomy.

Conclusion

The *Autonomous Revolution* has begun. Artificial intelligence, the IoT, robotics, and cryptocurrency are converging to deliver a new long-wave economic cycle. Understanding the long-wave economic cycle and what the key technological innovation is will make you a better investor. If you could have been investing in Internet infrastructure early in the Age of Information, you would have delivered superior returns as an investor. Understanding the technological revolution and where we are in the cycle would have kept your investment pointed "true north." Likewise, this new long-wave cycle will be about autonomous operations. Autonomy is the ultimate competitive advantage because it reduces operational cost and increases potential leverageable opportunities. Business founders and investors who focus their strategy on building autonomous infrastructure will reap the rewards. Those who don't will be left behind.

10

Clusters of Innovation in the Age of Autonomy

Ephemeralization is the ability of technological advancement to "do more and more with less and less until eventually you can do everything with nothing."

— Buckminster Fuller

This concept of ephemeralization is key to understanding where we're all headed. The Age of Autonomy is just one phase of a larger process. If we look back in history, we can get a sense that this ephemeralization process has been going on for a long time. One way to express ephemeralization is the past idea of automation and the future idea of autonomy.

I was searching around Twitter and saw that Harry Belafonte had a Twitter account. It was clear that two things were true: both that Harry Belafonte did have an official Twitter account and that he was absolutely not tweeting. Perhaps the account is an assistant and in the future it may be a bot. Present-day online personas, and with other social media accounts, are an evolution of us becoming more autonomous. Mr. Belafonte didn't need to actually do the tweeting to have an online persona. I saw that Elvis Presley has an official online Twitter account – the King himself! Having more autonomy doesn't always require AI or robotics. In these cases, you can see how. It's not just about technology – society is moving to a more autonomous future.

In his book *Rise of the Robots*, Martin Ford lays out a case where, in our not-too-distant future, there will be a major shift in employment and the social contract we have around full-time work.[1] He suggests that we're headed toward a transition that will put a major stress on the economy and society. This transition is going to have a heavy pricetag, as robots and other automation reduces the need for human labor and employment. So what is going to be the solution? I suspect labor will play a lesser role in family income and the broadening of capital ownership is the innovator's solution to lost income. Participation in the Age of Autonomy will come from a new kind of ownership – an investor class that participates by using their capital through the crypto economy. A new cluster of innovation sparks these revolutionary technologies to be combined in such a way as to offer a solution to the problem that, at least initially, requires less human labor to produce for society.

Innovation in new technologies is altering the means of production. Artificial intelligence, IoT, robotics, and cryptocurrency are changing the requirement of labor and our relationship to it. Concepts like a corporation in a physical location, full-time employment (or just the concept of employment), salaries, unions, holiday schedules, and all the infrastructure we have around labor are changing. It may take five decades to fully realize. But, that's why they call it a long-wave economic cycle. It is the utility of crypto assets that are transforming the future. It is the understanding and investing in crypto assets and participating in crypto networks that will generate value for early investors who see this novel trend coming.

Parallels to the Internet Technological Revolution

I earned a degree in computer science from the University of Texas at Austin in the 1990s. I had started programming when I was nine years old back in the early 1980s, but the degree was still hard for me. You can call me an overachiever; I think I ended up with a 0.70 higher grade average than I needed to graduate. Yeah, that's a 2.7.

My first job out of school was working for MCI Communications as a VisualBasic programmer, having never seen VisualBasic. I must have been coming into a great jobs cycle because we (software engineers) all had a great starting salary, and I got to backpack across Europe for a month as my signing bonus. Those were the days.

Eighteen months later, I started at a consulting firm in Santa Monica, California, that brought me into the dot-com era. I was a software engineer working on several dot-com projects back then, building new web software that was bleeding edge for the time. It's that experience of the dot-com era that reminds me so much of what's going on today in crypto.

The first thing that comes to mind is a piece of software that shipped with Windows95 called WinSockets. What a piece of shit. This was the software that, theoretically, connected a PC to the Internet. To say it was user-unfriendly is a gross understatement. I think the whole meme (we didn't call them memes back then) of "blue screens of death" and comments like, "Did you try rebooting?" catalyzed from WinSockets. Honestly, I get a little annoyed thinking about it today. It reminds me exactly of using some of these software wallets today that try to interact with a blockchain.

This is also similar to the networking protocol wars that happened in the 1990s. There was a huge fight among several networking protocols like NetBIOS, TokenRing, and Ethernet. Never heard of Token-Ring? That's because they lost. It was the Primecoin of the Internet Age.

There are a lot of other similarities, too. Scalability was a huge issue back then. In 1992, most homes had a 14.4 kbs (kilobits per second) modem, which was quite an improvement from the 9600 baud modems of the 1980s. Over the decade, that improved to 28.8 kbs, then 33.6 kbs, then the 56k lines of the late 1990s. It was only then that people could connect to the Internet with "broadband" using the new ADSL line (asynchronous digital subscriber line). This allowed the network traffic to be moved digitally instead of over the old analog phone lines, and it was a major improvement. Now we see the same problem today with the transactions per second (TPS) most blockchains can deliver on a proof-of-work (PoW) consensus mechanism. The scalability gets improved upon with different consensus mechanisms like proof-of-stake (PoS), but it's still not clear what security trade-offs there might be with that performance improvement. Either way, it's easy to draw the scalability analogies between these two technological revolutions, and there are many more.

Although SSL (Secure Sockets Layer) came out in 1994,[2] it wasn't fully adopted until the late 1990s. That means for most of that decade we sent all web content unencrypted all over the Internet. If someone wanted to intercept and read your web content, it was not hard to do; privacy was somewhat of an afterthought back then. However, once SSL was finally adopted, we found a way to start e-commerce websites, which began in earnest in 1998 or so. I remember working on a few at the consulting firm where I worked. We were building some of the first e-commerce websites for Buy.com, Teleflora, and others. I think parallels can be drawn today in the blockchain world and what will happen again this time around.

Other parallels exist, too, like capital-raising efforts, creation of more sophisticated developer tools, personalization, and resistance to adoption. Yet, having gone through a technological revolution before, it's clear to me that all these issues will get addressed and resolved. Adoption is coming. It just takes longer than the visionaries and early adopters ever think it should.

Blockchain Infrastructure for the Age of Autonomy

Blockchain technology is the core infrastructure for the Age of Autonomy. It provides the glue for the other revolutionary technologies such as AI, robotics, and IoT. Inside the blockchain technology there are a few primitives and constructs I'll describe, so you can get a sense of how this transformation is going to take place.

Decentralized Autonomous Organizations

Decentralized autonomous organizations (DAOs) and decentralized autonomous corporations (DACs) are the blockchain primitives that will allow people and organizations of people to set policy, maintenance, and governance of a blockchain. They allow the reduction of human input while providing an interface for humans to provide input and govern autonomous processes and systems. They are themselves actually smart contracts, so they only exist on public blockchains like Ethereum that have smart contracts capability. They can hold crypto assets and execute autonomous contracts on the platform blockchain where they operate (e.g. Ethereum or Algorand). These entities are decentralized and can exist throughout the world under no single jurisdiction. DAOs do not have corporate charters, while DACs may. This is the level at which goals and objectives will be set in the Age of Autonomy. It's the implementation of code inside autonomous contracts that enforces and executes tasks, on behalf of the DAOs and DACs, to achieve the stated objectives.

There have been several of the early DAOs that have come together to invest in crypto projects and public blockchain infrastructure. One example of these DAOs might be MolochDAO. It's aiming to provide an efficient system for management on the Ethereum platform and invests in crypto projects that will advance that community. There are many investment-type DAOs in the marketplace.

There is even a platform that exists to provide an autonomous legal framework for DAOs and DACs. One such platform is Aragon, a crypto project that provides a platform for DAOs and DACs to implement legal templates like for LLCs, corporations, and foundations. Aragon has Aragon Court, which creates a decentralized legal jurisdiction and framework. It uses a jury of peers, which are Aragon token holders/stakers, to adjudicate within the Aragon platform. As of 2020, there were about 1,000 jurors. The system primitive of a legal court for dispute resolution will be critical for the Age of Autonomy to foster and grow. It's already here.

Other legal/governing type institutions are being built to support DAO communities and infrastructure. An example is the Decentralized Autonomous Organization Budget Office (DAOBO) created by Prysm Group, set to operate like the Congressional Budget Office in the United States. Its charter is to create an independent body that exists to support local and national democratic governments. Some of the DAOBO's services are to provide credible, unbiased assistance for economic impact proposals, network economy forecasts, and long-term treasury sustainability with financial reporting for DAOs.

The legal and policy infrastructure for DAOs is being built in 2020 and beyond. It will support these community functions for this new digital financial world. Right now, perhaps 90% of a person's total income comes from labor and perhaps 10% comes from income from investments/capital. In the coming years, income inequality will not be fixed with a change in labor; it will be fixed by expanding how many people get income from their capital. In the future, the average person's income will be more like 50% from labor and 50% from capital. Belonging to the right DAOs will be a big social endeavor. In the 2020s decade, we will see an explosion of DAOs and DACs to organize human involvement in the Age of Autonomy.

Autonomous Contracts

Autonomous contracts are self-executing smart contracts that run on smart contract platforms that do not require permission to execute. They are always on and always available for execution. They sit on global public blockchain infrastructure that can be accessed by anyone with an Internet connection.

Companies incorporating autonomous contracts already exist in the market today. Look no further than Compound Finance. They describe themselves as "an algorithmic, autonomous interest rate protocol." Here's how their service works. Users can earn interest on the crypto assets or borrow against them. You can lend or borrow crypto assets by locking them in the Compound protocol. Compound provides a market for borrowers and lenders of several crypto asset types and provides an interest rate for both parties. It's transparent, autonomous, and permissionless.

There is another company and protocol that takes it one step further, and that's Staked's RAY (Robo-Advisor for Yield) protocol. With this autonomous contract, a user can lend either ether or a stablecoin like $DAI or $USDC. The user locks up their crypto asset with the RAY autonomous contract. That contract will look at multiple lending service providers out in the crypto markets and move the crypto assets to the highest-yielding service. So if three lending service providers offer 2.0%, 2.5%, and 3.5%, respectively, the RAY contract will move assets to the last provider, who offers the highest interest rates. RAY users get the highest yield offered in the market without ever having to look for or shop for lending services again. It happens real-time, 24/7. How is a human-managed lending service going to compete with that? They aren't.

Decentralized Marketplaces

One of the first moves an organization will need to make in order to transition into the Age of Autonomy will be to build a blockchain marketplace. It will take all of its internal and external communications to a vendor, and around a specific organizational set of tasks, build a marketplace. A marketplace is one of the fundamental primitives in the Age of Autonomy. A marketplace is where multiple parties will come together to communicate requests/responses, set prices and coordinate economic activity, and determine capital allocation or a party's requisition of products and services.

For example, there is a Japanese conglomerate in the energy industry that is building a marketplace around their steel supply chain. They've set up a ledger of their inventory, use AI to predict demand, and then make bids on steel products and supplies they will need across multiple business units. The Japanese conglomerate has already tokenized all of their assets in inventory so that they can maintain a ledger of what they have and what they need. They have tokenized purchase orders and created a set of smart autonomous contracts to manage the entire supply acquisition process. All of this is managed algorithmically and autonomously.

By implementing a blockchain marketplace, this allows the Japanese conglomerate cross-boundary functionality as it is in a network of six companies that can be expanded to a much bigger network of companies that work inside this infrastructure. It allows them to take advantage of market prices to improve efficiency. This will also allow the conglomerate to see its entire inventory across the whole network, which is a cross-corporate boundary, and that's never been done before. Also, the conglomerate can confirm that account balances and ledgers are accurate, and that no manipulation has occurred through the blockchain's implementation of triple-entry accounting. Everything can be checked through a mathematical function.

This blockchain marketplace replaces several software tools and spreadsheets the conglomerates use to manage the process currently. Those tools are opaque and do not provide nearly the transparency that a blockchain marketplace does. Managers of this process have been able to reduce the steps from 600 clicks to 60 clicks for the process of acquiring metal for the department through a step in automation and autonomy. Vast improvements that include transparency, auditability, scalability, and performance are realized through the implementation of a blockchain marketplace.

The State of Artificial Intelligence

Artificial intelligence (AI) is a revolutionary technology that is at the forefront of our modern progress. It provides the decision-making capability that drives current automation and will drive future autonomous operations. I know a bit about AI from personal experience.

In 1992, I was a freshman at the University of Texas at Austin. I had no idea what I wanted to major in. I started thinking that I wanted to be an electrical engineer, but one of my classes, 301 Introduction to Logic, killed any notion of that. Then I thought about majoring in philosophy. I think it was then that my stepdad asked what kind of job would I get with that? I took a logic course offered from the philosophy department. It was called Predicate Calculus, and I found it far more interesting than the first class. The people taking this course were majoring in linguistics, philosophy, engineering, and computer science. It's that last major that caught my attention.

I started programming when I was nine years old in 1982 on a Mac Apple IIe. I programmed a 30,000-line program in the BASIC programming language. I went to computer camp when I was 12. I programmed in PASCAL in high school. I liked it, so it was clear that I had now found my major.

At the University of Texas, graduates don't have minors along with their majors; they have concentrations. With a computer science degree, you can choose one of five concentrations, with one of them being AI, and that's what I chose. I was "cramming" four years of college into five, so it was my second senior year when I took as one of my electives a graduate computer science course, which was the Internet as an OS (operating system). In that class, all we did was read graduate-level research work in distributed systems, the Internet, operating system theory, and applications of AI to the Internet. At the end of the course, we had to write a paper with a partner. I led the idea that we should apply using neural networks to cybersecurity.

It was a positive experiment and we got demonstrable results, so my partner and I decided to take it one step further. We decided to write a formal research paper detailing our experiment, and I enlisted the CS AI department chair to be our third author. We published our work in NeurIPS and the Association for the Advancement in AI – both were prestigious conferences at the time – and I presented as first author at both conferences. Today, that is one of the top most-cited works in the field of applying AI to cybersecurity.[3]

I write all this to set the context that I understand what's going on in the field of technology and specifically with AI. There's nothing quite like the *aha!* moment when you train a neural network on a specific task, and it finds patterns that you as a human couldn't even see. It's quite powerful. Using AI switches the programmatic modality from deductive to inductive reasoning, and that switch is about to explode what's possible from a machine.

Deductive logic is a process of reasoning where one or more statements reach a logical conclusion. An example might be a Boolean operation of evaluating whether "x < 10" is true or false. It's what is used in the conventional programming we've been doing for the past 70 years. It's the type of programming that has conditional statements like if/then and follows structures like object-oriented programming, and so on. Deductive logic solves a certain set of problems. Inductive logic is a process of reasoning from one or more statements to reach a logically certain conclusion. The approach uses evidence, or data, to drive the methodology. It is what artificial intelligence is based on, and it solves a whole new set of problems. An example might be: training a neural network to drive an autonomous vehicle using supervised learning methods to teach the correct behavior by learning from a huge dataset of past examples of driving. Inductive logic allows us to solve problems that were not possible with conventional programming. Problem domains like machine vision or autonomous motion are examples of using inductive logic. These new solutions using inductive logic are what's allowing the transformation happening with artificial intelligence. We're now able to deliver machine vision, robotics, and autonomous motion, image recognition/classification, decision systems, natural language processing, and evolutionary learning systems, in real-world solutions. This is a backbone technology in the Age of Autonomy.

The Intersection of Blockchain and AI

Some of the applications of AI with blockchain involve a wide array of solutions, ranging from helping with supply chain management, to solutions for identity and authentication, to AI bots for trading digital assets. While the conditional logic of smart contracts will lie in blockchains, it's the AI components' off-chain that will provide inductive logic for these complex smart systems. There are green shoots of growth at the intersection of blockchain and AI technology. Antonio Senatore, the CTO of Deloitte Global, runs the EMEA Blockchain Lab. He is researching what the technical infrastructure might look like for big data, AI, and blockchain in the future. He's one of many people making progress in the application of AI technology with blockchains. AI is a required technology for autonomous systems, so it's at the heart of the Age of Autonomy.

The Intersection of Robotics, AI, and IoT/Sensor Data Technologies

We've seen the application of robotic, AI, and IoT sensors all over the place starting about a decade ago. With computers getting faster and faster and with disk space getting larger and larger, we have now been able to solve some of the early AI problems we were attempting back in the 1990s. One area that's at the forefront is the application of AI for autonomous robots.

I'm on the board of advisors for an AI startup called Greenfield Robotics. Their mission is to remove chemicals from the food-creation process. They build small autonomous robots for broadacre field management using the process of weed-eating that removes the need for chemicals in the growth process. They use small robots with AI systems for machine-vision and real-time decision-making in the field along with sensors on the robot to aid in vision- and location sensing. This start-up is at the intersection of AI, robotics, and IoT, and I suspect in the not-too-distant future will be connecting with a blockchain as a part of a much bigger precision agriculture and supply chain process.

Another area that's growing is the rise of IoT and sensor data. As 2020 began, we saw an explosion in the IoT and the sensor data that generates. Much of the growth in IoT is happening in four main areas: smart homes with smart appliances; wearables like smart watches and VR goggles; industries with autonomous robots and factory sensors; and smart cities with cameras and sensors for traffic and public safety.

IoT sensors will be generating massive amounts of data. As I've previously stated, imagine a world where the amount of data is doubling every 12 hours. We're here. Artifical intelligence will turn that data into knowledge. Blockchain will provide the rails for this knowledge to turn into economic action autonomously. This is the rise of the Age of Autonomy.

Ephemeralization

As quoted, ephemeralization is the ability of technological advancement to "do more and more with less and less until eventually you can do everything with nothing." This has been going on throughout all technological revolutions. It happened during the process of electrification when we were able to send sound over radio waves or messages across an electrical wire with a telegraph. It happened during the oil and automobile technological revolution when Henry Ford invented the assembly line. That invention increased productivity massively and allowed Ford to do more with less. The Age of Autonomy is one period of a longer process of ephemeralization, and it will continue well beyond the end of this technological revolution.

We're seeing ephemeralization play a role during the pandemic. As businesses are forced to adapt, the ones that will survive are the ones that have a digital presence over a physical presence and have software and Internet capability over their competitors. The businesses that fail during this pandemic will be the businesses that could not adapt and could not do more with less. This points to the Age of Autonomy.

11

The Case for Investing in Crypto Assets

You never change things by fighting against the existing reality. To change something, build a new model that makes the old model obsolete.
— Buckminster Fuller

In the not-too-distant future, it will become obvious that blockchains and crypto assets during the Age of Autonomy will have 10 times the economic impact the Internet had during the Age of Information. This chapter lays out the case for investing in crypto assets.

Old Fiat Money Regimes Are Dying

From 2020 on, we must deal with the reality of a sovereign debt crisis. All US dollar–denominated assets will be affected. As a part of a diversified portfolio, it makes sense to invest in non–US dollar–denominated assets. Since all fiat currencies are connected to the US dollar from the Bretton Woods agreement, all fiat currency, or capital built on top of those currencies, is not safe if the US dollar either devalues or defaults. That leaves commodities, gold, and bitcoin.

Bitcoin is an insurance policy against global central manipulating fiat currency's ability to be a store of value. If central banks inflate the money supply, they will be destroying the future purchasing power of that currency. It will lose its value as supply of the US dollar increases. If people start to lose trust and faith in a currency like the US dollar, it will lose its value as demand for the dollar will shrink. Since bitcoin is scarce and the total amount of minted bitcoin is known, it's the perfect kryptonite to the US dollar. If the US dollar were hands, then bitcoin would be the Chinese finger cuffs ahold of them. The more the US dollar wriggles and manipulates, the stronger bitcoin's grip gets.

Possession Is 9/10ths of the Law

The old adage "possession is 9/10ths of the law" is about to come back in vogue. When contracts break, when parties default and when the music stops, those who have a chair and those who physically control their assets are going to be the winners. We haven't needed physical control in a long time because we're a "civilized" society. When social contracts start to break, you're going to want to control your assets. Bearer assets are the key to this. Crypto assets are bearer instruments. Control your assets and control your future.

Old Investment Strategies Are Becoming Antiquated

Over time, strategies begin to not work like they used to. The information leaks. The market adapts. Over time, there is a new state of play. When the state of the game changes, it's time to rethink strategy.

Risk Parity Is Dead

Over the last 20 years or so, risk parity has become a dominant strategy. The risk parity investment strategy involves managing an asset allocation of stocks and bonds like a 60/40 portfolio. With 60% stocks and 40% bonds, the idea is that when volatility is up and the stock markets are down then the bond allocation will go up and dampen volatility. In addition, the bond portfolio will generate yield that will help improve total performance. So if the bond portfolio yields 5% and dampens volatility and the stock portfolio generates the growth, the risk parity strategy will provide an improved, risk-adjusted return.

Risk parity is used all over the investment markets. Sometimes hedge funds use this strategy but add leverage. They aim to generate market-beating returns and use risk parity as a hedging strategy, along with leverage, to generate alpha (i.e. above-market returns). Ray Dalio's Bridgewater Associates employs this strategy. Risk parity is used by millions of retail investors, too. If an investor is using some type of robo-advisor, they are most likely using risk parity. If a family office is using a certain software solution, they are using a risk parity strategy.

We saw the first chink in risk parity's armor in 2009. Financial advisors employing risk parity saw their customer funds cut by 40% like everyone in the market. We saw it again in the big drawdown of March 2020 when the market dropped 35% in a month. Risk parity did not help.

There are a couple reasons why risk parity isn't working anymore. First, the strategy assumes the bond portfolio will yield something like 5%, which helps performance at the end of a year. With rates less than 2%, the portfolio isn't getting much protection from the yield performance. Second, decelerating earnings, because of increased debt service payments, hinders the stock allocation in the portfolio. Price-to-earnings (P/E) ratios are increasing each year. Value is no longer present in the stock market. Third, risk parity doesn't do well in a deflationary crash when all asset prices go down. Other strategies do well when you're in this new phase of the cycle.

Fake Diversification Exists Everywhere

Many investors think they're diversified if they have both stocks and bonds or if they have growth stocks and value stocks. Or perhaps they have domestic stocks and international stocks. That is not true diversification. A truly diversified portfolio would comprise many types of asset classes including stocks, bonds, and alternatives like commodities, real estate, gold, private equity, and venture capital.

During a sovereign debt crisis, especially like the one we're about to have given that all currencies are interlinked, another type of diversification is required. They need to look at other strategies like commodity-trend strategies for long-volatility strategies as well. An investor also needs non–US dollar–denominated assets in their portfolio like bitcoin and gold. Since a sovereign debt crisis involves a gradual, then total breakdown of trust, they need assets that do not require trust to transact: crypto assets.

Risk Management Favors Antifragility and Ephemeralization

If you had a physical, capital-intensive business during the pandemic like a restaurant that required a physical space or an industrial company, you got screwed. The businesses that did much better were those that are more ephemeral. Restaurants that could quickly adapt and provided online delivery services embodied the ephemeralization principle. Ephemeral businesses are antifragile because they can quickly adapt and, relative to a physical business, they can earn market share in a downturn or a black swan event. Moreover, the financial markets are getting more and more brittle. In 2020, there were $692 trillion worth of currency and credit derivatives.[1] Warren Buffett called these "financial weapons of mass destruction." As the legacy financial system, built on fiat currency and leveraged with opaque exotic credit derivatives, gets more fragile, the newly built decentralized financial system, built on sound money with transparent blockchains, gets more antifragile. The more antifragile your assets, the more you can adapt and thrive. This adds to portfolio diversification.

Seizure-Resistant Assets Have a Premium

One of the big factors in the downfall of any currency is starting the use of capital controls. You saw it in the list I covered at the end of Chapter 6. When a sovereign currency default or devaluation is coming, the state can be counted on to implement capital controls. We see it time and time again. If you can remember 12 words of a seed phrase, which is the basis of your private keys, you can control $1 billion or more in crypto assets that are seizure-resistant and that can cross any border you want. Crypto assets could be a tool used against the state's implementation of capital controls. How much is that going to be worth in the future?

Blockchain Immutability Solves Information Integrity

Starting in 2016, we started to hear more and more about "fake news." It's hard to know what is true anymore. While blockchains aren't a silver bullet, they do provide a piece of the solution puzzle. Since blockchains are immutable, meaning that they cannot be edited once a transaction is committed, they are an invaluable data structure when trying to solve information integrity issues (aka fake news). Voting system solutions can be built and trusted because of blockchain technology. Sourcing and verifying information is now possible because of blockchain technology. As I talked about in Chapter 4, the news problem can be solved. As with any computer system, it's garbage in, garbage out, so blockchains still need good information flowing in to properly solve the problem. However, with other structures like token curated registries, which we'll talk about in Part III, users can vote up or down on entries' value/validity in such a way that a list can be curated by its users. Self-managing, autonomous systems can utilize ratings and reviews, like Amazon utilizes this user-generated content, to curate and maintain valuable information. Investing in today's technology can solve its current real-world problems.

The Gold versus Bitcoin Argument

One day, I was minding my own business walking around Town Lake in Austin, Texas. This was a day like any other day. Often in the afternoon I like to take walks and listen to podcasts. It's a part of my workday. I was listening to the Pomp Podcast with the original discussion debate about gold and bitcoin.[2] From the setup and structure of the podcast it seemed like this was going to be a genuine debate. It would be Peter Schiff who would make the argument for gold and Anthony Pompliano who would make the argument for bitcoin. Peter Schiff is the chief economist at Euro Pacific Capital and a long-time gold investor. He's been on CNBC and many other financial news channels for almost two decades.

I know a little bit about setting up an argument. I went to a high school that had more than 2,000 students, with about 500 in my graduating senior class. Some people get voted "best looking" and some people get voted "most likely to succeed." I was voted "most argumentative." The first half hour of the podcast was informative and going along fine, but soon it would take a turn. It was clear that Pomp was going to be more host than debater. I'm one of those people who yells at screens and yells at the TV during the football game. This was the first time I was yelling at a podcast.

The first thing you learn in debate is to attack your opponent's premise and base argument. You learn to sweep the leg. On the podcast, Schiff's argument for gold went untested. Schiff's premise was that gold has value because it has an alternative use. He states that gold has value because it can be used in jewelry. Schiff has fallen into a *post hoc* logical fallacy. I believe the entire Latin phrase is *post hoc ergo propter hoc*: after this, therefore because of this. *Gold is not valuable because it's used in jewelry. Gold is used in jewelry because it's valuable.* The entire jewelry market was $285 billion in 2018 and it's supposed to support the $10 trillion gold market?[3] That seems like the tail wagging the dog. Jewelry has been around long before the coinage of precious metals as a store of value. People used to store and wear their value as transport and protection. They are in fact called valuables when talking to insurance companies.

Let's think of a colloquial example. Say it's February 11 and Mr. Schiff wants to buy some jewelry for his special someone. It's a sunny, crisp cold day in Connecticut (scratch that) . . . it's a humid, moderately warm day in Puerto Rico and Mr. Schiff walks into a jewelry store. He's presented with two options. Option one is a beautiful gold choker necklace. Option two is still beautiful as it's the exact same choker necklace, but it's made of plastic. Both are jewelry. Both are used to express adoration. Both are a gift. Assuming Peter wants to impress his special someone, which one is he going to choose? Let's take it one step further: Which of those two choker necklaces is more expensive, the gold or plastic? If you say the plastic one, you're wrong. If you say the gold one, then the next question is, Why? Is the gold necklace more expensive because it has more uses in jewelry and cell phones? Gold is used in *fine* jewelry because it's a precious metal and rare.

If I buy a Monet painting, it's not valuable because it's beautiful or because it has a use as home decoration by being hung on the wall. If that were true, then the copy or print of the Monet would be just as valuable because it has the same utility (e.g. beauty and can also be used for home decoration). However, we all know this to be absurd. The Monet painting is valuable because it's rare, or in other words, *scarce*, and because the art world has *accepted* it as such.

There are two types of value that can be created: monetary value and utility value. For something to create monetary value, it needs to embody the six characteristics of good money. Moreover, it should not be consumed for anything. This is why oil or cows are not great as money, as they lack durability. In most cases, there is an indirect relationship between monetary and utility value. If something is consumed through utility, then it loses some of its monetary value. This can be proved through the stock-to-flow model as described in Chapter 7. Note that things can have both monetary and utility value. Remember that platinum has monetary and industrial (utility) value, but due to its stock-to-flow ratio, its value and price is less than gold's. Consumption reduces stock and decreases the stock-to-flow ratio. We see this with metals that are both monetary and industrial in nature, that have both monetary and utility value. Platinum's utility value destroys its monetary value. So in fact Schiff's argument is entirely ass-backwards. *Reductio ad absurdum.*

Schiff went on to make several more points about what creates value, and specifically why gold is valuable and bitcoin is not. He continuously conflates monetary value and utility value. Utility value is derived from how much the utility is worth in the market while monetary value is derived from the six characteristics of good money outlined in Part I of this book and outlined by economist Ludwig von Mises.[4] And let us not forget that economic value is subjective. Schiff mentioned that he could make a piece of Peter Schiff artwork that would be more scarce than gold, but not more valuable. While I agree that Peter Schiff's art is worthless, that's not due only to the dimension of scarcity. Good money, therefore, the creation of monetary value, needs to derive from being portable, divisible, scarce, acceptable, durable, and uniform. Monetary value is derived from these characteristics. Gold is both scarce and acceptable; Peter Schiff's art is scarce but not acceptable. Gold is also divisible, portable, durable and uniform. I suspect Peter Schiff's art is deficient when graded by these factors. Over the millennia, gold has been accepted as money. Herein lies the main risk with Bitcoin: it needs to become more widely adopted, and therefore accepted, to secure its role as good money. If it does, its fate is locked in because it has the other five characteristics of good money in spades. Bitcoin creates monetary value.

Schiff continued his argument against bitcoin: he mentioned seashells and that they were used as money because they were useful in that, again, you could make jewelry out of them. As I mentioned, people wore their valuables to store and transport them. Seashells were used because of their natural scarcity. It takes longer for larger seashells to form and many large seashells get broken or destroyed over time. Big seashells were therefore rare and hard to counterfeit. That's what made them good for money, not because they are used for jewelry. Schiff then asserted that bitcoin is not a hedge against inflation or government monetary policy, but a bet against gold itself. But again, that dog doesn't hunt. If that were true, then there would be an inverse correlation between the accumulation and performance of gold and the accumulation and performance of bitcoin. If that were true, bitcoin would be going up when gold was going down and vice versa. The data does not show this to be the case. Investors are buying both gold and bitcoin. For the past couple of years, gold has outperformed the US dollar and bitcoin has outperformed gold. Same for the past decade. While I don't think Bitcoin is a bet against gold, I do think it does a better job at most of the characteristics that make gold good money, as stated in Chapter 7.

Parts of Schiff's argument don't work because he doesn't really understand the revolutionary aspect of both Bitcoin, the blockchain network, and bitcoin, the currency. He argued that anyone could just as easily make another cryptocurrency and that it's just a digital set of characters. Everyone who was in the crypto universe in 2017 saw how many people tried to create a "better" version of Bitcoin and saw them all fail. The Immaculate Conception of Bitcoin is unique and is partly why it will never be replicated. Moreover, bitcoin is not just something created with a few keystrokes (like fiat currency is today). To mint a bitcoin, work has to be completed. To give you an idea of how much work, based on the hash rate in July 2020, assuming standard prices per kilowatt and some other assumptions for capital expenditure and maintenance, it costs an estimated $7,800 to mint a bitcoin. There's provable work required for a miner to mint a bitcoin and there's provable scarcity through its implementation of triple-entry accounting.

There are also benefits that Schiff was not realizing. For one, he mentions that you need trust and that a free market is about trusting counterparties, and that free markets are about building a trustworthy reputation. As we've mentioned, Bitcoin does not require trust and therefore has no counterparty risk. He explained that throughout history, governments have used their power to move from gold to paper currency because the paper bills are more portable. While that's true, the flipside is that this time a government cannot make that claim about bitcoin because bitcoin is more portable than physical paper bills. Additionally, Schiff argued that gold is very portable because he doesn't need to actually transport the gold, he can just transfer the rights to the gold. If the gold is stored in a vault in London or Hong Kong, then he can transfer the ownership rights to the new owner and the gold can stay in the vault. Well, how many people are happy about owning gold in Hong Kong right now? What risk and expense are they now incurring because their gold is now in a politically unstable part of the world? With bitcoin, you don't have to worry about storing it in a bad physical location with political risk or about trusting a third party. Finally, think about all the gold that is counterfeit.[5] I'm thinking about the largest Chinese gold fraud in history where 4% of Chinese gold reserves, valued at more than $2 billion, was found to be counterfeit. Bitcoin doesn't need to be assayed, audited, and insured, because it's easy and inexpensive to prove its scarcity and its ownership due to triple-entry accounting.

There's more that Peter Schiff doesn't realize about Bitcoin. Bitcoin is a reserve asset for the next digital financial system. Capitalism starts with base money and collateralized loans. It starts with having capital that you can borrow against. That is how capital and then loans and cashflows are created into existence. In the new digital financial system, the decentralized financial system (DeFi system), autonomous financial protocols and smart contracts won't take gold as collateral. Technically, they won't even take US dollars as collateral. Users have to convert dollars into stablecoins. This is one reason $1 worth of a USDC stablecoin is worth more than a US dollar even though it's a digital version of that very same dollar. It can be used as collateral to generate much higher interest rates than a US dollar sitting in a bank and with less risk taken. The new DeFi financial system, and all the power that it will unleash, requires digital reserve assets. As we'll see, this argument alone is quite compelling.

Both bitcoin and gold are hedges against monetary policy inflation. I like Peter Schiff and I'm glad he's out there speaking against bad monetary policy and its ill effects on the markets. I'm not arguing against Peter Schiff personally, I'm arguing against his position on bitcoin. I'm not arguing against gold. I'm arguing against the position that bitcoin isn't a digital commodity and that it isn't sound money. It is. *QED.*

A Set of New Innovations Is Affecting Everyone

As circumstances change throughout the world, the pendulum is starting to swing from aggregated to fractured once again. Individuals are going to experience a world where they cannot count on corporations for careers or even jobs. They are going to have to deliver something to the world economy on their own. As we see the new waves of innovation going on with AI, IoT, robotics, and blockchain technology, we're going to see new ways for people to come together to generate economic activity. They will join decentralized autonomous organizations (DAOs) and decentralized autonomous corporations (DACs), become more participatory with their capital, and build autonomous operations. Investing in crypto assets is investing in the new public digital financial infrastructure.

Revolution in the Means of Production

Financial wealth isn't just about money, whether it be fiat currency, gold, or bitcoin. Wealth is about production and generating cashflows. The Age of Autonomy is a revolution in how we produce – it will redefine the instruments and mechanics for ownership and the means of production.

Ask any wealthy person and they will tell you the same thing: you want to own nothing and control everything. That provides all of the upside and none of the downside. All of the benefit and none of the liability/responsibility. With crypto assets, it's possible to generate cashflows without owning a corporation. With a new digital economy comes new forms of capital and capital systems. In the future, a person will become a member of a DAO, which is just a smart contract, hold crypto assets, and set objectives and work to generate cashflows through crypto assets and autonomous smart contracts. Imagine a world where you have fractional ownership with partial control of a DAO that controls smart contracts used in everyday digital finance. There will be some autonomous contracts valued higher than any factory in existence. These contracts could be used to process insurance or provide hedged derivatives exposure or control peer-to-peer commerce transactions. Each time a client uses your smart contract, the DAO gets a small piece of the cashflow. Without partial ownership of a corporation, which carries regulatory and legal risk under certain jurisdictions, a participant can generate cash flows without the risk described. This new model may test and revolutionize the entire means of production and the legislation and regulation that goes along with it.

Public Financial Infrastructure

As an investor, there was no opportunity to invest in the Internet protocols that were created in the 1990s. Imagine if you had frational ownership of HTTP or SSL, and every time they were used, your investment generated a return either through yield or capital appreciation. Some of these protocols haven't been maintained or updated properly because there is no financial incentive to do so. This is one thing we got right during this newest revolution: an alignment of incentives.

Crypto assets are analogous to fractional ownership of these public blockchains. Public blockchains are permissionless, as we've described in previous chapters. If one (or many) of these blockchains really takes off and becomes widely adopted, how valuable would that fractional ownership be? The opportunity presented here is an investor's ability to obtain fractional ownership of public financial infrastructure that will power the next digital financial revolution.

Invest in Scarcity

When trust starts to erode in a system, provably scarce assets do considerably well and perform better than productive assets. There has been one asset class that has outperformed the stock market after the Great Recession of 2008 – rare collectibles. Rare, collectible wines, cars, and art have outperformed the S&P 500 since 2008.[6] This trend continues, not because rare wine or rare cars have more utility, but because they are provably scarce and each has a specific market with specific buyers that accept them as assets. This has been established over centuries, but even more so recently. In the 2010s, banks started to see rare collectibles as an asset class and started to provide collateralized loans against the assets. Family offices, ultra-high-net-worth individuals, and other sophisticated investors all had some asset allocation in rare collectibles. They are considered a safe store of value. We have seen new investment products developed where an investor can get fractional ownership in rare cars or fine art. This financialization of the asset classes allows for greater diversification and improved risk/reward investment in the asset class. They are considered a store of value because they have the two most important characteristics of good money: *scarcity* and *acceptability*.

Innovation Creates Asymmetry

Because of the nonlinear nature of the technology adoption curve – the S curve – investment in early innovation can produce asymmetric returns for investors. Just think about some of the revolutionary technologies of the past 100 years.

Time it took to reach an audience of 50 million:[7]

- Radio – 38 years
- TV – 13 years
- Internet – 4 years
- iPod – 3 years

- Facebook – 2 years
- Pokémon Go – 19 days

We live in exponential times. Google currently has 31 billion searches performed every month; it was just 2.7 billion 14 years ago. The top jobs in 2010 were invented in 2006. There were one billion Internet devices in 2008; there are more than seven billion now. Amazon had 1,000 robots working in their warehouses in 2013; now they have 100,00 robots working in 26 of their warehouses. With knowledge doubling every 12 hours in 2020, an investor must apply autonomous operations if they are to stay competitive. This growth- and user adoption pattern applies to crypto as well. Coinbase, a premier US crypto exchange started in 2012, had more accounts than Schwab by 2017.[8] They are one of the first crypto economy businesses slated to go public via IPO (initial public offering) in the United States.[9] If an investor can invest in the right technology at the right time in its adoption curve, an innovative investor can generate 10×–1,000× returns. We are still in the Early Adopters Phase of blockchain technology's S curve, with a global penetration of less than 2%. This makes crypto assets the ideal candidate for early investment in innovation to generate asymmetric returns. Every diversified portfolio needs an allocation like this.

Crypto Assets: A New Asset Class

Crypto assets represent a new asset class for investors. There hasn't been a new asset class developed in a few decades other than some financial derivatives. One of the most revolutionary aspects of crypto assets is that they replace legal rights with immutable programmatic rules. The transparency of execution can make enforcement of contracts fundamentally different than how business contracts are managed and enforced today. This notion alone can transform the entire capital system.

Crypto assets are not correlated to stocks, bonds, or gold. They have their own legal and regulatory risk set. They can increase in both price and value without the economy growing. They are distinct. Owning crypto assets helps a wise investor diversify by providing an asset class that is not US-dollar denominated. As we've seen, this is going to become more and more compelling in the years to come. Crypto assets create value via both monetary value and utility value. The monetary value is accrued in bitcoin and stablecoins. Utility value is accrued in other crypto assets that we define in Part III.

In the digitization analogy, crypto assets are Netflix and the US dollar is Blockbuster. As I have stated, the US dollar is in entropy – the slow and inevitable degradation of a system. The group of people who think that the antiquated fiat currency system will continue have a failure of imagination. We can look at this crisis as an opportunity. We can rebuild the financial system digitally and with sound money principles – side by side with the traditional financial system as we watch the struggle. In that pursuit, as investors we have the chance to participate in investing in a new asset class that will deliver asymmetric returns. We are building wealth – with the new digital gold and the new means of production.

As a sophisticated investor, allocating some capital to invest in crypto assets is a prudent move. In the future, investors who don't have an allocation to crypto assets will be in breach of fiduciary duty. It's your choice to invest now or later.

PART III
CRYPTO INVESTMENT
STRATEGIES

It'd be a lot cooler if you did.
— Wooderson (from the movie *Dazed and Confused*)

In Part III of this book, we aim to take what we've learned about money and economic cycles, coupled with the major technological trends we see coming, to formulate sound crypto asset investment strategies. We're building a new digital capital system. I outline systems and processes that guide you, as a retail or professional investor, in building your own customized crypto investment system. In Part III, we first want to get the basics about crypto asset investing from a contextual viewpoint. A fundamental principle in economics is that people respond to incentives. This is also a primitive in crypto asset investing. Crypto assets are themselves incentive structures. Later, we drill down on ways to evaluate which crypto assets are worth investment and which are not. Finally, I outline an investment methodology that will help you generate top risk-adjusted returns from this asset class.

Part III lays out a crystal-clear roadmap for constructing a crypto portfolio using strategy, themed-based investing, risk management, and tactics designed to optimize portfolio construction, asset selection, and managing market timing and market evaluation. I give you, the investor, a comprehensive plan for becoming a crypto investor. This section includes a framework for how to think about crypto investing, systems for evaluation and analysis, along with event-driven action plans to react to changes in the market. In this section, you will learn how to understand and use core investing concepts such as: evaluating tokenomic models, evaluating fundamentals of crypto assets, managing a portfolio with crypto asset allocation, using rebalancing, running an event-driven investment plan, and more.

12

A Primer on Crypto Asset Investing

Show me the money!

— Jerry Maguire (from the movie *Jerry Maguire*)

Bitcoin is the first crypto asset created and it's the first crypto asset discussed. We spent some time on this topic in past chapters. Fundamental analysis, technical analysis, macroeconomic analysis, and a good understanding of bitcoin provide the first steps for being able to evaluate and analyze this new asset class.

Once we have built a thorough framework for analysis, it is then time to delve into the details of investing in crypto assets. Most crypto assets are worthless, so it's important to have a system of analysis and to be selective. We review some of the basics about what crypto assets are, what some of their characteristics are, and why they are beneficial to have as part of any total portfolio. Adding crypto assets into a total portfolio improves portfolio diversification, so let's begin with an understanding of the mechanics, structure, and value proposition of crypto assets.

What Are Crypto Assets?

Secured by cryptography, crypto assets are the coins and tokens that operate within a system on a blockchain, or more broadly, a distributed ledger. The bitcoin coin is the crypto asset that runs on the Bitcoin blockchain.

Similarly, the ether token is the crypto asset that runs on the Ethereum blockchain. For the generalized purposes of this discussion, it is important to distinguish between coins and tokens. I distinguish them in the following manner: coins are transacted and accounted as the primary asset on a blockchain, and tokens can be created on a blockchain. They are managed within their own tokens, contracts, services, and infrastructure but do not interoperate or manage the blockchain they run on. For example, the 0x (pronounced *zero-X*) token, $ZRX, is a governance token that runs on the Ethereum blockchain. It has a set of smart contracts that manages and operates with the 0x token to provide a set of protocols for decentralized exchanges; however, that token has nothing to do with the management or operation of the Ethereum blockchain.

Governance

Governance is a core framework primitive that is a part of a blockchain. Blockchain governance deals with how the crypto asset is going to be managed, upgraded, and maintained and how issuance, and potentially burning (i.e. destroying), will occur. Many crypto assets handle governance off-chain, meaning it's handled in chatrooms or email by the holder, developer, and mining communities of that asset. Other crypto assets have instituted on-chain governance, which means they've built transparent software systems on the blockchain for managing governance on that blockchain. As an example, Ethereum is a blockchain that is managed with off-chain governance. It uses a system of voting on Ethereum Improvement Proposals (EIPs), that get managed, voted on, and implemented through the Ethereum Foundation and through the Ethereum developer community. Tezos, on the other hand, is an example of a blockchain that manages governance on-chain. It manages maintenance and upgrades through an on-chain proposal and voting mechanism that is transparent to all token holders involved. For example, users and holders of Tezos coins can delegate to a baker for baking (the Tezos process for staking, which will discuss later) and voting through a Tezos wallet. If you own Tezos coins, then you can participate in the governance process. This will become a key component as crypto assets mature.

Monetary Policy, Supply Schedule, and Inflation Rate

Monetary policy is the governance policy related to a crypto asset's supply schedule and inflation rate. It is a subset of the total governance of a crypto asset. This is a key attribute of a crypto asset because it affects the supply/demand dynamic, therefore the token's price elasticity. If the supply schedule and inflation rate are set too high, then token value will abate, not accrue. Conversely, if the supply schedule and inflation rate are set too low, it may affect developers' and users' ability to use the blockchain or may not properly incentivize early adopters. The supply schedule is critical because it is the equation that sets the scarcity for the crypto asset.

Value Accrual – Value Creation and Value Capture

One of the most important aspects of a crypto asset is how it captures and accrues value over time. That's what you want in an investment where you're looking for capital appreciation. In 2017, most of us, including me, conflated the idea of value creation and value capture. Most of the investors in this new asset class were looking for crypto projects that were creating value with some new service offering whether that was decentralized file storage or a new way to send remittance payments. What everyone from the ICO bubble missed and consequently learned is that it is more important to find crypto assets that capture value rather than create value. An investor wants to hold assets that accrue, not just create, value. If an investor is analyzing a token, then they will be analyzing for value capture. If an investor is analyzing a token model, she must consider both value creation and value capture to see how value will accrue to her token.

Generation 1, 2, or 3?

Crypto assets were developed in waves. The first generation of crypto assets were blockchain projects that were developed before 2017. Some examples of these are: Bitcoin, Ethereum, Litecoin, Monero, NEM, NEO, and Dash. These have value primarily because of the networks they've built. The next generation of crypto assets, those that deployed roughly from 2017 to 2019, are considered second-generation crypto assets. They improved on the first generation, but for the most part they didn't acquire a network of users. Some examples of these are: Cardano, Stellar, and Tron. Then finally, there is the third generation of crypto assets, which started in late 2019 and beyond. These crypto assets may not have the biggest network of users yet, but they have the best/latest technology on the market today. The battle will be fought between crypto projects that have the best tech and the projects that have the biggest networks.

	BTC	ETH	XLM	NXT	^SPX	^VIX	^GLD	^TNX	1
> BTC	1	0.85	0.75	0.79	−0.15	0.16	−0.13	−0.04	
ETH	0.85	1	0.72	0.77	−0.10	0.13	−0.06	−0.08	0.5
XLM	0.75	0.72	1	0.78	−0.08	0.12	−0.07	−0.09	
NXT	0.79	0.77	0.78	1	−0.17	0.15	−0.12	0.03	0
^SPX	−0.15	−0.10	−0.08	−0.17	1	−0.74	0.31	0.4	
^VIX	0.16	0.13	0.12	0.15	−0.74	1	−0.14	−0.53	−0.5
^GLD	−0.13	−0.06	−0.07	−0.12	0.31	−0.14	1	−0.16	
^TNX	−0.04	−0.08	−0.09	0.03	0.4	−0.53	−0.16	1	−1

Figure 12.1 SIFR data provided in 2019 on its website in 2019, https://sifr.com/.

As investors, we're looking for the best networks of users and the best technology. If a crypto asset isn't in the top tier of network users, which provides network effects, or in the top tier of technology, then as an investor we should take a pause. For the most part, as a crypto investor you're going to want to steer clear of second-generation crypto assets. In most cases, they have neither the technology nor the network to win out in the end, though, of course, there may be exceptions. That will also preclude investing in any first-generation crypto assets that don't have a large network of users or have a dwindling user base. For utility token model crypto assets, the size of the network and its network effects are key.

Crypto Assets: A Noncorrelated Investment

Crypto assets are not correlated to the stock or gold markets. As you can see in Figure 12.1, crypto assets are noncorrelated or slightly negatively correlated to stocks, bonds, and gold. This makes them a prime candidate for any portfolio because this new asset class is adding diversification. Asset managers far and wide are always looking for alternative assets that are noncorrelated. As Mark Yusko of Morgan Creek Digital touts, "Get off zero." What he means by that is that an investor may not be sure how much she should allocate to crypto assets, but the number isn't 0%. Crypto assets deserve some allocation to a total portfolio.

Crypto Classification: Security versus Commodity

There's been a big debate going on in the crypto markets about how to classify crypto assets and to which regulatory body they belong. Are crypto assets securities and therefore governed by the Securities and Exchange

Commission (SEC), or are they commodities and therefore regulated by the Commodity Futures Trading Commission (CFTC)? During the ICO Bull Market of 2017, many investors were interested in distinguishing a utility token from a security token. This would free it from the jurisdiction of the SEC, and in some cases, there was merit to the argument. Broadly speaking, a security token represents a tokenized version of a financial security. If it represents ownership and generates financial returns, and if an investor has invested cash in exchange for units of fractional ownership, then it is considered a security. You can think of real estate or equities that are tokenized assets as being security tokens, whereas a utility token is a token used to power a blockchain network. Utility tokens, conversely, exist to allow users to transact on their network or use their service. An example of this might be the Basic Attention Token ($BAT), which is used with the Brave web browser, which monetizes attention.

In the ICO craze of 2017, many tokens were issued under the premise that they were utility tokens – and therefore not subject to securities laws – but were later determined to be classified as securities. As an investor this is important because if a crypto asset is not registered as a security and it is later deemed to be a security, then it could cause the entire project to be devalued or worse. We saw this in 2020 with Telegram.

Howey Test

The basic framework used to determine whether a crypto asset is a security or not is called the Howey Test. It gets its name from a 1946 Supreme Court case between the SEC and the W. J. Howey Company of Florida,[1] which was an important case for determining applicability of the federal securities laws. Basically, the test consists of three questions used to determine classification:

1. Is there an investment of money with the expectation of future profits?
2. Is the investment of money in a common enterprise?
3. Do any profits come from the efforts of a promoter or third party?

Securities produce a return to a common enterprise, which I think can be argued is a central organization. The spirit of the law is to capture an agreement, "I'll give you some money for a percentage of the potential profit the enterprise generates." Securities represent ownership in the enterprise capital structure whether that's equity or debt.

That is not, however, what's happening with most crypto tokens. Crypto tokens are not generating a return that is then divided by the owners via dividends or share repurchase, though some tokens do split returns generated from fees. Most expectation of future returns would be generated by price appreciation through scarcity of supply and demand of one of the outlined token models. There may be an expectation of profit, but that's where it gets tricky.

Consideration – Similar Analog Assets

There are plenty of assets that people buy with this expectation of a return. Most of them revolve around scarcity of the asset playing into a tight market of supply and demand. Some examples include:

- Commodities
- Tickets for concerts
- Numismatic coins
- Precious metals
- Collectibles
- Rare art

None of these properties or assets are considered securities. Even assets that produce income like mortgages are not securities. Therefore, there are going to be many crypto assets that expect a future return but are still not securities. All three factors of the Howey Test need to be considered collectively.

Commodities – Looking at the "What"

Commodities are goods or assets that can be bought or sold on an exchange. They are typically raw materials or agricultural products. Commodities don't produce a return from a common enterprise. They are goods or property that get mined or grown where their value is intrinsic, based on market supply and demand. This distinguishes commodities from securities.

Crypto Assets – The "What" and the "How"

If you just evaluated a functioning crypto asset, like a crypto currency or a utility token, it would generally be classified as a commodity. Where an issue arises is in how a crypto asset project comes into existence. It's much more about the "how" than the "what."

If a crypto asset comes into existence via an initial coin offering (ICO) or a token-generated event (TGE) where the offering is a token in exchange for money up front before a working network or product yet exists and where the investor expects to make a return, then there's a problem. Anything that falls into this category is most likely going to be classified as a security and it's going to have to follow securities laws.

I like to think of regulatory risk as a continuum. As an entrepreneur or an investor, it's important to assess where you are with your project or crypto asset on this continuum. I use a set of factors for your consideration. The goal of this process is to quantify regulatory risk for investing.

Security or Commodity: Seven Factors to Consider

These are the seven factors I consider when I evaluate regulatory risk for any particular crypto asset:

1. Is it a coin or token?
2. If it's a coin, is it mineable?
3. If it's a coin, is it decentralized?
4. Is it functioning in production?
5. Was there an ICO, IEO, or some token-generation event (TGE)?
6. Was it offered in the United States in a public or private sale?
7. If it was offered in a public sale in the United States, was there Know Your Customer/ Antimoney Laundering (KYC/AML) paperwork completed?

Okay, so let's evaluate the answers to these questions and see where we land on the continuum of regulatory risk. The least risky crypto asset is a mineable coin running on a functioning decentralized blockchain network. A coin is slightly less risky than a token, generally speaking, because it's running its own blockchain and network. Further, if the coin is mineable, it has different economics than if people bought it in an ICO (or other means) because, in this case, miners received coins for work. This notion came out when the SEC announced that bitcoin is not a security.[2] As such, coins that are mined are inherently less risky than coins that have been premined or established in total at a project's inception.

If a coin is premined and centralized, it's the riskiest type of coin. Chances are good that it has high regulatory risk of being classified as a security. (One particular coin comes to mind.) Now, if it's a token instead of a coin, then the first question to ask is: Is its network functioning? If the token has a functioning network, protocol, utility, or product, then it's less risky. This notion came out when the SEC announced that Ethereum is not a security.[3] If the network is not currently functioning, then it bears much more regulatory risk.

The last set of questions regarding regulatory risk revolves around how the crypto asset came into existence. Was there an ICO? If so, there may be more regulatory risk. If it was airdropped or came into existence another way, then there might be less risk. If there was a public sale in the United States, then it's riskier than a private sale. If that public sale did not do KYC/AML, then it's much riskier than if they did. If you have a token that did an ICO, and it's not currently functioning, and you did a public ICO in the United States with no AML/KYC, then you have the greatest regulatory risk and you will most likely have to deal with an enforcement action from the SEC in some way.

As an entrepreneur or investor, you must evaluate the regulatory risk of your crypto assets. The SEC is going after bad actors, not people who are trying to do the right thing. If you're on the least risky side of the spectrum, there is less reason for concern than if you're on the most risky side of the spectrum. If that's the case, then there's work to be done.

Regulatory Risk – Yield Through Staking

Some crypto assets employ staking, which generates a yield as a part of their consensus mechanism, called proof of stake (PoS). Staking is when an investor uses their crypto assets to help secure the network in a PoS consensus model. While an argument can be made that this makes an asset a security, I believe that regulatory risk is greatly reduced because the asset holder must do something in exchange for the yield. This is an ongoing debate. They are both executing an action, which provides value in the form of helping to secure the network, and they are taking a risk by staking their assets in case something goes wrong. I believe this active approach to generating yield will be classified as something different than producing passive income will be, though I suspect a regulatory body will step in to make a determination at some point. We will need to hear more from our regulatory bodies before a full decision can be made. One aspect to think about, similar to staking yield, is whether the burn process, or removing tokens from a network, will be considered to be a share repurchase action within the equity context. Again, we'll need to wait and see.

Passive Investing and the Crypto Index Fallacy

For new crypto investors, I think it's important to lay out the two main approaches to investing and why one may not be what it seems. We'll discuss active strategies later in this chapter; however, let's first set some context with what typical investors think of when using a passive investment strategy.

Passive Investment Approach with Stock Indexing

Most people are familiar with passive investing using a stock index. Individual investors, family offices, and institutional investors often use this investment strategy. The indexed investments have low fees because they passively follow a particular index and adjust their holdings based on that underlying index. Probably the best known example is the S&P 500 Index and the various ETFs that follow it, such as $SPY and $VOO. They work well, particularly in efficient markets like US equities.

One of the components of an equity index that strengthens its value proposition is diversification. This diversification is achieved in a variety of ways. The index tracks the top 500 US companies by market cap, which is made up of 10 sectors. Each sector is comprised of many similar companies, for example, the technology sector. This gives investors exposure to companies with various sensitivities to economic growth, interest rates, inflation, and commodity prices as each sector will react differently to various market dynamics. Furthermore, each of the companies was started privately and grew into its position in the index. Each of these companies helps create diversification because each company has its own teams following their own systems and processes. They are atomic pieces making up a whole. All of these factors help to create a truly diversified investment vehicle.

Passive Approach with Crypto Indexing

When taking a passive investment approach in the crypto space, there are several options available. Most of them track an index of the top 10, 20, or 30 crypto assets by market cap (technically network value). You could think of the top 10 as the large caps and the top 20 or top 30 as the mid-caps, if comparing to an equity index. There are several indices to choose from but the top three are: Hold 10 Index (from Bitwise), the Bloomberg Galaxy Crypto Index (from Bloomberg), or the CCI30 Index (from the CryptoCurrencies Index, CCI30). Each tracks the crypto market using slightly different calculations. As with any index investing, you're getting lower fees than compared to an active strategy.

A lot of very smart people are building solid investment products in the crypto space. In no way am I refuting that. It is certainly possible over a long period of time, the passive approach may end up beating most active strategies, just like in the US equity markets once it becomes more efficient. Only time will tell since crypto is such a new asset class.

The Crypto Index Fallacy

The crypto index fallacy is that diversification can be achieved within the crypto asset class alone. For me to better illustrate the point, let's take a walk down Crypto Memory Lane.

In the beginning, in 2010, there was only bitcoin. Then slowly over time, many more crypto assets were created. Many started by copying the Bitcoin open-source software and adding some variants to create their own crypto asset. Since they were copies of Bitcoin, they had a similar regulatory risk. Once bitcoin was deemed not to be a security, it allowed its copies to infer that their regulatory risk, too, was reduced. As such, many of the early copies of Bitcoin were added to popular exchanges of the day, like Coinbase, and this drew new crypto investors to those crypto assets.

This is a function of the open-source nature of these networks. Open-source software is a powerful trend that's been building over the

Top 100 Cryptocurrencies by Market Capitalization

Cryptocurrencies ▾	Exchanges ▾	Watchlist				USD ▾	Next 100 →	View All
# Name		Market Cap	Price	Volume (24h)	Circulating Supply	Change (24h)	Price Graph (7d)	
1 ◎ Bitcoin		$71,751,818,959	$4,077.23	$9,315,719,476	17,598,187 BTC	1.31%		⋯
2 ♦ Ethereum		$14,796,440,950	$140.51	$4,289,939,234	105,303,684 ETH	0.92%		⋯
3 ✕ XRP		$13,269,107,048	$0.320261	$677,009,071	41,432,141,931 XRP *	1.13%		⋯
4 Ⓛ Litecoin		$3,690,030,161	$60.54	$1,759,540,782	60,953,886 LTC	1.10%		⋯
5 Ⓔ EOS		$3,419,334,027	$3.77	$1,273,864,807	906,245,118 EOS *	0.86%		⋯
6 ▨ Bitcoin Cash		$2,870,842,089	$162.37	$460,666,321	17,681,300 BCH	0.32%		⋯
7 ⊘ Stellar		$2,217,980,085	$0.115377	$286,142,188	19,223,800,319 XLM *	2.06%		⋯
8 ◇ Binance Coin		$2,211,390,594	$15.66	$224,750,171	141,175,490 BNB *	0.66%		⋯
9 Ⓣ Tether		$2,035,525,570	$1.02	$8,156,573,979	2,001,684,593 USDT *	0.54%		⋯
10 ▼ TRON		$1,539,408,286	$0.023086	$164,284,256	66,682,072,191 TRX	0.95%		⋯

Figure 12.2 CoinMarketCap of Top Crypto Assets

past 15 years. It means, as the name suggests, that the human-readable code is public code, and anyone can access it, review it, and if they want, copy it to start their own project. This is a powerful feature in blockchain as a technology, but it changes how a crypto asset might accrue value over time. No longer is having the best technology a defensible moat of this investment. With open-source software, ingenious entrepreneurs can make a copy of that software and start their own project, or in this case, launch a crypto asset.

To date, there are more than 5,000 various crypto assets. I distinguish crypto currencies as a subset and crypto assets as the superset in Chapter 14, Understanding Crypto Asset Classes. Of the 10 top crypto assets, four are crypto currencies and five are smart contracts platforms (see Figure 12.2). There is only one utility token in the top 10 and that just happened quite recently. There are no dApp, commodity, or security tokens in the top 10 indices (unless you count $XRP as a security token). Moreover, the concentration increases when you include the fact that three of the top 10 crypto assets are open-source software copies of either Bitcoin or XRP.

If we look back at the top 10 crypto assets, Litecoin and Bitcoin Cash are copies of Bitcoin, and Stellar is a copy of XRP. Just a year ago there was also Ethereum and Ethereum Classic, but the latter has fallen out of the top 20 crypto assets by market cap. There may be distinguishing features of each, but ultimately 50% of the top 10 crypto assets are similar and that does not help an investor who's looking for a diversified investment in the crypto space. *Therein lies the fallacy – that crypto index investing is a diversified approach to investing in crypto assets. It's not.*

The counterargument to this false notion could be that since the technology is open-sourced the only truly defensible moat for crypto assets is their networks. Network effects build moats for assets, that is true. However, if a crypto asset is a mere eight-hour coding change from Bitcoin and it was purchased because it was one of the first crypto assets to be listed on exchanges, does it really have any network effects?

There are more factors that contribute to the crypto index fallacy as well. Since crypto assets are mainly software projects, team members can work on multiple projects. Moreover, not all sectors of the crypto markets are represented in the index. For example, there are no governance tokens and there is only one utility token in the top 10. Finally, the fact that 80% of the total market cap is held by the top 10 crypto assets is a *bug, not a feature,* for current passive index investment. In time, as the market matures, I expect this will change, but today it stands the case.

Summary of Investing Approaches

Both passive and active strategies in the crypto markets are valid and serve different investor profiles. The only consideration is that assumptions made from investing in other markets may not hold for the crypto markets. Indexes may not be diversified. In terms of fees, active management is still expensive, compared to passive management, However, active management is an approach that may deliver superior returns because crypto markets are nascent and inefficient, and slightly more knowledge may deliver asymmetric returns. Likewise, passive investing still follows an index and reduces expenses. The index may not be diversified, which is typically one of the major strengths to passive investing. This will change, however, as both crypto markets and indexes evolve. For now, *caveat emptor* and know what you're investing in.

Investing from First Principles

Using first principles, we as investors look at the fundamentals and construct a reasoning and then test outcomes along the way to see if our conclusions hold. Good investors invest based on first principles. Our main thesis grows from a broader context: *Technological revolutions drive long-wave economic cycles.*

Understanding and applying first principles to investments in this context is essential to success. When you examine events and trends through the filter – that the world is going autonomous – you'll be amazed by how many events begin to fit together. One hundred years of proven economic theory guide how we identify investment themes and determine what types of investments we should consider. Using an investment thesis as a context, these first principles below help us identify the best assets for investment consideration or consideration for investment. These are the first principles we're thinking about when it comes to investing.

The fundamental tenet of investing is to make your money work for you. Most investments are looking for a passive return, meaning the investor is not working alongside her money to produce the return. It's the money that's producing the return through investment. The ultimate investment is one that produces a positive, predictable/forecastable return without the need for human intervention.

Money Goes Where It's Treated Best

As the old adage goes, "Money goes where it's treated best." Conventionally, that has always been taken to mean that money will flow to jurisdictions that are friendly to it and to investing. The converse is true as well – *money leaves where it's treated poorly.* If certain jurisdictions have onerous restrictions or taxes, money tends to flee. This also applies to money as a store of value. The currencies that best hold their value will see inflows while the currencies that least hold their value will see outflows.

Premium for Liquidity

Illiquid assets, seizure-able assets, and capital-controlled assets are worth less than liquid, seizure-resistant assets. Super-liquid, global, seizure-resistant assets are worth a premium. Our investment thesis focuses on liquid assets because we see that these assets demand a premium, especially in times of distress or during times of global instability.

Continuous Improvement

Many successful organizations follow a Capability Maturity Model that allows the organization to strive to become definable, repeatable, measurable, and therefore continuously improvable. Because decentralized autonomous organizations, or DAOs, can mostly be expressed and transacted in software, they minimize the requirement of human intervention. The more they minimize this requirement the closer to autonomous they become. Likewise, investments that are continuously improvable are self-optimizing. Crypto assets with on-chain and decentralized governance mirror this capability. If companies and organizations deliver operational success through these fundamental tenets, so, too, will governing bodies, like DAOs, who are providing similar tenets. It's the transparency and continuous improvement that create value.

Network Effects

The network effect is a phenomenon whereby increased numbers of people or participants improve the value of a good or service. The Internet is an example. Initially, there were few users of the Internet. It was of relatively little value to anyone outside of the military and some research scientists.

If we're to use the fact that network activity is the key to understanding the derived value of crypto assets, then we need to understand Metcalfe's Law. This law states that the value of the network is proportional to the square of the number of connected users. Simply put, as more and more people use a crypto asset, the higher the value rises because of the network effect.

As the number of users grows linearly, the value of the network grows geometrically, though it grows asymptotic once the network is of a certain size. Generally speaking, if the number of connected users of a network doubles, then the value of the network goes up by four. This is why it's key to understand network activity, so that we can take a fundamental approach to valuing Crypto assets. Linear growth producing nonlinear returns is a powerful investment first principle.

Platforms Dominate

In terms of business models, platforms beat pipelines. Based on the book *Platform Revolution* by Geoffrey Parker,[4] the pipeline business model is one in which the flow of value is linear from producer to consumer. It's called the legacy business model. The platform business model instead uses technology to match consumers and producers in a multisided marketplace. It's the disruptor business model. This business model has done most of the disruption of old business models over the past decade. Platforms like Uber, Airbnb, Amazon, and GrubHub are killing traditional pipeline companies which have been the incumbents by providing platforms for interaction.

In his book, Parker explains that platforms win because:

- Platforms scale more efficiently by eliminating gatekeepers;
- Platforms unlock new sources of value creation and supply;
- Platforms use data-based tools to create community feedback loops;
- Platforms have network effects.

Bitcoin and other certain crypto assets like Ethereum, Tezos, or Algorand are platforms. They eliminate middlemen and reduce friction. Applying the concept of the platform business model will help an investor ferret out which investments may be disruptive to their respective markets.

Antifragility

Centralization creates a single point of failure. Decentralized architecture is more than resilient; it gains in value from chaos and disorder. Looking for assets that are antifragile add to a portfolio's diversification.

Bearer Instruments

Bearer instruments, held properly, reduce investment risk. Bearer instruments do not have counterparty risk, default risk because the asset isn't someone else's liability. Secured properly, bearer instruments cannot be confiscated or seized, and can be more private.

Power of Compounding Returns

Compound interest is the eighth wonder of the world. He who understands it, earns it … he who doesn't … pays it.

— Albert Einstein

Most of you know that compound interest is one of the most powerful concepts in the world of investing. Compounding is a process of making more returns on an investment by reinvesting the interest. Compound interest is possible by investing in crypto assets. Some crypto assets allow for the investor to participate in the securing and governing of the blockchain. The mechanism for this is called staking. An investor can stake her crypto asset, which is used as collateral to ensure the security and accuracy of the transactions being executed on the blockchain. Investors' risk of losing staked assets incentivizes good behavior and makes bad-acting an unprofitable action. For that service, they are paid an interest payment, typically called a "staking reward." Most of the crypto assets that generate interest through staking get paid in the same staked crypto asset. If that asset grows in value, an investor can generate compounding returns because their interest is being paid in the underlying crypto asset. Over time, this can make a huge difference in the returns. Using the investing first principle of compounding interest is a key long-term investment strategy.

Investment Vehicle Options for Crypto Investing

There are a lot of different ways an innovative investor can get exposure to crypto assets. The most common approach, like investing in an ETF in the stock market, is currently not possible. However, many other ways do exist. In the following, we outline several ways an investor can invest in crypto.

Where Are the ETFs?

Currently there are no ETFs that give exposure to bitcoin or any other crypto asset. There are some trusts that act somewhat like an ETF, but they do have drawbacks. There have been many attempts, from the Winklevoss twins to Van Eck to Bitwise Asset Management; however, all have been problematic. From interpreting communication from the SEC, we're not going to see a bitcoin ETF anytime soon.

Single-Asset Trusts

Single-asset trusts are a compelling way to get some exposure to the crypto markets and there are a couple of companies that provide these products, which allow investors to pick one asset, say bitcoin, and invest via the trust. If you don't want to deal with managing, storing, and custodying the crypto asset, this might be a solution for you. With these trusts, you'll need to be an accredited investor to be able to invest. Some of these products are available to nonaccredited investors, but the trust, or investment vehicle, may have a discount or premium to the net asset value (NAV). This means, for example, if a trust like $GBTC or $ETHE were available to a nonaccredited investor through their brokerage account, those products might trade at a significant premium to NAV. As an investor, you'd be taking a risk on both the underlying asset's price move as well as the premium. If the premium fell dramatically, even if the underlying asset did not move, an investor could experience significant loss. I can remember a time in 2020 that the Ether single asset trust offered by Grayscale was trading at a 400% premium to NAV. At one point, if all the premiums had been pulled out of the vehicle, investors could have experienced an 80% loss even if the underlying asset price did not change.

Indexed Products

Several firms offer indexed products to provide exposure to the crypto investment universe. Some products may follow an index that is the top 10 or top 30 crypto assets based on market cap. I would be careful about considering these products until the market is much more mature. See the section on the Crypto Index Fallacy.

Bitcoin Futures

Bitcoin futures are available on the Chicago Mercantile Exchange (CME). There are futures contracts that allow an investor to buy one contract, which is equivalent to five bitcoins. At present, there is only one regulated futures contract and that is for bitcoin. This product does allow an investor to employ leverage. There are also plans in the works for an ether futures contract though it is not available as of this writing. Investing in futures contracts requires an investor to be accredited and able to get a commodity account and has the same risks commonly associated with commodities.

Crypto Options and Derivatives

There are several options for options investing in crypto assets (pardon the pun). Options are available via the Chicago Board of Options Exchange (CBOE), which is the only regulated vehicle for investors in the United States. There are also options contracts available by a firm like LedgerX, which provides a full set of options contracts for bitcoin in a regulated environment. All options trading employs leverage in the investment product. An investor must be an accredited investor to be able to use these investment vehicles.

Crypto Venture Funds

There are also crypto venture funds that specialize solely in early-stage venture investing within the crypto space. These funds invest in companies to get both equity and tokens in crypto enterprises. Ventures funds typically have a 7- to 10-year time horizon with a 5- to 7-year lockup, and investors must be not only accredited but also qualified. A qualified investor has a net worth of two-million-plus in assets, excluding their primary residence.

Crypto Hedge Funds

There are many crypto hedge funds that focus on investing in liquid crypto assets. My firm, TRADECRAFT Capital, is one such crypto hedge fund. These investment vehicles are private and unregulated investment with limited partners who invest in the fund. There are many different investment strategies that a crypto hedge fund might employ, just like in the traditional hedge fund world. Some include investment strategies like: volatility, arbitrage, long-only, long-biased, long/short, quant, discretionary, and opportunistic. Like crypto venture funds, crypto hedge funds require investors to be qualified investors. Crypto hedge funds typically have a lockup of 12–24 months and are more liquid than their venture counterparts, though both have longer-term investment horizons. Again, a qualified investor has a net worth of two-million-plus in assets, excluding their primary residence.

Direct Crypto Asset Investment

The intention of this book is to educate investors and build a strong argument for direct investment. The primary way to invest in crypto assets is through direct investment. Opening an account at an exchange like Coinbase or Gemini and investing or trading direct crypto assets gives anyone that chance to get exposure in crypto. This approach is going to take more education because there is a lot to learn about crypto asset investing. Because of its low regulatory requirements and its superior liquidity, along with the ability to profit from several investment strategies, direct investment provides opportunities that will be available no other way.

13

Quantitative Analysis Frameworks

Never tell me the odds.

— Han Solo (from the *Star Wars* series)

One of the top abilities good investors must have is the ability to determine the value of an asset. You could be a swing trader and focus solely on technical analysis, but that is trading, not investing, and that's a different book. Informed and reasonable investment decisions can be made once an investor has price and value in hand. In this chapter, we focus mostly on fundamental analysis and come at it from the notion that blockchains are networks. Investors have a lot of experience with various mechanics of how to value a network – it comes down to usage and utility. We cover other quantitative analysis frameworks within analyzing crypto assets, but we discuss topics that relate to crypto assets, like macroeconomics. From an investor's perspective, crypto assets are currencies, so actions that happen in the currency markets are going to affect the crypto asset class.

Fundamental Valuation Using On-chain Metrics

Approaches to fundamental analysis are well-known with traditional asset classes like stocks or bonds. Those methods would be either insufficient or inappropriate to apply to Bitcoin. The core process of determining value with crypto assets stems primarily from their usage and utility since they are networks. In 2020 and most likely over the next decade, we're in the Frenzy phase of the technological revolution cycle, as defined by Dr. Perez.[1] Later, once the market matures, we'll achieve mainstream adoption, and once we enter the Synergy phase from Dr. Perez's model of technological revolution, only then will fundamental analysis of each crypto asset be truly meaningful.

For now, what works is to use the Bitcoin blockchain as a proxy for the entire crypto market because most crypto assets are highly correlated to bitcoin – where bitcoin goes, so goes the market. If Bitcoin is seeing increasing usage and utility, then a savvy investor can infer that the entire crypto market is trending higher (though this does not mean that every crypto asset will appreciate – it's just an indicator for value due to use). Additionally, it becomes more effective to measure usage and utility in relative terms versus notional terms. As investors in crypto, we're looking for trends and relative changes. Again, the crypto market isn't mature enough yet to say X usage or Y utility calculates to an exact value.

As a member of the crypto investor community, I can say there's been a lot of discussion on how an investor should go about fundamental analysis for crypto assets. We see a lot of discussion about technical analysis all over the Internet from Facebook groups to Reddit to #CryptoTwitter. Chris Burniske's book *Cryptoassets: The Innovative Investors Guide to Bitcoin and Beyond*[2] was among the first to use "cryptoassets" instead of "cryptocurrencies" to describe assets using blockchain and other distributed ledger technologies and it was the first book that took a deep dive into fundamental analysis of crypto assets.

Fundamental analysis revolves around measuring network activity. Most of these crypto assets are networks either logically or physically. Some blockchains are a collection of decentralized nodes running the same open-source code. These nodes communicate with one another to keep all the same information in lock-step so that all nodes record the same data and in the same order. These are blockchain's physical networks. Other crypto assets are tokens running protocols. Their users are networked together, providing some protocol or service. They run on a smart contract platform blockchain like Ethereum or Algorand, but the tokens themselves aren't coins directly affected by the blockchain they utilize. These crypto assets still run on networks, though they are logical networks.

Regardless of whether a crypto asset is a logical or physical network, a primary value of a crypto asset is derived from being a network. Crypto assets generate value from network effects. A network effect is

the positive effect described in economics and business that an additional user of goods or services has on the value of that product. Because
crypto assets are networks, Metcalfe's Law helps us determine how to
value these assets.

While we use technical analysis and macro risk analysis in our total
model, fundamental analysis of the Bitcoin blockchain is all that is
required to inform your investment plan. You can build on this later by
adding other crypto assets that have meaningful usage data. But for now,
we'll focus on being able to analyze the Bitcoin blockchain with the
metrics, indicators, and ratios I lay out for the model.

Many of us who were around during the Internet boom of the 1990s
remember trying to come up with a new valuation model for New
Economy businesses. In many cases, there were no profits yet, and in
some cases, there wasn't revenue. If you wanted to try and value a dot-
com company at that time, a discounted cash flow model would not
have helped you. At that point, you could have either not invested in
the new technology or you could have come up with a new framework
for valuing those assets. Investors started to think about *eyeballs* and *page-
views* as key metrics to determine value.

Global Macro Risk Management Models

During the summer of 2019, I was running my crypto fund and I needed
to make daily determinations about portfolio asset allocation and how
much I should have in cash. Technical analysis on August 25 showed that
the price in bitcoin was still above the 200-day moving average, and it
was making higher lows. Trading volume was low, but the analysis was
basically benign. Fundamental analysis showed that there was value present based on the ratios, but it was mixed. Over the coming weeks, technical analysis showed the market was getting worse, but the fundamental
analysis was still mixed. From August to November the price of bitcoin
plummeted as it's known to do. Sometime in late September I started to
hear that there were global macro problems in the overnight repo markets here domestically and problems in the Eurodollar markets overseas.
I started to hear more about credit issues and inter-bank overnight loan
problems along with high interest rates for overnight loans. There was a
shortage of Treasuries in the markets.

That's when I realized that the Eurodollar market is a quadrillion-
dollar market. Any problem in that market is going to affect a $250

billion digital currency market. I started to add some metrics that measure macro indicators, which would give me a picture into what was going on globally in the credit, gold, and currency markets. It became clear I needed to watch various indicators to get a picture into the global macro market.

As crypto investors, we hear and say that bitcoin is a safe-haven asset. That's partially true. Sometimes it trades like a safe-haven asset and sometimes it trades like a risk-on asset like stocks. Likewise, though crypto assets are uncorrelated to stocks and gold, at times they can trade like risk assets. To answer the question of whether bitcoin is trading like a safe-haven asset or not, you have to measure it. First, a savvy investor needs to check if there's volatility in the stock, bond, and gold markets. Then she needs to check if the risk-on assets like stocks are falling. If there's volatility and risk-on assets are falling, then the investor must check how bitcoin is trading. As a general rule, if bitcoin's price is falling, along with stocks, then it's trading like a risk-on asset. However, if it's holding or rising when other risk assets are falling, then it's trading like a risk-off, or safe-haven asset. Going forward, I'll use *risk-off* and *safe-haven* interchangeably. We can now determine whether bitcoin is trading like a safe-haven. Over time, I've found that it oscillates between trading like a safe-haven or risk-on asset. In all of January 2020, it traded like a safe-haven asset. In February, it oscillated back to trading like a risk-on asset. This determination becomes an important factor in your investment plan because an investor needs to know when their crypto portfolio is protected and when it's not.

In addition to risk-on/risk-off classification for bitcoin, there are some other market indicators that are helpful to follow. Stock market volatility, captured by the ticker ^VIX, is not very helpful in determining if a big drawdown is coming because it's often volatile and it is a current, not future, indicator. However, bond market volatility index, captured by the ticker ^MOVE, is helpful because it's not commonly volatile, and when it is, it can be a leading indicator. Bond market volatility measures the global markets' brittleness. The bond market can signal a problem is near better than the stock market. The gold volatility index, ^GVZ, is also a helpful indicator to follow. If you see volatility in gold markets and bond markets, then there's a good chance risk-on assets are at risk of a drawdown. That information, coupled with the safe-haven classification, will help a savvy investor mitigate risk by altering the percentage of cash their portfolio should be in.

A Model for Fundamental Analysis

In this section I outline a model to be used as a starting point for fundamental analysis based on on-chain blockchain data. Crypto assets are a network good. As such, they have network effects and measuring the *relative* network activity should provide a framework to value the network. The goals are threefold: to be able to spot trend reserves and new trends forming; to be able to quantify *relative* trends of usage and utility along with cash flow generated to miners for securing the blockchain; and to be able to track relative valuation, both current and long-term. The model uses Directional Indicators to help inform whether there is a trend-reversal, or a new trend beginning. Then, there are Current Indicators, which track relative trends of usage, utility, and miner's cash flows. Finally, there are two types of valuation ratios, current valuation ratios and long-term valuation ratios, that help determine if value is present based on current price.

Directional Indicators

These indicators show continual direction of two short-term indicators. These are the most time-sensitive and transitory of the five indicators. They are:

- **NVT Directional Indicator** – This shows the relative trend direction of the NVT Ratio. Either it's heading toward adding relative value or losing relative value in the NVT Ratio.

- **Correlation Directional Indicator** – This shows whether the crypto assets are getting more or less correlated to one another. If crypto assets are getting more correlated, that generally means a bearish trend while assets getting less correlated means a more bullish trend.

Current Usage Indicators

These indicators measure direct blockchain network usage and utility. These indicators show that current network utility in the form of: (1) number of daily unique users; (2) daily transaction value (in USD); (3) mining fees, which are the revenues the network is generating. If the crypto network is being used by more people per day and is being used to move more value, then its intrinsic value is increasing. Again, the focus is on relative trend over absolute nominal quantification. They are:

- **Unique Addresses** (Daily) – This counts the unique addresses used in transactions per day. This data is being used as a relative indicator. If the unique addresses trend is increasing, that's bullish for the crypto markets.

- **Transaction Value** (Daily) – This counts the estimated US dollar transaction value daily. This data is being used as a relative indicator. If the amount is increasing, that's bullish for the crypto markets.

- **Mining Cost** (Daily) – This metric averages the fees that the miners are generating for processing transactions on the blockchain. This is distinct from the block rewards miners are paid for generating the next block of transactions on the blockchain. If the fees are moderate, that's bullish for the crypto markets. If the fees are really low, like below 20 cents, or really high, like above $20, that's a red flag and is indicating something is wrong and requires further investigation.

Current Valuation Ratios

These ratios track current relative network value. The NVT ratio is similar to a P/E ratio in the equities markets and is one of the core valuation metrics in crypto analysis. It measures network value to transactions (NVT). The MVRV ratio[3] is market value by realized value (MVRV) and is a similar yet more complex ratio to the NVT ratio. Realized value tracks the trade price at which the last trade was executed. The ratios used in the framework are:

- **NVT Ratio – Undervalued is <65 and Overvalued is >95**
- **MVRV Ratio – Undervalued is <1.1 and Overvalued is >3.5**

Long-term Valuation Ratios

These ratios track long-term relative network value. The Mayer Multiple[4] calculates price against the 200-day moving average, which gives a ratio relative to time and past trading prices. The P/BE ratio[5] shows the value ratio of price to miner's breakeven cost, which yields a ratio of price relative to production cost. The ratios used in the framework are:

- **Mayer Multiple – Bullish is <1.0 and Bearish is >2.4**
- **Mining P/BE Ratio – Bullish is <1.2 and Bearish is >3.2**

Interpretations of the Model

The metrics I've talked about above are used daily in the core model of the quant system we use at my crypto fund. We use other, more sophisticated metrics as well, but these initial nine metrics grouped together in four categories give a good base for a model to determine value within the bitcoin blockchain.

    Below, I've pulled out a few events that happened throughout 2019. I show charts of the price in bitcoin as well as what the model was showing for that day. The goal is to help give you some idea how to interpret the metrics.

A Downtrend with Early Stage Indicator of a Possible Trend Reversal

Figure 13.1 shows that usage of the bitcoin network is falling. You can see that in the Current Indicators. It might, however, be close to a trend reversal in usage. A trend reversal to the upside is reflected in the model the first day both Directional Indicators are green. Here you see the NVT Directional Indicator is green, which means either usage is going up or price has gone down enough that the NVT Ratio is starting to show more relative value. The Correlation Directional Indicator is not quite green, but when it gets there, when both are green, that's an indication a new uptrend may be beginning.

    In the ratios, all ratios are either light green or dark green showing relative value is present. You won't get dark green in the Long-term

Figure 13.1 Dashboard Showing Metrics as of July 28, 2019

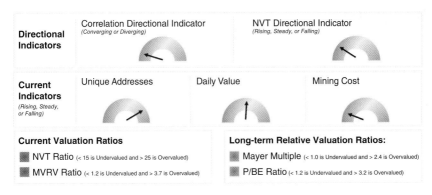

Figure 13.2 Dashboard Showing Metrics as of February 10, 2019

Relative Valuation ratios unless you're at the end of a bear market cycle, there's blood in the streets, and the cycle is bottoming. *We saw dark green in early 2019, but we're not likely to see that again until the next big drawdown.*

Overvalued After a Big Correction

Figure 13.2 shows a market that has already crashed. Looking at the price of bitcoin at the time, the asset has already seen a big drawdown in price but is still overvalued and is still in a bear cycle. We see this by looking at the NVT ratio and the MVRV ratio, which both are showing that bitcoin is overvalued. It may, however, be reversing due to increased usage. The Correlation Directional Indicator is showing a market downturn because crypto assets' correlation converges during a drawdown. At the end of a bear cycle, you will finally start to see deep value in the long-term ratios. They may stay deep green for a while until valuation ratios are finally signaling value through price decline or usage increase. You'll know when to get into the market when the Current Valuation ratios signal value.

Bull Market – An Uptrend in Network Utility and Deep Value

As an investor, you're seeing an ideal market to enter when you see these three things: a new uptrend forming; usage and utility increasing; and current and long-term value present. That's the point when you want to

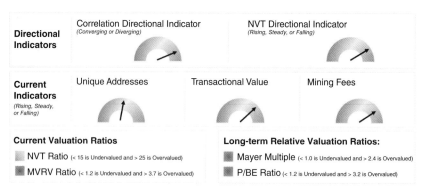

Figure 13.3 Dashboard Showing Metrics as of March 11, 2019

be fully invested. Figure 13.3 shows a market that has bottomed because a new uptrend is beginning based on the Directional Indicators being green. It's showing the market is undervalued, and the Current Indicators are showing network usage and utility are increasing. Finally, value is present in all the ratios. The price of bitcoin has gone down so much that all the ratios are showing relative value based on current utility.

Overvalued Due to Price Rising Faster Than Usage

Figure 13.4 shows a market that's growing usage and utility, but price is rising faster. We see that as the Current Indicators are green, but the Current Valuation ratios are yellow. That means value is leaking because price is rising faster than utility. You'll also notice that the NVT Directional is showing that as well because the trend of the NVT ratio is falling.

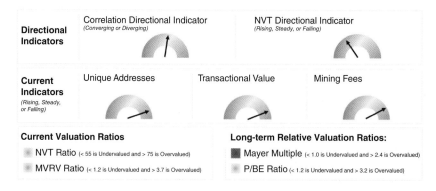

Figure 13.4 Dashboard with Metrics Showing June 26, 2019

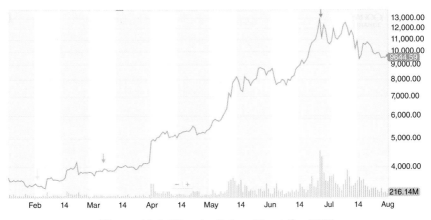

Figure 13.5 Bitcoin Price Chart for 2020

Bitcoin Chart YTD for 2019 for Comparison

If you look at Bitcoin trading history, you can see that the fundamentals would have helped your trading. Fundamental analysis of the Bitcoin network will show when there's deep value (typically from a major correction during a long bear market), when there's an increase in usage, or when price has risen too far, too fast. Checking the dates of the network metrics on the price chart of bitcoin (Figure 13.5) illustrates the point.

Other On-chain Metrics

The indicators I provided earlier should only form the basis of your quantitative model. You want to layer in additional on-chain metrics to provide more views into what's happening within a blockchain. Some other on-chain metrics include:

Financial Metrics

- Sharpe Ratio – A measure that indicates the average return minus the risk-free return divided by the standard deviation of return on an investment.
- Sortino Ratio – A measure that indicates the risk-adjusted return of an investment asset; it is a modification of the Sharpe ratio that penalizes only those returns falling below a target or required rate of return, whereas the Sharpe ratio penalizes both upside and downside volatility equally.

- ROI, one-year – A measure of a return on investment (ROI) over a one-year period.
- Volatility – A measure computed by finding out the square root of the variance of a daily (periodic) price.
- Market Capitalization – A measure of market capitalization colloquially, though network value more specifically, which is computed by multiplying the price and the total supply.
- Daily Trading Volume – A measure of the dollar value of an asset traded daily.
- Realized Capitalization – An alternative calculation of market capitalization derived by multiplying the price of each coin last traded by the size of each trade.

Transaction Metrics

- Transaction Count – A measure of the number of transactions per day on a blockchain.
- Transaction Value (USD) – A measure of the amount of US dollar value that is transacted/transferred in a day.
- Active/Sending/Receiving/New Addresses – A measure of counting various actions per day.
- UXTOs (Profit/Loss/Created/Spent) – A measure of Unspent Transaction Output (UTXO) actions per day.

Production Metrics

- Issuance (USD) – A measure of value in US dollar terms of how much bitcoin was issued or mined for a period, typically a day.
- Current (Circulating) Supply – A measure of how many coins have been mined and are in use; distinct from total supply, which is how many coins can possibly be issued by the end of the scheduled supply.
- Mean Difficulty – A measure of the average mean of how hard it is to find a hash below a given target.
- Hash Rate – The measuring unit of the processing power of the crypto asset blockchain network.
- Mining Profitability – A percentage calculation that determines income after expense consideration based on mining difficulty, exchange rate, power costs, and hash rate.

Ratios

- NVT (Network Value to Transactions) Ratio – A crypto asset valuation metric that takes the market capitalization (network value) of an asset and divides it by the transaction value, which is how much is being transacted, exchanged, or transferred each day in USD.
- NVT (Network Value to Transactions) Signal – A valuation metric that improves on NVT ratio by using the same NVT ratio and adding a smoothing mechanism of a moving average.
- Mayer Multiple – The current price of bitcoin divided by its 200-day moving average (named after Trace Mayer).
- Metcalfe's Ratio – Like the NVT ratio except that it relates to Metcalfe's Law; calculates price divided by $n \log n$ of the number of UXTOs; can be a relative valuation ratio.

Social Metrics

- Tweets per Day – A measure of the number of tweets per day that contain crypto-related hashtags.
- GTrends (Google Trends) – A measure of the number of Google searches per day of crypto-related search terms.
- Sentiment Data – A measure of sentiment on the crypto markets using Twitter as a data-set and using some machine-learning to qualify sentiment.

Advanced Ratios and Metrics

Once you as an investor get some of the fundamental metrics and indicators working, you may want to add more advanced versions. Most of the advanced ratios and metrics are combining complex metrics or adding time as a dimension into the measure. This could be a long section, but here are just a few terms for your consideration:

Bitcoin Days Destroyed – A measure of transaction volume of bitcoin. It is calculated by taking the number of bitcoins in a transaction and multiplying that by the number of days since those coins were last spent. This is used as a better metric to value economic activity; thus, 1 bitcoin that hasn't been spent in 100 days (1 bitcoin

$\star$ 100 days) counts as much as 100 bitcoins that were just spent yesterday (100 bitcoins $\star$ 1 day).

Liquidity Coverage Ratio (from Messari) – A ratio of real daily volume/daily dollar-value of newly mined crypto asset where the real daily volume eliminates fake and wash trading from the metric. From that, a ratio of "Liquidity Coverage ratio" is obtained for a given blockchain network. This gives you a sense of whether there is enough exchange liquidity on a daily basis to handle new liquidations. Low Liquidity Coverage ratios may lead to steadily grinding lower price in individual markets.

UXTO Age Analysis – Basically an accounting system used in a variety of blockchains like Bitcoin. Every transaction creates a new UXTO and the age of that UXTO tells in which block that transaction was first included. Analyzing UXTO Age can give a savvy investor an idea of when that bitcoin was last transacted and, in aggregate, can give a window into historical and pricing patterns.

NVTG Ratio – Compares to the PEG Ratio in equities. This is a ratio of NVT to Growth. A lower value indicates a better value. This is a relative valuation ratio as well.

There are several resource websites where you can get public data including: CoinMetrics, Glassnode, and Woobull Charts. There is so much information that I could spend a whole book just discussing quantitative valuation of fundamentals. I will leave you, the savvy investor, however, with a foundation you can use to build your own fundamental analysis model and also give you the tools to expand upon it. CoinMetrics does an amazing job outlining valuation, metrics, and ratios in their blog post – https://coinmetrics.substack.com/p/coin-metrics-state-of-the-network-6f5[6] and https://coinmetrics.substack.com/p/coin-metrics-state-of-the-network-c37.[7]

Summary of Other Valuation Models

Crypto assets represent innovation and experimentation in the evolution of money and the store and transfer of value. Frameworks and methodologies are only now being investigated and tested. Valuation models will continue to be hypothesized, implemented, discussed, and continuously improved in the coming decades.

There are many other valuation models for experimentation that have sprouted up over the past two years. There are some great Medium articles and other blog posts that go into specific detail about complex and sophisticated models and frameworks. Following is a summary of a few of those sets of models.

Metcalfe's Law

As we've previously discussed, blockchains are inherently networks and as such follow properties like Metcalfe's Law, which states that the value of a network is proportional to the square of the number of connected users of the system. Using this law coupled with certain usage metrics creates a set of valuation models that focus on the nonlinear value creation that happens from the linear addition of users in a network. Models from this set have been used for tasks ranging from predicting price values to identifying suspected market manipulation.

Equation of Exchange

The most notable equation for money supply and monetary dynamic is probably the Fisher Equation of Exchange. The core idea is simple: the equation of exchange is MV = PQ where M equals the money supply, V equals the velocity of money, P equals the price level, and Q equals the index of real expenditures or goods purchased. Time is a variable component for V, P, and Q. This valuation model is applied to cryptocurrencies. To be noted, this was one of the first areas of study that was applied to token valuation with the idea of velocity. This valuation model was discussed extensively in Burniske's book.[8] There have been many models built on top of this framework, but some have drawn a fair amount of criticism, which has surfaced from posts by CoinMetrics and others. We study this more in subsequent sections of this chapter.

Price Regressions Models

Price regression models refer to valuing crypto assets where price is regressed over time. Kevin Lu and CoinMetrics team have written, "While some practitioners may dismiss this family of models because of its simple approach, we believe it is a mistake to ignore them entirely – early models have had remarkably accurate out-of-sample results, have reliably identified historical periods of over- and undervaluation, and still receive considerable attention from market participants."[9]

The Stock-to-Flow Scarcity model detailed in Chapter 7 is one such price regression model. It has had an enormous capability to predict the price of bitcoin over long periods of time based on the stock-to-flow model outlined by PlanB, which built upon the model from Saifedean Ammous. In 2020, with the Bitcoin Halvening Event in May, we see another chance for this model to be tested when the Halvening doubles the scarcity value of bitcoin. I recommend everyone read the Medium article by PlanB titled "Modeling Bitcoin's Value with Scarcity."[10]

Discounted Future Utility

The discounted future utility is a set of models that determines valuation using a total addressable market, a discounted cash flow analysis, and the equation of exchange. Discounted Future Utility models were introduced by Chris Burniske in his book, *Cryptoassets*.[11] These models are based on usage and utility and are heavily driven by quantitative approaches using nominal/absolute numbers and metrics. They originate from the traditional finance world and standard value-based investment approaches using discounted cash-flow modeling.

Other approaches have been based on bottom-up analysis using some version of a discounted cash-flow (DCF) model. I've read some great reports from top crypto funds that do a bottom-up analysis on how much revenue a specific crypto asset may generate based on a model and some assumptions. Crypto asset value will come from the supply/demand dynamic when investors make decisions of investment based on token models, relative valuation, and network utility – perhaps in the future, cashflow. As discussed, this set of models may be a good approach when markets have matured and are in the Synergy or Maturity Phase of Carlota Perez's model for technological revolution. In the Frenzy phase, however, using the hard data to calculate *relative* value is more beneficial.

Cost of Production

The set of models that fall under the cost of production is based on commodity and precious metals models from the mining industry. It focuses on the cost to produce certain crypto assets and on the breakeven prices of that production as well as mining profitability. This comes from classic economics that focuses on the price level relative to the cost of producing a commodity. Being able to calculate the natural price of a given commodity will help a savvy investor conclude value relative to current market price. These models work for certain crypto assets, but this area of work is mostly limited to commodity-like assets.

Token Models and Tokenomics

Tokens implement one of two main token models: *monetary* or *production*. I use "production" instead of "utility" token model to avoid historical confusion. A token model describes the value proposition of the crypto asset and how it derives its value: exogenously or endogenously.

Crypto assets with a monetary token model accrue value based on their use as money. For example, bitcoin derives its value from being a store of value, a medium of exchange, and perhaps eventually, a unit of account. Monetary token models create value by their scarcity and acceptability through wider use, adoption, and their network effects. Bitcoin is scarce because it's hardcapped at 21 million total supply. It's also the most widely accepted crypto asset. As such, with these two characteristics of *scarcity* and *acceptability*, it creates the most monetary value, which we see in the market today. Bitcoin and stablecoins, which we'll talk about more later, meet the demand for most of the monetary value creation. There may be incremental monetary value to add, but for the most part, bitcoin and stablecoins deliver the sound money aspect in the digital financial system.

Crypto assets with a production token model focus on adoption, functionality, rights to govern, and the overall cashflow they generate. For example, ether currently derives its value from utility – its value is exogenous, derived by the functionality it delivers into the market. Most of the current work in the crypto economy is focused on the production token model, where production value is created through new services, utility, and cashflow generation. In 2020, out of thousands of crypto assets, there are only a few examples of solid production token models. However, absence of evidence is not evidence of absence. Many falsely conclude that because they haven't seen uses for blockchains other than money (i.e. bitcoin) there must not be any other use for a blockchain. Furthermore, they conflate the concept of monetary and production value. The successful DeFi crypto assets are a good example of the production token model building on top of monetary tokens.

Token models and their economics, or tokenomics, play a key role in how a crypto asset accrues value. Token models affect the demand-side price elasticity by their use. Tokens create value through their use but accrue value through their tokenomics and token mechanics. This key characteristic of token model design will be used later to make investment decisions.

I hypothesize that the total collective value of tokens of monetary token models grows logarithmically while those with production token models grow exponentially. If correct, this too will play an important role in investment decisions.

Many in the crypto community have designed their own concepts of a token model with different monikers. I believe that abstracting two distinct layers of token models and token mechanics will lay a better foundation for crypto asset investing.

Token Mechanics

Tokens implement a set of token mechanics that aid in a token's design and its ability to create and accrue value. Token mechanics are a set of logically grouped actions that augment a token model and demonstrate how a token is going to create demand, utilize cash flow, and how/why it will accrue value. They mostly affect the price elasticity of a crypto asset by setting monetary policy, governing the supply schedule, and enforcing how revenues flow. Understanding token mechanics is a critical component to being able to evaluate which crypto assets are investable and which are not. We, as an investment community in 2017, learned the critical lesson that it takes more than just token usage for that token to accrue value.

In 2017, most retail investors thought a token utility would increase in value if the token was used or had big promise of usage. Many tokens were built and issued to meet a specific-use case. If a token was in use and provided a specific utility or access to a specific service, then the use would positively affect price, and tokens would accrue value over time.

The investor wave came because most thought a new investment model had been created through this new process known as an initial coin offering (ICO). Mass numbers of retail investors came to invest in early stage crypto projects where they thought they could expect a future return. The crypto markets turned into a frenzy with this perceived new model for venture investing. In general, we saw that investors were the only group coming to purchase tokens and without real usage, the crypto markets experienced a mania bubble where its popping was inevitable. Ultimately, the design of a token's mechanics can be the key to whether it can and will accrue value over time.

Classic Token Mechanic

The classic token mechanic is the most basic token mechanic – use through supply and demand. It's applied in all token models of all crypto assets today. It can only be effective if a large ecosystem is built around a token, which means that most tokens that only employ this token mechanic are not successful. If a good token ecosystem is created, the participants should expect to have good price elasticity, which will create an upward pressure on price. Tokens can create that dynamic pricing pressure either through limiting supply, creating sufficient and increasing demand.

Bitcoin utilizes the classic token mechanic well by limiting the total supply of bitcoin to 21 million. Investors hold this asset because they expect it to increase in value based on its scarcity, its network effects (acceptability), and the other properties that make it sound money. Production tokens aim to create a specific incentive structure within their token model.

Reserve Token Mechanic

The reserve token mechanic is one of the strongest token mechanics. It is powerful in that it allows holders of crypto assets to generate a return by holding it in reserve to create an entirely new crypto asset. That is the basis of capitalism – digital, decentralized capitalism. Savvy investors will continue to hold reserve assets through volatile markets because they are generating a return, and this is noteworthy. This token mechanic accrues value from this special property. It applies to just two crypto assets today, bitcoin and ether, though some open finance services allow for smaller tokens to be used as reserve assets. For example, the MakerDAO service allows for the $BAT token (Basic Attention Token) to be used as a reserve asset within its contract platform to mint $DAI stablecoins. For now, I'm going to reserve (pardon the pun) the use of this token mechanic for the base crypto assets, bitcoin and ether, as the core crypto assets that use the reserve token mechanic.

Lending Token Mechanic

The lending token mechanic is another of the strongest token mechanics. It's a token mechanic that focuses on a crypto asset, many times a cryptocurrency, which investors lend in order to generate interest income. This token mechanic is slightly different from the reserve token mechanic in that the crypto asset is generating income versus being used to create an entirely new crypto asset. It is powerful because it's one of two mechanics that currently generate an income stream. Investors will want to hold these crypto assets as long as the interest they can generate remains high relative to other options. This token mechanic is somewhat unique in that it's not a mechanic that gets designed into the token per se but rather is created by services and exchanges that lend out assets, and it is based on the supply and demand of that market.

Incentive Token Mechanic

The incentive token mechanic is one of the stronger token mechanics. It provides an incentive, in the form of tokens, for all value-added activity a user might perform within its ecosystem. This token mechanic transfers value to a user in the form of issuing tokens. However, for a token design to accrue long-term value, it must incorporate this token mechanic wisely within its overall design. Otherwise, value may be created but not accrued. This token mechanic is relatively new in the space, with some of the first implementations coming from the DeFi sector.

Burn Token Mechanic

The burn token mechanic is yet another strong mechanic for a crypto asset because it reduces supply, which should affect price. This mechanic has built into the blockchain system to programmatically set aside a percentage of the token's cashflows to buy and "burn" the token, meaning to destroy the token and decrease the total quantity in circulation. By reducing supply, and assuming that demand remains unchanged, price will be pushed higher, and value should accrue to the token due to price elasticity.

An example of this might be Binance's BNB token. This token uses multiple token mechanics to increase supply price elasticity by using governance, discount, and burn token mechanics. With the burn token

Figure 13.6 Binance Burn Chart for 2020

mechanic, Binance commits a portion of the fees generated from using BNB for transaction, trading, and transfer fees on the Binance exchange. In March 2020, Binance announced their 11th Burn Process, which burned 3,373,988 BNB tokens amounting to $52.5 million USD at the time (Figure 13.6). Binance took ~3.3 million BNB tokens out of circulation on that 11th burn process. At the time, it was the biggest burn in USD and in BNB terms.

The burn token mechanic is somewhat analogous to the share repurchasing process with equities when companies commit profits to buy back their stock. As we see more and more tokens consider this mechanic, it's typically combined with other token mechanics like governance. Tokens with multiple tokenomic mechanics are going to strengthen their potential to accrue value.

Governance Rights Token Mechanic

The governance token mechanic is a strong mechanic to help a token accrue value. Token holders who own and control crypto assets that have a governance token mechanic are allowed to vote on the management and governance of that blockchain. This is compelling because crypto assets may not be wholly complete in their design and development at the time of their launch. Blockchains, and their services and features, will need to be governed, maintained, and managed along the way. On-chain

governance is a very effective and transparent tool that allows the owners of those tokens to make the decisions and choices that are in the
best interest of that particular blockchain. Now, governance mechanics
aren't perfect just yet, but they are representative of what's possible currently with shareholder voting. That shareholder voting allows items to
be voted on and is a "one share for one vote" model like many of these
current simple on-chain governance models.

Governance mechanics will get more sophisticated and complex as
the investor community sees the value of on-chain, decentralized governance. The governance rights token mechanic is valuable to the crypto
asset, we assert, because as the value of crypto assets increases, so, too, will
the governance rights. Because token holders must hold the crypto asset
to be able to continue to vote in the interests of that particular blockchain, investors are going to want to hold more tokens. This mechanic
should therefore accrue more value to the token.

Staking Token Mechanic

The staking token mechanic figures as another strong token mechanic.
Staking tokens is a process used in blockchain systems that utilize a
proof-of-stake consensus mechanism. Owners of the tokens can stake
their tokens, which helps secure and manage the blockchain network
and confirms transactions within the system. For this effort, token holders are issued a staking yield, which is like an interest payment. Staking
yields are analogous to dividend payments in the equity asset class with
the caveat that they are considered active, not passive income. There's
also risk associated to staking because if you generate an invalid block,
your staked assets could be at risk. It's this very risk that creates incentive
for token stakers to validate and confirm the correct transactions. This
intrinsic property of a token is valuable to investors because it generates a financial return in the form of a yield. Most yields are somewhere
between 6% and 18%, so they can be quite lucrative, especially within
this current low rate interest environment.

Discount/Feature Token Mechanic

The discount/feature token mechanic provides holders of the crypto
asset specific discounts or access to services. Holders of the token can
get discounts on fees like exchange trading fees or access to services like

identity verification services. This token mechanic has value equal to the value of the discount feature provided, but I would estimate this to be one of the weaker token mechanics.

Service/Work Token Mechanic

The service/work token mechanic provides the holder of a token a commodity or service in exchange for the token, for example, getting computer power or networking service in exchange for a token. We see this type of token mechanic in blockchains, for example, Filecoin. For value to accrue via this token mechanic, the value of the service/work completed needs to increase relative to the token supply. The value of this mechanic may come from price elasticity, the tension of supply and demand of the particular service provided. This may become a strong token mechanic, but as of 2020 we have yet to see a lot of users with a crypto asset utilizing this token mechanic. Neither has there been a lot of value getting transferred with such a system, so we don't yet have great examples of this token mechanic.

Conclusion on Models and Frameworks

There is a lot of discussion around token mechanic design and tokenomics. Since crypto assets are truly in the experimental phase, there is a lot of dialog and conjecture without a firm taxonomy for the entire crypto investor community to follow. At this point, the important feature to understand about token mechanics stems from token design, which is what creates the ability for a token to accrue value. Some token designs with layered mechanics will accrue more value over time because of their design. As savvy investors, our job is to continue to look at the most current thinking and include this aspect in our decision making around portfolio construction. Both asset selection and portfolio construction are key factors in building a crypto asset portfolio that generates superior returns. Understanding token design, token mechanics, and tokenomics is critical to crypto asset investing and will give savvy investors the needed edge.

14

Understanding Crypto Asset Classes

Blue Horseshoe loves Anacott Steel.
— Bud Fox (from the movie *Wall Street*)

Classifying and categorizing crypto assets well gives an investor an edge in portfolio construction. Along with market timing and asset selection, strong portfolio construction provides the capability of delivering market-beating returns. To that end, understanding crypto asset classes will give a savvy investor a leg up on her tools to building and managing a portfolio.

I come at the process of organizing information like a software engineer, through encapsulating and abstracting, but with the knowledge of an investor knowing standards from the traditional investing world. I classify the mutually exclusive subsets of crypto assets based on logical groupings with similar attributes and market reactions as well as similar legal, cashflow, and asset structures. Each asset within a class has similar functional goals and reacts to the market in a similar fashion, which means they're correlated. Each crypto asset within a class has similar token and valuation models, compete with one another in some form, or operate similarly within their set and have similar regulatory risk. Finally, each crypto asset class defines the broadest subset under the umbrella of crypto assets. I utilize 11 distinct crypto asset classes: reserve, currencies, platforms, utility tokens, governance tokens, security tokens, asset-backed tokens, crypto-commodities, appcoins, nonfungible tokens (NFTs), and stablecoins.

Fundamentally, I'm coming at this as an investor and so are you. I want to have an asset allocation strategy and then have multiple positions of the coins I think will best produce a return for that crypto asset class. I want to be able to manage target asset class percentages. I don't want to commingle currencies, utility tokens, platforms, and appcoins in the same asset class because that does not provide me with a satisfactory level of precision to allocate across the total market. The asset classes may have similar valuation models, but their stated goal and their functions are different. Assets within a crypto asset class should be correlated and respond similarly to market conditions. Finally, crypto asset classes should have a similar set of token mechanics where tokens from a particular class implement similar token mechanics as other tokens within the class. From an investor's perspective, it makes sense to create 8–12 classes that are generally mutually exclusive while also being exhaustively comprehensive to classify members in the entire crypto asset superset.

Reserve Crypto Assets

The reserve crypto asset class contains just two assets – bitcoin and ether. While bitcoin and ether are different in many ways, they both have a market quality similar to one another and not shared by any other crypto assets. Along with stablecoins, they are considered the base crypto asset an investor typically converts from fiat currency before buying any other of the 5,000-plus crypto assets. Bitcoin and ether share many other characteristics. They are both mined and have set monetary policies. They both act as reserve crypto assets in the market by being reserved, or locked up, to create other financial assets and services. Both of the reserve crypto assets employ the classic and reserve token mechanics presently.

Both ether and bitcoin crypto assets are used as reserves, which can be borrowed and can produce income for the lender. Both are used in the decentralized finance (DeFi) or open finance markets for borrowing and lending. Bitcoin is seen more as *the* reserve asset for the crypto markets and for investors who are focused on store-of-value investment characteristics. Ether is a reserve asset because its locked up in order to back loans, derivatives, insurance, and monetary issuance in the decentralized world. Ether is a reserve asset but it's not sound money.

Cogent arguments have been made that bitcoin is its own distinct crypto asset class because it is *the* deflationary/disinflationary cryptocurrency with hardcapped supply, making it a much harder form of money and truly built as a store-of-value (SoV) asset. Ether's prime utility is not as an SoV asset as it exists to power the decentralized Ethereum world computer, which runs all Ethereum-based smart contracts. The Ethereum network is a platform with different supply/demand mechanics than bitcoin. Furthermore, Ethereum is in the process of moving to proof-of-stake (PoS) and will employ the governance and staking token mechanics as well, which we discuss later in the book. However, as long as these two crypto assets hold special characteristics within the marketplace as base crypto assets, I consider them both reserve assets.

Reserve Asset Traditional History

Let's take a page from the traditional financial analog. The entire current global capital complex is built first with a reserve asset as base money that has no counterparty risk. Initially during a sound money period, gold was used as the first reserve asset. Banks formed and began issuing credit based on deposits of reserves. Collateralized loans are the first product built in a capitalist system. Countries to this day still use their gold reserves as collateral, stored mostly in the United States, for trade and finance.

The use of gold started thousands of years ago. Gold was the first decentralized form of money because it is not issued, managed, or controlled by a central authority. As such, it does not have counterparty risk. From gold during past historic periods of sound money, countries managed their fiat money supply through their central bank, which was limited based on their gold reserves. Central bankers still borrowed and created debt, but it was limited based on gold reserves and ability to pay back the loan. Central banks then create a new asset class, sovereign bonds, which include an interest rate, setting the price for money. It's this rate that sets the entire fixed-income asset class complex in terms of interest rates based on duration risk and credit risk for the rest of the bond complex. So, as you can see, the entire financial capital complex is beginning with an asset that is used as a reserve currency, and it's that reserve currency that is the base of lending, banking, insurance, derivatives, and on which all financial services are built and on which all capital is built: equity, debt, and other assets.

While gold is classified as a commodity (for legal and other reasons), it is treated as both a commodity and a currency. It is a reserve asset. It has special properties that convince asset allocators and investors that gold is an asset class of its own. The same is true for bitcoin. It is like gold in the traditional financial world, and all other assets are built upon them.

Cryptocurrencies

Cryptocurrencies' core benefit to the market is to be a digital form of payment. The fundamental question to test the validity of a coin as a currency asks, "Is the primary use of the coin as a medium of exchange and/or a store of value?" That is, does it digitally fulfill on a currency's ability to be:

- a medium of exchange;
- a store of value;
- and ultimately, a unit of account.

Each cryptocurrency is at various stages of delivering on the functionality of a currency, which is the primary goal or function. The classic token mechanic is employed in most of the older cryptocurrency crypto assets while some of the newer assets also employ the governance and staking token mechanics. Cryptocurrencies collectively have similar regulatory risk as a collection compared against other crypto asset classes, that is, utility tokens, depending on how they came to market. Ideally, they would legally be considered currency, not property, to improve tax problems and improve usability. There has been legislation introduced into the US House of Representatives, dubbed the "Crypto-Currency Act of 2020," that treats cryptocurrencies differently from crypto-commodities and crypto-securities.[1]

Cryptocurrencies are all trying to address the same issues of value transference whether it's remittance, supply chain, or consumer payments. Cryptocurrencies are grouped logically, and there is no broader, more generalized grouping; therefore, cryptocurrency is its own crypto asset class. Dash, decred, and monero are all examples of cryptocurrencies.

Platform Crypto Assets

Smart contract platforms, or platforms, are blockchains with one of the most interesting crypto assets because these are where smart, autonomous contracts and programmatic money exist. If a blockchain implements smart contracts in some form, then it's in the platform asset class. Fundamental change in innovation has already transformed what's possible with the digital accumulation, transference, and store of value. Programmatic processing of legal and financial contracts will transform the shape and velocity of what's possible globally.

Crypto start-ups are building a decentralized finance digital infrastructure. Prediction market smart contracts have been built, which could be the building block of insurance and hedging products. De-Fi start-ups are building stablecoins run by DAOs, which determine monetary policy for the digital stablecoin. From there, all sorts of digital finance products can be built for lending and borrowing. We're in the early stages, but we're starting to see autonomous functions occur without the need of human intervention, and it's happening inside smart contracts on these platform blockchains.

As I illustrate in Part II of the book, let's paint a picture of the future in 20 years. Most corporations will effectively become a set of smart contracts governed by a DAO or DAC. Governance, voting, supply chain, and contract enforcement will fundamentally change because we will be able to programmatically store and transfer value based on some previously agreed-upon logic. Value will be created globally just from the transparency and predictability of contract execution. We will be able to see exactly where our food comes from and how it's handled along the way. We will be able to trust that there has been no tampering with digital voting because of the immutability of a blockchain. If land titles are securely registered and managed on a blockchain, land title disputes will rarely occur, and if they do occur, they will be adjudicated quickly. Proof of ownership, a clean record of transfer, and the fundamental characteristic of immutability will exist because of the way blockchains are designed.

Platforms, such as smart contracts, immutability, and decentralization, provide some of the building blocks of blockchain. However, they are distinct from cryptocurrency in their stated goal and function. They have different regulatory risks than other crypto asset classes, depending on how they were created (e.g. based on regulatory region and whether they are a public ICO or a private presale governed sale, etc.) and how they transfer value back to token holders/owners. If platforms have a functioning network in production and are sufficiently decentralized, then they have less regulatory risk than other types of crypto assets based on communications from the SEC. Platforms are closer to legal contracts than money in the analog paradigm. Their valuation model is primarily based on network effects, which is described by Metcalfe's Law – the value of the network is proportional to n^2 users of the network – whereas cryptocurrencies are valued on the velocity of money and the equation of exchange. They are typically utilizing governance, staking, and service token mechanics along with classic and ultimately reserve tokenomics once they're really being used and adopted. Platforms are distinct from all other crypto asset classes from these perspectives, and thus they are a crypto asset class of their own. Some examples of platform crypto assets are Algorand, Ethereum, and Solana.

Utility Tokens

Utility tokens focus on providing a service layer. They typically implement the classic, discount, and service token mechanics. They provide a function or a resource to address a specific need. They have partners and contributors that create applications on top of the protocol or create applications that use the utility token. An example of this might be earning the Brave Attention Token (BAT) that's given for using the Brave browser. Instead of an advertiser model, the Brave browser blocks ads and pays users for their attention, or it allows users to pay for content. The utility tokens valuation model is primarily based on network effects and is influenced by price elasticity from the classic token mechanic. Utility tokens run on a platform blockchain they do not directly manage or control. To date, most run on the Ethereum platform. They are distinct from platforms in that they aren't providing a lower level or horizontal functionality built on top of a blockchain like a protocol, and they are distinct from appcoins because their stated functional goal is not limited to one application or service. Currently, utility tokens are tied to a particular blockchain and therefore only work on that blockchain. In the future, however, the utility tokens may operate on multiple networks to serve multiple appcoins. Some examples of utility tokens are Basic Attention Token and Orchid.

Governance Tokens

Governance tokens are a subset of utility tokens, and they manage, govern, and report on their blockchain's crypto assets. Like the name implies, they implement governance rights token mechanics, though they will typically have staking, burning, and other ancillary token mechanics as well. Governance tokens provide transparency and a mechanism for managing and governing a system or community with shared assets of that community. Many times, governance tokens represent ownership in a DAO. Voting and governance both occur on the blockchain by holders of the token.

An example of a governance token might be Binance's $BNB token. It allows holders to indirectly participate in the revenue stream created by Binance exchange trading fees. It does this by burning, or destroying them, which reduces the overall outstanding supply. Many governance tokens work in a similar fashion. Other examples of governance tokens are: $ZRX and $MKR.

Security Tokens

Security tokens are tokens that are classified as securities by the SEC here in the United States and other relevant regulatory bodies globally. Currently, there are not many security tokens. They need to trade on regulated exchanges and the parties involved in the transaction need to be whitelisted. However, there may be an SEC decision, enforcement action, or legislative update that will provide more clarity around digitally native crypto assets that are also securities in the future. These will implement the previously discussed burn and yield token mechanics, which are two ways to pass ownership and cashflow rights to their holders. Tokens that aren't yet classified as security tokens, but act like securities now through providing income, may be reclassified as security tokens by various regulatory bodies. We'll have to wait and see. An example of a security token might be $BCAP, which is Blockchain Capital's first digital asset fund.

Asset-Backed Tokens

Asset-backed tokens are different from utility tokens and platforms by their functional nature and goal as well as by their regulatory risk profile. Asset-backed tokens represent assets in token form and do not leverage tokenomics per se. The asset-backed tokens derive their value from being linked to an external asset and will likely be subject to federal securities regulations here in the United States.

These tokens will have a much bigger play in their growth stage in 2022 and beyond. I predict that by 2023, there will be illiquid companies or real estate projects that want to have their equity trade as security tokens on a regulated crypto exchange. We will see real estate secured on a blockchain with a security token. Asset-backed tokens are distinct from all other crypto asset classes because of their link to an external, real-world asset.

Crypto Commodities

It is commodities' aim to provide a direct consumable resource. This is distinct from the platform asset class in that it's vertical/industry-specific, and it seeks exchange based on a specific subset of resources. Those resources might include disk space, computing power, or other consumable services. Commodities are distinct from utility tokens in that their valuation model is mostly influenced by the supply and demand of a given resource. Crypto-commodities run their own blockchain. This is different from utility tokens' operation and is one of the main mechanics of how supply and demand affect price. Crypto-commodities may be more affected by price surges and other scarcity risks than other asset classes, such as utility tokens or appcoins. They will, nevertheless, have less regulatory risk because of the work or resource exchanged, assuming appropriate measures were followed in their presale.

Crypto-commodities mostly employ the classic and service token mechanics. Their valuation model is influenced by network effects, but it's important to think about both demand and supply price elasticity and how that will affect the commodity offering. They are different than currencies, which are mostly valued by the velocity of money, and utility, which are valued mostly by use. Examples of crypto-commodities are STORJ, Filecoin, and Golem.

DApps (Decentralized Apps)

DApps work on one specific network to provide a specific vertical application service. They are distinct from commodities in that their supply is not constrained like a commodity or resource that is consumed. They are different from platforms because they are vertical- and application-specific. They aren't providing a platform or protocol for others to build upon. Their goal and utility are distinct in focusing on their own narrow ecosystem. They have a many-to-one relationship in their network model, whereas utility tokens have a many-to-many relationship. They implement the classic, discount, and service token mechanics. Appcoins are the narrowest applications and are therefore levered to a specific use case as being a "pure play" to a particular application or service. As a result, their valuation model will be distinct from commodities, currencies, or platforms. Examples of appcoins are Steem, Civic, and SALT.

Nonfungible Tokens (NFTs)

Nonfungible tokens, or NFTs, represent a unique digital item. The fundamental property of NFTs? They are unique and that unique structure may provide some compelling investment opportunities in the future. They might be used as claims to unique art or virtual items inside games that represent something of real value to the players. At present, we haven't seen a lot of examples of NFTs, and their token mechanics are mainly focused on the classic token mechanic and whatever they represent as a unique digital asset. These types of tokens are in a nascent stage, but their idea could unlock a lot of value in the digital world to come. An example of NTF tokens is CryptoKitties, which was a game released on the Ethereum platform in 2017. The Worldwide Asset Exchange (WAX) blockchain is offering many new NFTs that are selling out.

Stablecoins

Stablecoins are present to provide a stable store of value. Currently, there is one major player within this crypto asset class, and that is Tether. New stablecoins like $DAI, $USDC, and $PAX are, however, gaining market share. Currently there are several projects pursuing various methods as to how to achieve a stablecoin. Stablecoins themselves don't have token models, though there may be governance tokens that are associated with them. One example of this might be MakerDAO with its $MKR governance token. This manages the $DAI ecosystem and the $DAI stablecoin. This is a new and burgeoning asset class, and we will distinguish it on its own due to its stated goal and functional nature. Some examples of stablecoins are $DAI and $USDC.

Other Approaches

Many investors have attempted to describe, classify, and categorize the various crypto assets. Most fund managers have their own models. Some of the most common labels used to organize a collection of crypto assets include: security tokens, utility tokens, governance tokens, work tokens, cryptocurrencies, crypto-commodity tokens, platforms, appcoins, non-fungible tokens (NFTs), reserve crypto assets, and stablecoins.

Investors like Tom Lee of Fundstrat Global Advisors break the collections into cohorts based on how they trade – more like sectors. For example, Lee breaks the sectors into commodities, platforms, privacy, exchanges, and stablecoins. He does this because these cohorts trade similarly, and he can model trading action based on their collective attributes. Sector definition is important, but I think there's one higher level of abstraction needed. That's crypto asset classes. Commodities, platforms, and stablecoins are of a different classification type than privacy coins and exchanges, and I would separate them as such. That way, we have both asset classes and sectors like we do with traditional financial markets.

Other investors or investment firms, like the general partners at Multicoin Capital, break asset collections into three major cohorts: currencies (stores of value), security tokens (tokens backed by real-world assets or that generate return like securities), and utility tokens (work tokens). They've settled on this configuration because they think each has a separate and distinct valuation model. They outline a valuation model for currencies and work tokens. You'll notice that they don't distinguish platform coins from cryptocurrencies as they believe platform coins will be held for their own specific store of value. The CIO of Ikigai Asset Management, Travis Kling, uses sectors and subsectors to define the crypto asset universe. As you can see, each model has its pros and cons.

Some labels have lingered through nomenclature "inheritance." An example of this is the moniker "altcoins." It can be confusing as to exactly what an altcoin is and whether it can mean every other coin that is not bitcoin. Such a large subset really doesn't help an investor in their portfolio construction and management and should be thrown out of the investor vernacular.

Conclusion

As investors, we're in the very early stages of thinking about portfolio construction for this new asset. Our thinking and grouping could change. Ultimately, the concepts here should help you as an investor think about how you want to classify crypto assets to aid in your portfolio management efforts. It is possible ether could fall out of the reserve asset class and be reclassified under the platform tokens asset class. It is possible appcoins could merge with utility tokens or crypto-commodities merge into platforms.

My goal is to help investors build a portfolio with the ability to use asset allocation to improve your risk-adjusted returns. To achieve that, we need a good framework that provides a logical way to think about crypto asset classes. If Modern Portfolio Theory (MPT) suggests a return can be made only three ways – portfolio construction, asset selection, and market timing – then we want a structure that helps guide and reinforce our thinking about asset allocation. A comprehensive crypto asset class model will help in this effort by providing investors a way of diversifying a crypto portfolio across multiple crypto asset classes just like a traditional equity portfolio.

15

Investment Themes

The most valuable commodity I know is information.
— Gordon Gekko (from the movie *Wall Street*)

Investor conviction is a key determining factor for generating positive, outsized returns. An investor must have conviction to stay in a trade when volatility spikes, and that happens often in crypto asset investing. The antidote to volatility is conviction.

One of the ways to achieve conviction is to have an investment thesis and then investment themes that fit within that thesis. In this chapter, I outline three investment themes for crypto asset investing. They are sound/self-sovereign money, decentralized governance, and autonomous contracts. Sound money as an investment theme provides an insurance policy against the greatest monetary experiment in history, which is going on today with quantitative easing and modern monetary theory. Decentralized governance will outline a case for why crypto assets that have on-chain governance will increase in value more than assets that don't, and I explain what on-chain governance is. The thesis here is that as crypto assets increase in value so do the governing rights around those assets. Finally, this chapter outlines how autonomous, smart contracts as an investment theme lead the way during the Age of Autonomy.

We based our investment themes on our investment thesis to target where we think value will get created and where value will accrue.

We invest from first principles we outlined in previous chapters. Finally, each of the investment themes is derived from some aspect of the Age of Autonomy thesis.

Sound Self–Sovereign Money

One investment theme is to invest in digital, scarce, hard, nonpolitical, nonsovereign decentralized money. One of the most important justifications for investment in crypto, specifically bitcoin, is to have an insurance policy against the global central banks and their manipulation of the money supply. This is a hedge against the largest monetary experiment in history, which began with quantitative easing as an intervention to the 2008 crisis but has morphed and expanded since then. Central banks around the world have lowered interest rates to 0% or even negative rates. They've all continued to expand their balance sheets. There is no end in sight.

As a Hedge

As of 2020, Japan's central bank, the Bank of Japan (BoJ), now owns more than 80% of Japanese equity ETFs. The "Lost Decade" was a term coined to refer to the decade-long economic stagflation (disinflation) crisis in Japan. That term was coined in 2001, and the ongoing crisis is now almost three decades long. That's the problem with a deflationary spiral – it goes on for decades. It ends when the central bank ends up buying back all bonds, and the currency collapses.

On the other end of the spectrum, you have Venezuela. In 2019, their inflation rate was 9,586%. That's high. The money was debased until it was worthless, and the currency collapsed.

Either way, it's the government intervention that causes both of these outcomes. Money and state must be separated. Since we do not have the political power to complete this goal on our own, the next best thing is to buy insurance, or a hedge, against fiat-denominated assets, including currency, debt, and equity. That hedge is gold and bitcoin. Both are highly liquid and have no counterparty risk. Bitcoin, as previously described, has many attributes that make it a superior hedge to sovereign-based fiat currency. Sovereign money without the attachment to a government is going to be critical in the future because it removes all the political risk associated with a particular country and that's crucial in the next-generation of global reserve assets.

Global Central Bank Backdrop

As we've discussed throughout the book, global central banks are implementing more and more exotic forms of monetary intervention. Interest rates around the globe are set to 0%, or in some cases negative interest rates are implemented. Central banks are in the process of using various forms of balance sheet expansion. Japan's central bank, the BoJ, is in the most advanced stages of its country's balance sheet expansion. It buys Japanese corporate debt as well as Japanese equities in the form of buying ETFs. The European Central Bank, too, has had many discussions about buying equities. Here in the United States, former Fed chair Janet Yellen has also commented that the Federal Reserve doesn't need to buy equities now but Congress should reconsider allowing it.[1]

The coronavirus only accelerated global central banks' efforts. During the early spread of the pandemic in March 2020, the Federal Reserve started with $700 billion in quantitative easing. With the economy basically shut down, markets went into freefall. Then, the Fed initiated a second effort which was $1.5 trillion – a balance sheet expansion available, which was their *bazooka* moment.[2] On the government side, its $2 trillion fiscal stimulus bill was passed in an effort to help citizens, small businesses, and corporations deal with the pandemic, but that wasn't the end of it. The Fed then announced "QE to infinity"[3] and ended on April 9 declaring another $2.3 trillion of balance sheet expansion,[4] also announcing they could and would buy corporate bonds, which had never been done before here in the United States. All of this monetary and fiscal stimulus will have a future impact on inflation and the US dollar. Bitcoin, with its limit of 21 million bitcoin and its superior money characteristics, is ideal as an investment into a sound money vehicle.

A Digital Reserve Asset

Bitcoin is also a reserve asset in the new digital financial platform. It is the digital asset that provides a store-of-value. As such, it makes it the ideal digital candidate to be a reserve asset upon which other digital assets can be created. The book *The Bitcoin Standard* makes its case for this.[5] Building a digital financial system on sound money is a core principle to the Bitcoin revolution.

Surveillance-Resistant Asset

A part of the sound money investment thesis is that we need to build upon a surveillance-resistant asset. We have a choice of two worlds. Do we allow governments the power to watch every effort and action like in China? Do we allow corporations access to all of our data and allow them constant surveillance of our activities through our mobile phones like happens in the United States? One aspect of the crypto movement is to preserve some individual privacy. This sound money investment thesis builds upon this need.

Seizure-Resistant Asset

Finally, the sound money investment thesis incorporates the concept of a seizure-resistant asset. Since bitcoin no longer requires a third party to execute a financial transaction, it also removes the capability of the third party to interfere or intervene on a financial transaction. The concept of immutability is built into the bitcoin system. Coupled with cryptography and the use of keys, bitcoin provides a permissionless, seizure-resistant asset. Ultimately, the sound money thesis posits the market will put a premium on this characteristic.

Decentralized/Open Finance

The biggest thing to hit the crypto community after the ICO craze was decentralized finance (DeFi) or open finance. We saw a growth from $0 to almost $1 billion committed as collateral into the open finance system within a year through 2019 and into 2020. The desire is here.

What's so powerful about open finance is that it's permissionless and doesn't require a trusted third party. You don't need an account and you don't need approval from anyone. DeFi runs on a public blockchain that can be accessed by anyone with an Internet connection. This allows two things to happen. On the supply side, it allows investors to create new forms of capital. Under a sound money policy, investors can provide collateral into the system, through smart contracts, and print a new form of stable currency called stablecoins. This is a new decentralized money that is backed by other digital assets. On the demand side, investors can take that newly printed digital money to provide the first formation of capital, which is debt in the form of lending. This creates an interest rate for the currency. It creates banking services. The same investors or other investors can then take that borrowed money and invest it. This is the basis of a financial system.

Banking the Unbanked

Open finance aims to provide a new digital and permissionless version of traditional financial services that have the capability of reaching everyone. Only 1.5 billion people worldwide currently have access to checking accounts or financial services in general. Being able to provide financial services to the other 4.5 billion while reducing the friction of cost and time to existing consumers will create enormous economic activity. All of those 4.5 billion people could have access to accounts for money payments, savings, and borrowing.

Digital Currency/Stablecoins

But this is more than just banking the unbanked. Imagine the guy in Africa who has never had access to capital markets. The very first capital formation for a family typically happens when you can borrow against an asset like land. Most people who've gotten out of poverty have borrowed against their land to get cash to then be able to create some sort of business that produces cashflow. Well, that guy in Africa never had clear title to his land, couldn't prove he owned it, and therefore could never borrow against it. He never had the chance to create a business to start producing cashflow. Even if he had started small. Even if he had started with one satoshi (the smallest increment of bitcoin), the open finance system allows any person to get a collateralized loan on some digital asset and borrow against that asset. They can then put the borrowed money to work, create more economic value than the loan interest amount, and generate cashflow. Stored cashflow is equity. With money, debt, and equity, you've now got a full financial system that requires no permission and no third party. How powerful could that be unleashed across the globe?

Lending

Now that a decentralized bank has created digital money, more and more players can lend. To date, only collateral lending occurs through tying up digital assets in smart contracts and lending at interest rates. Borrowers get certain rates and lenders get certain rates, and the entire system that matches borrowers and lenders gets the spread. This is how traditional banking works and is now replicated in DeFi. All of DeFi's lending services are provided in the form of smart contracts. They provide for collateralized loans in a permissionless environment, which are provided for by public blockchains. Right now, Ethereum is the winner for a Layer 1 blockchain delivering DeFi services.

Derivatives

Speculators and investors will need derivatives to hedge positions or to speculate. DeFi provides several decentralized autonomous organizations (DAOs), or companies, which provide digital derivatives contracts, typically enforced in smart contracts. Companies, or DAOs, like Synthetix, FTX, Augur, and others provide derivatives in the DeFi space.

Insurance

Decentralized insurance has begun in 2020 starting with a *mutual* insurance entity like in traditional markets. Nexus Mutual and Opyn offer insurance on several different services and assets. This provides a value proposition by offering protection, hedging, or speculation service in a permissionless, decentralized format. This also provides benefits to its members with faster payouts and greater flexibility. This allows anyone to generate income by becoming an insurance company/individual, taking on certain structured risks for a premium. DeFi insurance also covers technical and financial risks that no other insurance companies provide and, coupled with other services, can provide more complex financial instruments. If an investor wanted to cover risk that comes from using a smart contract or risk on loan or other financial risks, they can do so with DeFi insurance services. More sophisticated users will use these services and more investors will come to DeFi now that they can hedge and insure against risk.

Decentralized Exchanges (DEXs)

In the future, investors won't log into an exchange and enter their market/limit orders to buy/sell their digital assets. It will be done inside a bigger framework that includes a user interface (UI) with defined goals and rules and will be managed within smart contracts. Furthermore, investors will be looking to put together more complex trades that include: assets, lending/borrowing, insurance, transference, and, potentially, the purchase/sale of derivatives, all-in-one transaction. Investors will want these more complex transactions because they reduce risk, increase return, and improve overall risk-adjusted returns. In fact, insurance is a key component that the average investor doesn't even factor into their investment plan because they don't know about it, it's not available, or it's too expensive. Furthermore, with the addition of programmatic money, there is an innovation that will transform how money is stored, processed, and transferred as units of stores of value. Decentralized exchanges, or DEXs, will change the game for how we invest and how that whole process operates.

DEXs are different than centralized exchanges, and there are many different flavors of them. Essentially, most DEXs do not take custody of their users' assets. Those assets stay within the users' wallets and interact directly with a set of smart contracts that manage the exchange process. There are still order books, market makers, makers/takers, bids, and asks, but they do not operate under one centralized exchange. This changes the regulatory game as well since DEXs aren't asset custodians. In five years, I predict there will be regulated centralized exchanges, regulated DEXs, and unregulated DEXs. It will probably be a decade before regulators can wrap their legal frameworks around how to regulate DEXs because, by and large, they are just software running on servers. Now, there are still regulatory chokepoints within the system and important regulations that must be followed both in spirit and by the letter of the law. The main point is that DEXs provide a world where the exchange of assets happens within smart contracts, and a savvy investor will start taking advantage of this paradigm shift.

Liquidity Mining/Yield Farming

One aspect to DeFi is building up network effects and users of DeFi crypto networks. Some crypto assets offer ways to generate outsized yields by participating in their network. Some tokens offer smart contracts to find the best interest rates and are crypto assets themselves. Some provide the collateralized loans themselves and want to attract more participants. Some are looking for market liquidity in whatever that market is trading. Liquidity itself is a product and, as such, it can be bought, sold, and traded. There's a market for it.

Decentralized Governance

Decentralized governance is the ability to manage a blockchain, its assets, and features on-chain. This allows for the management of voting and governance, lists the possible development upgrades, policy updates, schedules, and manages voting and reporting governance outcomes all on-chain, which creates value through its transparency. Decentralized governance stems out of the idea to be able to govern, vote, and manage the upgrading process of a blockchain on-chain. Community members vote their tokens on a list of potential change/upgrade options.

One of the core principles of this investment theme is that as the crypto assets of blockchains become more valuable, so, too, do the governance rights. Blockchains aren't going to be perfect in their version 1.0. They are going to require continuous improvement. How is that upgrade cycle managed? Is it managed by one central figure or in the virtual backrooms of various offices, garages, and/or bedrooms cloaked in opacity? Or is it managed transparently, out in the open, by the group of interested and vested parties having a say? If we all see the value of decentralized assets, then the next logical step is to see the value of managing those assets in a decentralized way. That is decentralized governance.

On-chain Voting and Governance

On-chain voting is one of the key aspects to decentralized governance. Each blockchain may do it a different way. Some of their approaches stem from their consensus architecture. For example, there are blockchains that use Delegated Proof of Stake (dPoS). This is analogous to a republic instead of a democracy. As a token holder, you can vote on who is going to be your representative, and then your representative votes and governs on your behalf. We see this type of architecture with EOS. Most of the other blockchains that support decentralized governance use a proof-of-stake consensus mechanism. Under this model, you can still have a republic or democratic model for governance. Some blockchains use tickets, and those tickets allow both a vote and also manage the staking yield payment. We see this model with a blockchain like Decred. Some other blockchains model straight-up democracy. Upgrades or policies get initiated and seconded, and then the whole community votes on the measure. We see that in Tezos and MakerDAO.

There's a real "aha!" moment to be had when you participate in decentralized governance. While the governance models are still basic "one coin/one vote," they will get more complex and more nuanced in the future. Right now, they are at least as good as the process for a shareholder vote in public stock whose traditional process is one share/one vote. However, by participating in a blockchain voting process, you get to see the real power of being a part of one of these communities. You see people playing different roles and providing various functions for the blockchain's community – miners, developers, investors, and token holders all with aligned interests. You see the power of transparency. The whole thing is done in the open and managed by software. There is no intermediary in the middle counting votes or creating opacity. It creates an active investor model and encourages participation. This is wholly different than what we've experienced as small investors holding stocks in a portfolio that is held and managed by our broker. As an investor, you feel like a participant involved in the creation of a community that's generating something new and something powerful. It's the act of being able to vote and govern on a public blockchain that everyone can see that makes the difference. As an investment theme, this aspect of good decentralized governance will help create more value for the token holder of assets.

DAOs and DACs

DAOs and DACs are the groups of people collectively involved to further a specific goal or objective. They come together in a group to act as a single entity and create rules, goals, and policies that advance the organization's interests. Once fully matured, a DAO or DAC will program all of their rules, goals, and policies into a set of smart contracts that operate in the decentralized world, over one or more blockchains, interacting with one or more accounts, and on one or more smart contracts, to advance the group's interests. In the future, the interface between human decision making and codifying policy will intersect inside a DAO or DAC. These are the groups that will participate in decentralized governance. Again, at first it may be human-led, but in the future it will all be driven by smart contracts managed by DAOs. DAOs aren't permissionless. You need to be approved to join. Some of these DAOs and DACs will be exclusive. Those who get into powerful DAOs early will have more power than those who lag behind. A savvy investor will learn about their power sooner rather than later.

The Age of Autonomy

The Age of Autonomy is a long-term investment thesis. The crypto assets that an investor might incorporate into this investment thesis will change over time. In the beginning of this investment thesis, platform crypto assets will play a critical role, as there is a race to establish what blockchains are used in which environments. Ethereum is a platform that's established itself in the DeFi space, but there are still other areas up for grabs. The core tenet is to invest in public infrastructure that will promote autonomy and autonomous operations.

It will take time for more of the public infrastructure to be built out. DeFi is a critical piece so that investors and operators can use autonomous contracts to interact with services that provide hedging, insurance, trading, lending, and other financial services. The next phase of the Age of Autonomy investment thesis is gluing all these services together to provide autonomous execution. Other phases will be to build out marketplaces for real-time interaction through executing autonomous contracts. Those marketplaces will most likely operate as decentralized exchanges (DEXs) where smart contracts move assets and money programmatically and not through a human computer user interface. Another aspect is governance of these crypto assets and the self-organization of humans in various DAOs and DACs to organize and synthesize knowledge into goals and actions. All of these ideas and instruments play a role in the Age of Autonomy.

Web 3.0 – Own Your Own Data

Web 3.0 is the next generation of the Internet. Web 1.0 was about static content delivered over the Internet as a web page. Web 2.0 was user-created content and dynamic content delivered to browsers and mobile apps where the provider delivered a service, typically for free, in exchange for access and ownership of user data. Web 3.0 will be about users owning their own data and being able to control who sees it, how much they see, and how long they can see it. They will be able to monetize their own data for themselves instead of for the service company. Web 3.0 is aiming to disrupt the disruptors.

Uber disrupted the taxi industry by providing a marketplace for real-time matching of drivers and passengers. With Web 3.0, this will eventually be possible using peer-to-peer commerce via a set of smart contracts that will eliminate the rent-seeker that now is Uber.

Decentralized Architecture

Web 3.0 has a decentralized architecture that is more peer-to-peer than centralized. Blockchain technology is a foundational protocol to deliver a decentralized web.

Identity

If Web 3.0 is going to be peer-to-peer, the function of proper identification and authentication will be required. Decentralized identity management solutions allow privacy and security of user data while also providing a second party in a peer-to-peer transaction the ability to confirm and verify identity without giving away more information that is needed to confirm a transaction. For example, if a person wants to get into a bar, they need to demonstrate they are at least 21 years of age. However, they do not need to give their full name, address, and date of birth to the second party, confirming that they are old enough. They don't really even need to give their full birth date. What they need to provide is yes or no to the question of, "Are you 21 or older?" Decentralized identity management solutions solve this problem.

Self-Sovereign Data

A user should be able to own and control personal data. That is not currently the case in the Web 2.0 world of 2020. Google and Facebook have vast amounts of user data, and the user has no control over how much access or for how long that data can be used. Web 3.0 looks to change all that. By allowing a user to maintain custody of their own data on a blockchain and by providing various levels of access to their data, along with duration of use, a user can take back control of their own data. Self-sovereign data will allow a user to maintain data privacy while also allowing them to share data when and how they so choose. This will also allow them more control over the monetization of their data. Web 3.0 makes all this possible.

P2P Commerce – Disrupting the Disruptors

Peer-to-peer (P2P) commerce is a part of Web 3.0, but I abstract and encapsulate it into its own investment theme because it has different factors going on when compared to Web 3.0. Most of Web 3.0 is focused on the infrastructure to deliver Web 3.0 while P2P commerce may or may not require the entire technology stack to deliver on the theme. The concept of P2P is what is powerful, and that is the idea of direct commerce between two parties. This is a paradigm shift from how commerce is typically done in the traditional sense.

Decentralized Commerce

Decentralized commerce, or P2P commerce, is that act of direct consumer commerce. Think of Uber with the company of Uber being a set of smart contracts. There is a smart contract for hailing drivers, there is a smart contract for payment settlement, there is a smart contract for finding riders, and finally, there is a set of smart contracts for people to plug in to help with customer service, issue resolution, reconciliation, and ratings/reputation. Most of what a company does can be codified. Human aspects can be managed through oracles, DAOs, and contracts that allow for employment on behalf of the DAC that manages the Uber smart contracts. Decentralized commerce is the leanest form of commerce, and, therefore, in the Age of Autonomy, it reduces rent-seeking to its minimum. What can be codified, is (codified).

Decentralized Commercial Governance

Way in the future as this technological revolution matures, we can envision an abstraction layer where governing commerce comes together in a series of smart contracts that help benefit the whole set of DAOs and DACs committed to similar commerce goals. This will be the mechanism for arbitration and communication between groups.

Token Curated Registry/Decentralized Reputation

A token curated registry (TCR) is a registry of reputation and reviews that is managed on a blockchain. In essence, it's a list that is curated, or managed, in a decentralized manner. You can think of Yelp or TripAdvisor, with their ratings and reviews, as potentials to become TCRs. As such, a built-in economic model exists to incentivize the curation of the list to optimal outcome. TCRs can also be used to weed out unwanted activity like spam or voter fraud. Token models exist to codify this structure.

Decentralized User Role Plug-In

Decentralized role plug-in smart contracts have yet to exist, but you can imagine a set of contracts that allow users or community members to plug into a DAO or DAC and provide service for economic benefit. A P2P car service to compete with Uber won't do a very good job without customer service. This could provide customer service or business development. Humans interface with smart contract plug-ins to provide human action and decision making within an autonomous economy. As we progress in the Age of Autonomy, there will be more and more code linking our economic behavior as we learn to systematize the corporation into a series of smart, autonomous contracts.

Digital Collectibles (Nonfungible Tokens)

An interesting investment theme that's up and coming is the digital collectible space. Just like unique items in the physical world can accrue value, unique items in the digital world can, too. More and more people are getting used to the idea of unique digital goods. Digital collectibles are not going to be very correlated to the main crypto market so they may have a position in an overall crypto portfolio.

I was on a Zoom call with William Quigley, who is the founder of the WAX (Worldwide Asset Exchange). He started WAX to trade virtual items that would be used and traded in certain online games. Recently, he started offering digital collectibles on the WAX platform. One such offering was unique digital content from William Shatner, who auctioned off a variety of items. One item was an X-ray of Shatner's teeth. Using NFTs, those digital items are now unique and cannot be reproduced. As such, they trade on secondary markets after the initial auction. Of the first half-dozen auctions Quigley has done, they've all sold out. Even more impressive is that many of these items were flipped in the secondary market for many multiples of their initial price at auction. This investment theme is gaining traction because there's a real demand out there. Some examples of other crypto projects related to this investment theme include OpenSea, Decentraland, and SuperRare. They offer digital collectibles via NFTs for art (both digital and physical), gaming, digital worlds, and unique real-world assets.

Passive Income

Passive income could be the next "killer app" of crypto by generating cashflow at much higher rates than offered in the legacy financial system. The passive income investment theme is not like any of the other investment themes. Its goal is to use stablecoins, like $USDC and $DAI, as cash-like equivalents and lend them out to produce an income return. Most of these cash-like equivalents can generate an interest rate of 2–8.6%. In the traditional financial system, we've destroyed the ability to generate risk-free passive income. There are several different risk parameters within the crypto interest-income markets, but let's look at two examples. If a savvy investor were to use $USDC and lend it out through a service, they would be taking minimal price risk since $USDC is pegged to the dollar. It's also backed by US Treasury notes and not inside a bank practicing fractional reserve banking. In essence, it's less risky than its traditional dollar counterpart sitting in a bank, and it's yielding 20×–200× yield interest. Investors inside the crypto world want to borrow $USDC, so there's actual demand for $ USDC, whereas the demand dynamics are different in the traditional markets right now. Another example could be lending $DAI, which is a truly decentralized stablecoin minted within a decentralized framework by MakerDAO. An investor can think of it as a *de*-central bank. At times, $DAI can fluctuate a bit more than the pegged stablecoins, so at times it can act more like a bond. This allows you to construct a risk-parity portfolio that helps absorb shock if there is a big drawdown in crypto because the price of $DAI typically goes up in a deflationary-type crash when everyone is scrambling for cash. It too can generate a healthy yield. You'll need to learn more about all the risks associated with these instruments, but there is a strong case for the fixed-income investment theme.

16

Building an Investment System

That was some of the best flying I've seen to date — right up to the part where you got killed.

— Jester (from the movie *Top Gun*)

The most important aspect to consistent investing is to build systems and processes that produce more positive, more predictable results. That's because investing really comes down to risk management. Systems and processes allow an investor to leave emotion out of the equation of investing. In this chapter we outline systems and processes for every aspect of crypto investing. These systems manage risk at their core.

Investing in crypto assets has many similarities to investing in equities, but it also has many differences. For example, technical analysis on a chart for a stock or for bitcoin is going to be roughly the same. There may be different time horizon aspects, but generally the analysis will work the same. However, other principles familiar to investors do not hold. For example, I do not recommend using stop-loss orders for investing in crypto unless you're trading, not investing. Investing requires conviction, a lower time preference, and correct asset selection. Some of these assets are thinly traded or have low liquidity and low volume, therefore price can be moved quite easily. I have seen many instances of "flash crashes" where a crypto asset moves down 50% for a few minutes, then goes back up. I can remember the terror of Black Thursday (March 12, 2020). The crypto markets are nascent and will need time and size to act more like a mature market.

There are many ways to approach crypto investing just like any other market. You could be looking for a quantitative model to inform a directional trading plan or a discretionary approach where you're looking to pick the best crypto assets for each crypto asset class or sector. The approach outlined in this book starts with a fundamental approach to investing. We're looking to develop an investment thesis we believe is driving the market. Under that thesis, we want to develop investment themes for how we think the long-term investment thesis is going to play out. Right now, investment themes are where the theoretical rubber meets the road of reality.

Investment themes are important because they will be used to govern one aspect of the portfolio. They provide an investor with what she needs most: conviction. Conviction is what is going to keep an investor on track even in the most volatile markets. That is critical to crypto investing. Remember, in Modern Portfolio Theory (MPT) an investor can produce superior returns through one of three ways: portfolio construction, asset selection, or market timing. Investment themes, along with crypto asset classes, will help us construct a framework for how we're going to build and manage a portfolio.

As a part of managing the portfolio, we will use time-interval rebalancing to adjust the investments per asset class and per position. Rebalancing helps an investor to manage diversification and is a systematic way to "buy low and sell high." The secret of this portfolio management framework is to always have a target percentage for cash. If the cash position is lower than the target, then an investor should be selling some assets to capture profit, and if the position is higher than the target, then the investor should be putting new money to work. As Harry Markowitz, the inventor of MPT, said, "Diversification is the only free lunch."

In our portfolio management framework, we use an event-driven model. We update our asset allocation model only when: (1) a strategic event dictates a percentage adjustment in asset allocation; (2) a market event dictates, through technical or fundamental analysis, a change in percentage allocation to each asset class.

We update our particular positions only when strategic decisions inform us to do so. We sell a position when one of three events happen: (1) we reach our target price; (2) asset allocation signals us to trim; or

(3) we've found a more strategic position to invest in that better expresses our investment theme. We never sell out of a position just because the price drops. With the portfolio management framework outlined, that still leaves us asset selection and market timing to discuss.

Once an investor has one or more investment themes and an initial asset allocation, she needs to start selecting some assets within that crypto asset class. In this chapter I outline 10 factors to consider when evaluating a crypto project/asset, and I provide some reference materials to help support an evaluation framework. In addition to the evaluation framework, an investor will want to use the fundamental analysis as a further criterion detailed within this book to help inform their asset selection plan. These tools used collectively will help an investor pick superior assets that should produce better risk-adjusted returns in the long run.

Finally, we want to consider market timing and how that will inform an investor's investment plan. In this chapter, I outline some simple technical analysis that helps an investor see the short-term and long-term trends of the market. Since bitcoin is the major reserve asset and the market is correlated to it, an investor will want to track bitcoin to make an informed directional trend decision. In this final section, I outline the three simple ways technical analysis governs an investor's decisions on market timing and how that feeds into the portfolio management framework. Additionally, this section covers global macro risk analysis and how that might fit into a total framework. If a trend is broken, that is a market event that should announce to the investor it's time to update the asset allocation percentages. Using this event-driven portfolio management framework, an investor will be able to bring a systematic approach to investing.

Portfolio Construction

Portfolio construction is a key aspect for building an investment framework. A savvy investor will want a way to segment their holdings in such a way that they can maximize benefit by the amount of a particular position and how that position correlates and responds to the market over time. A well-constructed portfolio will factor in correlation, position sizing, diversification, and target allocation percentages to help guide the rebalancing process. Good portfolio construction should see a portfolio respond well in different market events over time.

Crypto Asset Classes and Asset Allocation

Crypto asset classes are the core structure to use when constructing a portfolio, similar to how a traditional investor might go about building a portfolio with stocks, bonds, and alternatives. In our model, a savvy investor will select which crypto asset classes they want in their portfolio based on their investment thesis/strategy and then select which crypto assets to invest in from within those classes.

Once an investor has selected which crypto asset classes to have in their portfolio, they will then pick target percentages for each of those classes as well as for each position. Getting these percentages right, along with a system for what might change those target percentages, is a key aspect to portfolio construction.

Asset Correlation

The next consideration for each crypto asset class is to think about correlation between crypto assets. If each position responds exactly the same as, say, bitcoin, then your portfolio will be one big bitcoin portfolio from a correlation perspective. The goal is to consider correlation when tuning the position size so that you maximize noncorrelation within the portfolio. This can take time and trial and error to tune a portfolio with the correct position size based on each asset's correlation. (See Figure 16.1.) *Assets that are less correlated provide more portfolio diversification and diversification is the name of the game.*

Position Sizing and Volatility

We then need to consider portfolio volatility and how volatile each position is in the portfolio. If one position is twice as volatile as another, you may want to position size it smaller in the portfolio, so that the portfolio is balanced relative to beta or to volatility. You can use software to help do this, or you can calculate it yourself. In the early days, there was a site called Crypto TradeSmith that calculated a proprietary metric called the volatility quotient (VQ) for each coin. Volatility of each position and sizing that position is a key aspect to portfolio construction.

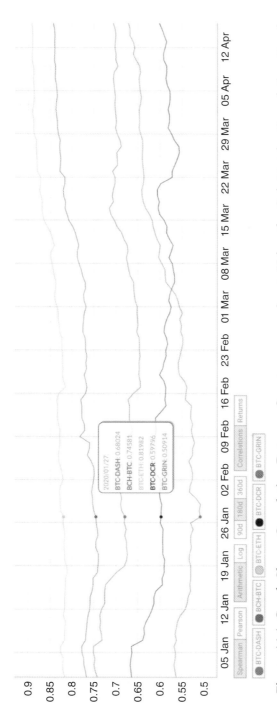

Figure 16.1 Graph Shows Correlation Between Cryptocurrency Assets Using the CoinMetrics Correlation Graph

	Position	Target %	Actual %	Position	Actual
Reserve	BTC	50.0%	45.3%	58%	54%
	ETH	8.0%	8.6%		
Currencies	DCR	2.0%	1.5%	4%	2%
	DASH	2.0%	0.0%		
Platforms	XTZ	4.0%	6.0%	12%	14%
	ATOM	4.0%	3.7%		
	ALGO	4.0%	3.4%		
Governance Tokens	BNB	2.0%	1.7%	5%	5%
	MKR	2.0%	2.0%		
	ZRX	1.0%	0.4%		
Utility Tokens	DATA	1.0%	0.3%	3%	
	OXT	1.0%	0.3%		
	SNT	1.0%	0.2%		
Fixed Income	DAI	10.0%	9%		
	USDC	5.0%	6%		
	USDT	0.0%	1%		
	USD CB	0.0%	4%		
Cash	USD Bank	1.0%	6%	18%	26%
	Total:	100%	100%	100%	100%
	Last Change:				

Figure 16.2 Asset Allocation Management Template

Portfolio Allocation Percentages

A savvy investor will take an investment strategy and will construct a portfolio by choosing crypto asset classes, determining a position under each chosen class, and then using correlation and volatility to help size each position. All the above will support an investor to come to a target asset allocation for each crypto asset class and each position.

An example might look like Figure 16.2.

Portfolio Management

Once a portfolio is constructed, it must be fine-tuned using back-testing and real-world events to optimize performance. An investor will have to play with asset allocation, correlation, volatility, position-sizing, and target percentages to get to an optimal portfolio. Once that's complete, training is over, and it's time to use the target percentages to help govern trading. When a position gets over its target percentage, an investor will need to sell some of that position. When a position gets under a target percentage, an investor will need to buy more of that position. Rebalancing is the core process of portfolio management for a long-biased or long-only investor.

Hedging with Insurance and Derivatives

If you're managing a sizeable portfolio and you're a sophisticated investor, you'll want some instruments to reduce risk. Just like in the traditional investing space, there are markets that provide the ability to hedge or lever up a position using options or other derivative instruments. There are also markets to insure certain crypto products and services. You can use regulated exchanges that offer futures or options contracts on crypto assets like bitcoin. Or, you can look to the DeFi space with its many offerings for insurance and derivative exchanges. Two examples of insurance offerings might be Opyn or Nexus Mutual. Two examples of options markets might be FTX or Deribit. You'll need to check your jurisdiction and its regulations to know which products and services are available to you.

Advanced Risk Management Concepts

Risk management is the key to investment. Here are some concepts you should be aware of but that are beyond the scope of this book:

- Convexity – Convexity is a risk management tool used to measure a portfolio's exposure to market risk. It's typically used to calculate and manage exposure to interest rate risk. As the crypto asset market matures, this will become a more prevailing concept, especially in the DeFi market as it matures and develops.
- Reflexivity – Reflexivity encompasses the nature of feedback loops where investors' perceptions affect market fundamentals. Compared to other asset classes, bitcoin, and crypto assets in total, is/are an extremely reflexive asset with high highs and low lows.
- Liquidity Constraints – An asset's liquidity is an important factor for investors to consider, especially when investing larger sums. If an asset is illiquid, prices move up or down in higher variation when money is moved in and out. This is especially important to consider when there is a market dislocation and investors are trying to get out

of positions in a shallow market. Institutional investors want liquidity so they can deploy larger amounts of capital without incurring price slippage. A conservative threshold for a liquidity constraint might be an investor will not own more than 5% of the daily transaction volume of a crypto asset.

Asset Selection

A crucial component in being able to produce alpha, which is above-market returns, is *asset selection*. Security selection with stocks has many frameworks. An investor could be a value investor or a growth investor, and each strategy has its own rubric. With crypto asset investing, there is a framework, too, and I outline one such framework that I think will be helpful in determining an asset selection process. This is distinct from creating your own investment thesis or strategy – the asset selection is tactical.

Crypto Project/Asset Analysis (PAA) Framework

When investing, it's important to develop a framework for evaluating potential investments. Crypto assets are not unlike investing in other asset classes like venture capital. If you want your investments in crypto to go the distance, they'll need to do well in the following categories:

- Product/Function: Do they own a functional niche? Do they have a defendable product and unique functionality?
- Size of Community/Adoption: Do they have a rabid following of users? Do they have an invested and interested community? Is the community growing rapidly?
- Technology/Moat: Do they solve a problem with a unique method? Do they implement interesting, defendable technology?
- Governance/Aligned Incentives: Are the investors systematically aligned with incentives? Are there proper systems and process for governance? Is there mining and/or other incentives or did they generate all the coins at once?
- Monetary Policy/Issuance: Does the project have a coin or token? Is it pre-mined? How much has been set aside for the internal team members? What is the issuance or inflation rate? How do they go about governing monetary policy?

- Market Opportunity: How big is the problem that is trying to get solved? What is the total addressable market?
- Development: How much work is being done on the crypto project? How many developer "commits" are there in the current period? How many full-time/part-time developers are working on the project? And how many people are "starring" or following the project in GitHub?
- Token Model: What is the "business model" for the token?
- Token Mechanics: What are its revenue streams or value propositions?
- Decentralization Strategy: Is this a centralized project with no intentions of becoming decentralized or does it have a roadmap to ultimately become a DAO or DAC?

I suggest starting off by using an unscientific rating from 1 to 10 for each of these factors. Later, an investor may build upon this PAA framework to improve its sophistication. I recommend creating a spreadsheet and going about a quantification approach to all of these qualities of a crypto project.

Token Models and Monetary Policy

Whether a token can accrue value or not comes down to, in no small part, the design of its token model and its monetary policy. There are two main factors to evaluate. First is the token model or how the crypto asset will accrue value. It can be determined by cash flow and how the token will accrue value. Second is the monetary policy and token issuance, which can determine how each token unit could be affected by monetary policy on the circulating supply and total amount of tokens available.

As discussed previously in the book, the token model determines its why and how its value will accrue, by creating monetary or utility value, and its monetary policy. If a token is premined and has an issuance model that creates high inflation, then that's going to be less appealing than a coin that is not premined and does not leave a substantial quantity of tokens to the internal team. Of course, there should be some thought as to how the community will pay for upgrades and maintenance, so a portion of the inflation should probably be planned for the developer team. There are many ways crypto projects construct their tokens, so it's important to understand the nuances of how the token accrues value and how the token incentivizes all the different community members. A token that tilts toward solely providing investor incentives will probably not grow its user base. A token that focuses solely on developers and users will probably not grow its investor base. All these factors must be considered.

Token Mechanics Evaluation

Token mechanics create the demand-side price elasticity for the crypto asset. These various token mechanics build the incentives for why investors should hold the tokens. A crypto asset with several high-quality, well-defined token mechanics, such as burn, high staking yield, and governance, is going to prove more valuable than tokens with poorly defined token mechanics or ones that are unable to capture value. If a token simply provides access to a dApp and perhaps a small discount on services, that's not as likely to inspire an investor to hold. An investor wants to see a sound token model, with good tokenomics and strong token mechanics that incentivize investors, developers, and users alike.

Using Technical Analysis

Technical analysis works well in the crypto markets. I don't know if it's because of all the algo-trading or what, but crypto trading seems to follow patterns and respect the lines. Now, entire books are written on technical analysis and the topic is far beyond the scope of this book. However, I do want to give a beginning framework that you can build upon.

Moving Averages (Daily and Weekly)

Moving averages give a rolling average of an asset's trading price over a period of time. They provide a look into price levels with resistance or support. The standard daily moving averages in stock that are used are the 20-/50-/200-day moving averages. In the crypto asset world, assets trade 24/7 and are more volatile; I see the 14-/40-/200-day moving averages working the best, though you can use any daily moving averages that you find useful. The 20-day and 50-day moving averages are still useful in determining support or resistance. Finally, the 200-week moving average has held for bitcoin every time – tested twice (minus

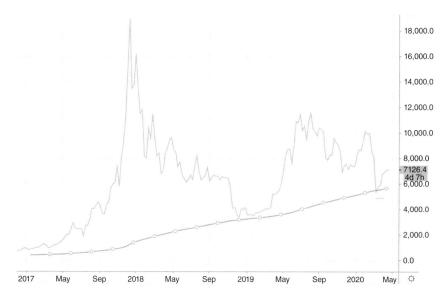

Figure 16.3 Bitcoin's 200-Week Moving Average Using TradingView

a four-hour trading period during Black Thursday). (See Figure 16.3.) This is the major level of support an investor can rely on for bitcoin.

Relative Strength Index (RSI)

The Relative Strength Index (RSI) is a metric of momentum that measures the magnitude of recent price changes to evaluate overbought or oversold conditions in the price of an asset. The metric is 0 to 100 with 50 being the middle, which means neither overbought nor oversold. A measure of, say, 30 or below indicates oversold, and 70 or above indicates overbought. This is a basic momentum indicator, which oscillates.

Trading Volume

Trading volume measures how many units of an asset traded in a 24-hour period. Low trading volume may denote less conviction, and price can be moved easier. High volume may denote more conviction, and it may take more to move the price. Typically, an investor wants to see higher volume before committing to a trade.

Other Advanced Metrics

There are many other advanced indicators and metrics. I invite you to research and check out more as you expand your technical analysis framework. Some of them include:

- MACD (Advanced Oscillators)
- Exponential Moving Averages
- Bollinger Bands
- MA Cross (Golden Cross/Death Cross)
- Stochastic RSI
- VWAP

Advanced Technical Analysis

There are many other advanced technical models that are beyond the scope of this book but may be worth exploring. These include:

- Ichimoku Cloud
- Fibonacci Retracement

Event-Driven Portfolio Management

The point of any portfolio management system or investment system is to remove emotion from the investment process so that an investor can make rational decisions based on sound data. Here I outline an event-driven system that allows a savvy investor to react to market forecasting and real-time data. The basic structure of the system is to create a portfolio with set target asset allocation percentages, then adjust those percentages based on feedback from the system in the areas of global macro events, technical trading analysis, and fundamental analysis. We use a green, yellow, and red indicator for each of the areas of the model. I'll outline a set of criteria that may drive state change within the model, but you can improve on this base model.

Global Macro Risk Events

The set of global macro metrics is measuring what's going on in the global currency and credit markets. For example, the euro-dollar market is a quadrillion-dollar market. If events and crises show up in this market, it's going to affect the crypto market. Watching a metric like the ^MOVE Index, which is the bond volatility index, will measure the total market's brittleness. If the ^MOVE Index is below a set threshold, that can indicate the global market for credit is stable and the market is not brittle. If the ^MOVE Index is outside the thresholds set, that can indicate instability in the credit markets and market brittleness. Supporting volatility metrics like the gold volatility index (^GVX) and the stock volatility index (^VIX) will measure the volatility in the gold and stock. If there's volatility in the bond market, we're going to see volatility in other markets.

Additionally, the ^DXY, the US dollar index, is an index that shows the strength of the dollar relative to a basket of other fiat currencies. Because of the way global FX markets work in relation to the US dollar, which is the world's reserve currency, the strength of the dollar can have effect on whether a market is inflationary or deflationary. In 2020, though the thresholds may be slightly different in the future, if the ^DXY is 96 or below, that is inflationary because the reserve currency is buying less of everything, relatively. If the ^DXY is over 104, that may warn of trouble and indicate a market is deflationary. When the rate of change in the ^DXY is high, that may warn of a crash in risk assets. Deflation is bearish for risk assets and a deflationary crash can affect all asset classes. As they say, in a deflationary crash, all correlation goes to 1.

Technical Events

The set of technical metrics used in our technical analysis framework will indicate potential market events that we want to capture in our Technical indicator. We've outlined the 20/50/200-day moving averages above as levels of support or resistance as well as trading volume and RSI (Relative Strength Index). We also track whether the price of bitcoin is putting in higher highs and higher lows for a bullish pattern and lower lows and lower highs for a bearish pattern.

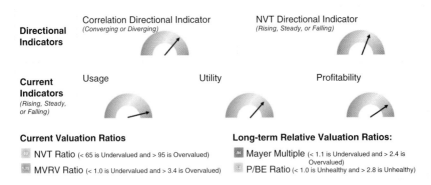

Figure 16.4 Dashboard with Metrics

If you want to set your Technical indicator more conservatively, then you might set it to be red if the trend breaks below the 200-day moving average and yellow if RSI rises above 70 or trading volume is too low, or the trend breaks the higher highs' and higher lows' trend. The objective is to set up metrics and thresholds to watch Technical indicators and adjust asset allocation based on pre-programmed parameters and events.

Fundamental Events

The Fundamental indicator is driven by measuring the utility (how much money is being transacted daily), the usage (how many unique addresses are being used daily), and the profitability (how much the miners are making per transaction to process a transaction). The Fundamental indicator also factors in valuation ratios, like the NVT ratio and the MVRV ratio as well as the Mayer multiple, to determine whether value is present at the current trading price of bitcoin. I've shown an example in Chapter 13. For example, look at the Fundamental indicator on April 23, 2020 (Figure 16.4) , the first day all the areas (*macro, technical, fundamental*) flashed green after "Black Thursday" (March 12, 2020) to see what the metrics were illustrating:

The price of bitcoin on that date was around $7,250. As you can see, in the following days and week, bitcoin traded higher.

Strategic Target Allocation Adjustment

The prime mechanism that drives changing target asset allocation from the macro, technical, and fundamental analysis is adjusting the asset class target allocation and the position target allocation based on a model. If the model determines there's a benign investment landscape (green in the model), then an investor should adjust the asset allocation for each asset class and position to take advantage of the marketplace, reduce the cash allocation, and get fully invested. If the model determines there's a cautionary investment landscape (yellow in the model), then an investor should adjust the asset allocation toward much more cash and reserve asset classes, readjust the target total allocation, and rebalance. If the model determines there's a risky investment landscape, then the investor should allocate mostly to cash in their strategic target asset allocation and rebalance.

Rebalancing

Once you have the mechanism for adjusting the asset allocation, then the prime mechanism to actually drive trading is the rebalancing. If the actual allocation percentage is off from the target allocation by some predetermined amount, say 2%, then once the actual and target percentage differences are wider than that, an investor will buy or sell a position to get the portfolio asset allocation back into its strategic allocation. It is rebalancing that solely drives the buying and selling of a position.

Strategic Adjustments to the Portfolio

There are three reasons why an investor might sell. One reason to sell is that they've reached their target price. Another reason to sell is that an investor finds another investment that the investor believes will generate a better return. A final reason to sell is that an investor has reached maximum pain on an investment and is unwilling to lose any more to the point the confidence is lost. Any of these strategic reasons may drive an investor to sell a position and alter the strategic asset allocation.

Investment System Summary

This investment system is event-driven and removes emotion from the decision-making process. An investor can pick a strategic asset allocation and then choose which crypto assets are going to express their investment theme under various crypto asset classes. An investor will rebalance and then buy or sell once the actual position percentage drifts from their target allocation. This creates a systematic way to *buy low and sell high*. A position may be sold off for one of three reasons. Other than that, the investment plan is driven by using a model for evaluating the macro, technical, and fundamental environment. If the investment environment looks promising, a savvy investor will alter the asset allocation toward investment in her themes. If the investment environment looks challenging, an investor may allocate more to cash in the portfolio and rebalance as determined by the target asset allocation. This is the base of the framework for a long-only or long-biased portfolio. However, there are many additions and improvements that I'm sure can be made. I think a smart investor can take this investment system and its core tenets and make them their own.

Thresholds

In this chapter, I've outlined an investment system you can use for crypto investment. Now that I've provided a template for the technical, functional, and macro aspects of the model, it's time to set the thresholds. Thresholds are the measurements' conditions where the state of the model changes (e.g. a measurement that changes a model from red to yellow to green). These metric thresholds have been backtested to provide optimal outcomes, but they may change over time. As a smart investor, you're going to have to test and perhaps do similar adjustments over time. This, however, gives you a good understanding of the mechanics of the model.

Technical Model

- Green: If the price is above the 200-DMA, RSI within its threshold, and volume is above its threshold, then the model turns green.
- Yellow: If any of the cases above don't hold, then the model turns yellow (warning).
- Red: If the price breaks below the 50-DMA, then the model turns red.

Fundamental Model

- Green: If usage, utility, and profitability are trending green and NVT is below its upper threshold, then the model is green.
- Yellow: Any other case, the model is yellow.
- Red: If the NVT is above its upper threshold and trends of usage and utility are falling, then the model is red.

Macro

- Green: If ^MOVE is under threshold and DXY is within its threshold, then the model is green. You can use ^VIX and ^GVX instead of ^MOVE but watch other markets' volatility.
- Yellow: Any other case, the model is yellow.
- Red: If either ^MOVE or ^VIX is above threshold or ^DXY is outside its threshold, then the model is red.

Asset Allocation Thresholds and Event-Driven Management

Setting the Conditions for a Required Rebalance

In your portfolio management, you will need to set the threshold for when a rebalance is required in your portfolio. In general, this system sets the need for rebalancing when the crypto asset class has drifted 2% or more and then when a position has drifted 1% or more. Also, since the correlations inside each crypto asset class should be high, I would not rebalance until the whole crypto asset class is 2% off the target, even if a position is off by 2%. For example, say the reserve class has a target allocation of 40% with a bitcoin position target of 30% and an ether position target of 10%. Let's say bitcoin has drifted to 32% but the total reserve asset class is still at 41%. This case would not require a rebalance, even though the bitcoin position has drifted by 2% because the asset class target hasn't drifted by at least 2%. This can happen often in an asset class where you may have four to five positions. This saves an investor from having to rebalance more often though an argument can be made for more rebalancing. For now, the system outlined here still recommends not rebalancing until the class is off 2% or more.

Event-Driven Adjustments to Strategic Portfolio Asset Allocation

The last piece of the investment system is altering the portfolio asset allocation based on readings of the model. If the model has mostly greens, you can set the cash allocation to 10%. If the model is mixed with yellows and greens, then set the cash allocation to 40%. If any of the model is red, then set the cash allocation to 80%. You can use the fixed income investment theme as cash as well for the purposes of this asset allocation. Using this model in such a way should help you avoid taking big losses when the environment is not in your favor and press your investing when it looks like circumstances are in your favor.

Putting It All Together

All right, now you have all the components needed to build a top investment system. Let's walk through an example of how you might use various aspects of the system to drive an event-driven investment plan. You need to think about how frequently you're going to check in and update the system. We'll call this *attributed system cadence*. Since this is an event-driven investment model, the cadence can affect many aspects of the system itself. An investor can set the system cadence to be one to two times per day or one to two times per month or anything in-between. The number of times you're looking to update the models can then also affect some of the levels you may be looking at within the model. For example, if you've set the system cadence to once per week, it makes more sense to focus on the 20-day moving average rather than the 200-day moving average in that portion of the technical model. Conversely, if you set the cadence to monthly, then you may not want to have the 20-day moving average in any aspect of your model because that may require you to respond quicker than what you've allowed for in your system.

I'll walk through an example of an investor who is fairly sophisticated and who has done her homework. She wants to set her system cadence to twice per week, so she's going to be a fairly active trader. She's gone through a lot of research and wants to invest using four investment themes – *Sound Money*, *Age of Autonomy*, *Governance*, and *Fixed Income*.

Now, she's completed her PAA framework and has selected 10 crypto assets in total (asset class and investment theme):

- $BTC – Reserve asset class with sound money and fixed-income (using BlockFi)
- $ETH – Reserve asset class with AoA theme and fixed-income (using a lending service)

- $DOT – Platforms asset class with AoA theme and governance (using staking for income)
- $ALGO – Platforms asset class with AoA theme and governance (using staking for income)
- $ATOM – Platforms asset class with AoA theme and governance (using staking for income)
- $COMP – Governance token with DeFi theme
- $LINK – Governance token with AoA theme
- $MKR– Governance token with DeFi theme
- $DAI – Stablecoin with fixed-income theme (using the Staked's RAY Smart Contract)
- $USDC – Stablecoin with fixed-income investment theme (using BlockFi to lend)

Based on her investment themes, she decides to construct her portfolio and allocate to specific crypto asset classes. She decides to invest 40% in the reserve crypto assets, 20% into platforms, 20% into governance crypto assets, and 20% in stablecoins (generating income). She sets up her analysis model to track and analyze technical, fundamental, and global macro events. Based on her initial portfolio allocation, if her model warns with *yellow* collectively, then her allocation will go to 20% reserve assets, 15% platforms, 15% governance crypto assets, and 50% stablecoins. She will then rebalance based on the new target percentages. Then, if her model turns *red*, she will have 15% reserves, 10% platforms, 5% governance, and 70% stablecoins, again rebalancing. Once the model turns back to *green*, indicating tailwinds and beneficial backdrop for crypto investing, she will reset her portfolio allocation to her original targets and rebalance. Along the way, she may find a better investment for governance tokens. Perhaps she decides for strategic reasons to divest of MakerDAO ($MKR) and invest in Binance Chain ($BNB) because it is now more decentralized, and it allows investors another avenue of generating a return. She will set the target allocation for each, and once sold, she will remove $MKR from her portfolio.

Portfolio management is entirely driven by a system. The model governs risk management. Trading is driven by events that inform the investor an action needs to be taken. Of all the analysis and information gathering that happens, the action that results from that process is to change the target percentages of the portfolio. Then, the trading that happens is entirely driven by rebalancing the portfolio based on the target weights and the comparison of target percentages to actual.

Risks and Disclosures

Crypto asset investing is very new. Over ninety-five percent (95%+) of crypto assets are worthless and do not accrue value. Markets are nascent. The entire concept of crypto assets is experimental. The industry is somewhat regulated but there are many aspects that are unregulated. Follow the regulations of your jurisdiction. When something goes wrong, there is no customer support to call. These bearer assets are *use at your own risk*. When you take back your autonomy and your control, you're going to have to deal with the fact that it's now on you to secure your assets. Using untested smart contracts is risky. Investing in speculative crypto assets is risky. The entire crypto space should have a big explosive warning sign around it. Do your own research. Build your own systems and processes to mitigate and manage risk. Move slowly. Test things. *Circumspicio.*

Conclusion

A system similar to this, but slightly more advanced, is what I use at my crypto fund. The various areas of the Analysis Model have alerted me before the price of bitcoin has made its moves. When the price of bitcoin breaks below its 200-day moving average, that's been a good time to get out of the crypto markets. When there are major issues in the eurodollar FX markets, our Macro model will pick it up and it has shown it's a good time to get out of crypto investing. Volatility and dislocation happening in a huge market like the global credit market of the world's reserve currency is going to affect the small crypto market with 100% certainty. When bitcoin trades with a low Mayer Multiple and when its NVT ratio is low and all the other fundamental metrics are green, it's been a good time to get back into crypto markets. Bitcoin dominates the crypto capital markets, so crypto markets aren't going to do well unless bitcoin is doing well. That's why a deep analysis of the Bitcoin blockchain network can be informative in any crypto investment system. I've learned that it's more important to look at trends and relative moves than it is to look at some bottom-up analytical approach to trying to value each crypto asset. There will be a day when that bottom–up quantitative approach yields more fruit than a qualitative trend approach, but I don't think it will be during this Frenzy phase of the technological revolution. Price decouples to value during this phase, so what a savvy investor wants to watch are the relative trends, not the absolute values from these blockchain networks.

We're in a new long-wave cycle of this technological revolution and we're early. As famed investor Mark Yusko says, "The greatest wealth is created by being an early investor in innovation. Making that investment requires believing in something before the majority of people understand it. You will be mocked, ridiculed, and criticized for your nonconsensus action. And, it is absolutely worth it!"

Crypto assets are the fundamental building blocks of a new digital capital system and the Age of Autonomy. While AI, the IoT, and robotics create value, it's blockchain technology implemented as crypto assets that are the rails of an entirely new type of system – a system that allows and promotes a greater level of autonomy. You can spin up compute services on Amazon's AWS system today, but it's not the same as designing and deploying a set of autonomous contracts that run without permission, 24/7, on public infrastructure that can execute and optimize, all without human intervention. As the world becomes more autonomous, it will become that much harder to compete without it. If you wait too long, you may become obsolete.

Crypto assets are transformational. They bring back more participation in the investment process because owners/holders of these assets need to participate in their governance. Participation is not required, but I think you'll find that if you choose to do so, the rewards are vast. I mean that both from a returns standpoint and from a sense of belonging. The entire world will be shifting over the next 40 years to take advantage of this key innovation. After reading this book, I hope you see why the opportunity exists, what the future holds, and how you as an innovative investor can reap the rewards from investing in crypto assets.

Notes

Introduction

1. https://usdebtclock.org.
2. Perez, Carlota. *Technological Revolutions and Financial Capital: The Dynamics of Bubbles and Golden Ages.* Northampton, MA: Edward Elgar Publishing, 2002.
3. "Worldwide Spending on Artificial Intelligence Systems Will Be Nearly $98 Billion in 2023, According to New IDC Spending Guide." IDC, Framingham, MA, September 4, 2019. https://www.idc.com/getdoc.jsp?containerId=prUS45481219.
4. https://em360tech.com/tech-news/tech-features/global-ai-business-value-reach3-9-trillion-2022-gartner.
5. Wikipedia. "Decentralization." 2020. https://en.wikipedia.org/wiki/Decentralization.
6. Taleb, Nassim Nicholas. *Antifragile: Things That Gain from Disorder.* New York: Random House, 2012.

Chapter 1: The Fed and You: A Brief History

1. DiMartino Booth, Danielle. "How the Fed Went from Lender of Last Resort to Destroyer of American Wealth." Excerpt published on LinkedIn (https://www.linkedin.com/pulse/how-fed-went-from-lender-last-resort-destroyer-american-booth) from *Fed Up: An Insider's Take on Why the Federal Reserve Is Bad for America.* Portfolio: 2017.
2. Amadeo, Kimberly. "Bretton Woods System and 1944 Agreement: How Bretton Woods Introduced a New World Order." *The Balance,* July 24, 2020. https://www.thebalance.com/bretton-woods-system-and-1944-agreement-3306133.

3. Maloney, Michael. *Guide To Investing in Gold & Silver: Protect Your Financial Future.* Scottsdale, AZ: Wealth Cycles, 2015.

4. Ibid.

5. Ibid.

6. Wikipedia. "Nixon shock." https://en.wikipedia.org/wiki/Nixon_shock.

7. McMahon, Tim. "Historical Inflation Rate." InflationData.com, August 12, 2020. https://inflationdata.com/inflation/inflation_rate/historicalinflation.aspx.

8. Lewis, Paul. "Nixon's Economic Policies Return to Haunt the G.O.P." *New York Times*, August 15, 1976. https://www.nytimes.com/1976/08/15/archives/nixons-economic-policies-return-to-haunt-the-gop-nixons-economic.html.

Chapter 2: Understanding Economic Cycles

1. Ammous, Saifedean. *The Bitcoin Standard: The Decentralized Alternative to Central Banking.* Hoboken, NJ: Wiley, 2018.

Chapter 3: The Long-wave Economic Cycle

1. Perez, Carlota. *Technological Revolutions and Financial Capital: The Dynamics of Bubbles and Golden Ages.* Northampton, MA: Edward Elgar Publishing, 2002.

2. Ibid.

Chapter 4: Safe Is the New Risky

1. Wikipedia. "United States Federal Government Credit-Rating Downgrades." https://en.wikipedia.org/wiki/United_States_federal_government_credit-rating_downgrades.

2. Congressional Budget Office. "The Budget and Economic Outlook: Fiscal Years 2012 to 2022." CBO.gov, 2012. https://www.cbo.gov/publication/42905.

3. "Federal Debt: Total Public Debt as Percent of Gross Domestic Product." Federal Reserve Bank of St. Louis and U.S. Office of Management and Budget, July 30, 2020. https://fred.stlouisfed.org/series/GFDEGDQ188S.

4. Haltiwanger, John. "America's 'War on Terror' Has Cost the US Nearly \$6 Trillion and Killed Roughly Half a Million People, and There's No End in Sight." *Business Insider*, November 14, 2018.

5. Gibney, Bruce Cannon. *A Generation of Sociopaths: How Baby Boomers Betrayed America.* New York: Hachette Book Group, 2017.

Chapter 5: Credit and Commodity Currencies

1. Menger, Carl. *Principles of Economics.* Braumüller, 1871.

2. Smith, Adam. *An Inquiry into the Nature and Causes of the Wealth of Nations.* London: William Strahan and T. Cadell, 1776.

3. Mises, Ludwig von. "The Principle of Sound Money." In *The Theory of Money and Credit.* New York: Skyhorse Publishing, 2013, pp. 413–428.

4. Ammous, Saifedean. *The Bitcoin Standard: The Decentralized Alternative to Central Banking.* Hoboken, NJ: Wiley, 2018.

5. Oldest coin: a 2,700-year-old 1/6 stater was discovered in Efesos. Fleur-de-Coin.com. https://www.fleur-de-coin.com/articles/oldest-coin.

6. Stella, Peter. "The Federal Reserve System Balance Sheet: What Happened and Why It Matters." IMF Working Paper, May 1, 2009.

7. "The Rise and Fall of Fiat Currencies." DinarDirham, October 12, 2018.

8. Ibid.

9. von Mises, Ludwig. *The Theory of Money and Credit.* New York: Skyhorse Publishing, 2013.

10. ———. *Epistemological Problems of Economics*, 3rd ed. Ludwig von Mises Institute, 2003. Reprint New York University Press, 1978; D. Van Hostrand, 1960 (trans. George Reisman); German ed., 1933.

11. Halton, Clay. "Debasement." Investopedia. Updated June 14, 2019. https://www.investopedia.com/terms/d/debasement.asp#:~:text=Roman%20emperor%20Nero%20began%20debasing,content%20was%20down%20to%205%25.

12. Wikipedia. "Edict on Maximum Prices." https://en.wikipedia.org/wiki/Edict_on_Maximum_Prices.

13. Desjardins, Jeff. "This Infographic Shows How Currency Debasement Contributed to the Fall of Rome." *Business Insider*, 2016.

14. Wikipedia. "The Great Debasement." https://en.wikipedia.org/wiki/The_Great_Debasement.

15. Ibid.

16. Martin, Felix. "John Law, the Gambler Who Revolutionised French Finance." *Financial Times*, August 30, 2018.

17. Ibid.

18. Maloney, Michael. *Rich Dad's Advisors: Guide to Investing in Gold and Silver: Everything You Need to Know to Profit from Precious Metals Now.* New York: Hachette Book Group USA, 2008.

19. Ibid.

20. Wikipedia. "Early American Currency." https://en.wikipedia.org/wiki/Early_American_currency.

21. Fergusson, Adam. *When Money Dies: The Nightmare of Deficit Spending, Devaluation, and Hyperinflation in Weimar Germany.* New York: William Kimber, 1975.

Chapter 6: The Fall of Credit Money and the Rise of Multicurrencies

1. Lewis, Parker. "Parker Lewis Gives an Overview of the Federal Reserve." The Pomp Podcast 321. (Interview: Anthony Pompliano.) June 24, 2020.

2. Perez, Carlota. *Technological Revolutions and Financial Capital: The Dynamics of Bubbles and Golden Ages.* Northampton, MA: Edward Elgar Publishing, 2002.

3. Trefis Team and Great Speculations Group. "Quantitative Easing in Focus." *Forbes*, November 15, 2015.

4. Engemann, Kristie. "What Is Quantitative Tightening?" *Open Vault Blog: Everyday Economics Explained.* Federal Reserve Bank of St. Louis, July 17, 2019.

5. Trefis Team and Great Speculations Group, "Quantitative Easing in Focus."

6. Wile, Robert. "The Richest 10% of Americans Now Own 84% of All Stocks." *Money*, December 19, 2017.

7. Wikipedia. "Pensions Crisis." https://en.wikipedia.org/wiki/Pensions_crisis.

8. Durden, Tyler. "Here Is the Stunning Chart That Blows Up All of Modern Central Banking." ZeroHedge.com, June 1, 2020.

9. MacroVoices.com. "Dr. Lacy Hunt: The Road Through Deflation Toward Eventual Hyperinflation." MacroVoices #217. April 30, 2020.

10. Ross, Sean. "Why Negative Interest Rates Are Still Not Working in Japan." Investopedia, updated October 12, 2018.

11. "ECB Ends €2.5tn Eurozone QE Stimulus Programme." BBC News, December 13, 2018.

12. Fergusson, Adam. *When Money Dies: The Nightmare of Deficit Spending, Devaluation, and Hyperinflation in Weimar Germany.* New York: William Kimber, 1975.

13. Redish, Angela. "Anchors Away: The Transition from Commodity Money to Fiat Money in Western Economies," *Canadian Journal of Economics* 26, no. 4 (1993) and Selgin, George. *Money: Free and Unfree.* Washington, DC: Cato Institute, 2017.

14. Wikipedia. "Terra (currency)." https://en.wikipedia.org/wiki/ Terra_(currency).

15. Podcastnotes.org. "Bitcoin, Central Bank Digital Currencies, and How Crypto Impacts the Financial Industry." Meltem Demirors on *Off the Chain*, hosted by Anthony Pompliano. February 19, 2020.

Chapter 7: A Digital Commodity: Bitcoin as Digital Gold

1. Popper, Nathaniel. *Digital Gold: Bitcoin and the Inside Story of the Misfits and Millionaires Trying to Reinvent Money.* New York: HarperCollins, 2015.

2. "An Interview with F. A. Hayek (1984)." The Jim Turney Collection. Interview at the University of Freiburg. https://www.youtube.com/ watch?v=s-k_Fc63tZI.

3. Taleb, Nassim Nicholas. *Antifragile: Things That Gain from Disorder.* New York: Random House, 2012.

4. Ibid.

5. "Hashcash." Bitcoin Wiki. https://en.bitcoin.it/wiki/Hashcash.

6. "Proof of Work." Bitcoin Wiki. https://en.bitcoin.it/wiki/ Proof_of_work.

7. von Mises, Ludwig. *The Theory of Money and Credit*. New York: Skyhorse Publishing, 2013.

8. Barber, Gregory. "The Cypherpunks Tapping Bitcoin via Ham Radio." *Wired*, June 27, 2019.

9. Suberg, William. "Binance Debuts Euro Pairs as CZ Says 180 Fiat Currencies Set for 2020." *Cointelegraph*, January 3, 2020.

10. Nakamoto, Satoshi. "Bitcoin: A Peer-to-Peer Electronic Cash System." Bitcoin.org. Whitepaper.

11. "The Beginner's Guide to Bitcoin." Part 9, Podcast #190: Altcoins, A History of Failure with Nic Carter. whatbitcoindid.com, January 31, 2020. https://www.youtube.com/watch?v=BUj_RZXdzQw.

12. Bitcointalk.org. Bitcoin discussion forum. https://bitcointalk.org/.

13. Mauldin, John. "Your Pension Is a Lie: There's $210 Trillion of Liabilities Our Government Can't Fulfill." *Forbes*, October 10, 2017.

14. Nelson, Danny. "MicroStrategy Buys $250M in Bitcoin, Calling the Crypto 'Superior to Cash." Coindesk, August 11, 2020. https://www.coindesk.com/microstrategy-bitcoin-buy-protects-against-fiat-inflation.

15. Henley, John. "Sweden Leads the Race to Become Cashless Society." *The Guardian*, June 4, 2016.

16. Isreal Goes Cashless – https://www.israelnationalnews.com/News/News.aspx/257054

17. Anand, Geeta, and Kumar, Hari. "Narendra Modi Bans India's Largest Currency Bills in Bid to Cut Corruption." *New York Times*, November 8, 2016.

18. Larry Summers says it's time to kill the $100 bill – https://www.washingtonpost.com/news/wonk/wp/2016/02/16/its-time-to-kill-the-100-bill/

19. Vaswani, Karishma. "China's Currency Move Upsets Markets." BBC News, January 7, 2016.

20. Stewart, Emily. "Soros Thinks We're Headed for a 2008-Like Crisis – Do Icahn, Cooperman and Others Agree?" TheStreet.com, January 7, 2016.

21. Ammous, Saifedean. *The Bitcoin Standard: The Decentralized Alternative to Central Banking*. Hoboken, NJ: Wiley, 2018.

22. Ibid.

23. "What Is the Value of All the Gold in the World?" OnlyGold.com. https://onlygold.com/gold-prices/all-the-gold-in-the-world/.

24. CoinMarketCap. Bitcoin. https://coinmarketcap.com/currencies/bitcoin/.

25. Frank, Jacqui, Chin, Kara, and Silverstein, Sara. "Top Strategist: Bitcoin Will Soar to $25,000 in 5 Years." *Business Insider*, October 18, 2017.

26. Wikipedia. "Metcalfe's Law." *Wikipedia*. https://en.wikipedia.org/wiki/Metcalfe%27s_law.

27. Silverstein, Sara. "Analyst Says 94% of Bitcoin's Price Movement over the Past 4 Years Can Be Explained by One Equation." *Business Insider*, November 10, 2017.

Chapter 8: Blockchain

1. Dictionary.com. "Blockchain." Dictionary.com. https://www.dictionary.com/e/tech-science/blockchain/.

Chapter 9: The Age of Autonomy

1. Perez, Carlota. *Technological Revolutions and Financial Capital: The Dynamics of Bubbles and Golden Ages*. Northampton, MA: Edward Elgar Publishing, 2002.

2. Ibid., p. 106.

3. Futurism, "The Age of Automation: Can Education Prevent Widespread Joblessness?". https://futurism.com/images/age-automation-welcome-next-great-revolution.

4. Google search on "age of automation." *Google*. https://www.google.com/search?q=age+of+automation&oq=age+of+automation.

5. Schumpeter, Joseph. Various works.

6. Kondratiev, Nicolai Dmitriyevich. *The Major Economic Cycles* (in Russian). Moscow, 1925. Translated and published as *The Long Wave Cycle* by Richardson & Snyder, New York, 1984.

7. Perez, *Technological Revolutions and Financial Capital*.

8. Martin, Felix. "John Law, the Gambler Who Revolutionised French Finance." *Financial Times*, August 30, 2018.

9. Wikipedia. "Hyperinflation in the Weimar Republic." Wikipedia.org.

10. Lewis, Tom. "The Failure of Fiat Currencies." *The Gold Telegraph*, February 28, 2018.

11. Toffler, Alvin. *Future Shock*. New York: Bantam Books, 1970.

12. CMMI Institute. "Appraisals." CMMIInstitute.com. https://cmmi-institute.com/learning/appraisals/levels.

13. Perez, *Technological Revolutions and Financial Capital*.

Chapter 10: Clusters of Innovation in the Age of Autonomy

1. Ford, Martin. *Rise of the Robots: Technology and the Threat of a Jobless Future*. New York: Basic Books, 2016.

2. Prodromou, Agathoklis. "TLS Security 2: A Brief History of SSL/TLS." *The Acunetix Blog >> Wordpress Security*, March 31, 2019.

3. Google. "Jake Ryan." List of articles published by Jake Ryan et al., and their citations by others. *Google Scholar*. https://scholar.google.com/citations?hl=en&user=Y7f6J54f-nsC.

Chapter 11: The Case for Investing in Crypto Assets

1. https://usdebtclock.org.

2. Schiff, Peter. "Peter Schiff, Chief Economist and Global Strategist." The Pomp Podcast (Interview: Anthony Pompliano). Off the Chain, October 27, 2019.

3. https://www.grandviewresearch.com/industry-analysis/jewelry-market.

4. von Mises, Ludwig. *The Theory of Money and Credit*. New York: Skyhorse Publishing, 2013; von Mises, Ludwig. *Epistemological Problems of Economics*, 3rd ed. Ludwig von Mises Institute, 2003. Reprint New York University Press, 1978; D. Van Hostrand, 1960 (trans. George Reisman.); German ed., 1933.

5. IANS. "China's Biggest Gold Fraud, 4% of Its Reserves May Be Fake: Report," July 2, 2020.

6. https://www.investing.com/studios/article-1012; https://www.cnbc.com/2015/08/25/scared-by-markets-maybe-you-should-invest-in-cars-instead-classic-cars-outperform-global-stocks.html; and https://www.fool.hk/en/2019/03/18/the-advantages-of-investing-in-fine-wine.

7. Free Working Tricks. "Did You Know (Officially updated for 2020) #2020." September 3, 2016. Youtube.com/watch?v=u06BXgWbGvA.

8. Buck, Jon. "Bitcoin Going Mainstream: Coinbase Has More Users Than Charles Schwab." *CoinTelegraph*, November 26, 2017.

9. Wilhelm, Alex. "Coinbase Reported to Consider Late 2020, Early 2021 Public Debut." *TechCrunch*, July 9, 2020.

Chapter 12: A Primer on Crypto Asset Investing

1. *Securities and Exchange Commission v. W. J. HOWEY CO. et al.* 328 U.S. 293; 66 S.Ct. 1100; 90 L.Ed. 1244, 1946. Supreme Court case proceedings transcript. https://www.law.cornell.edu/supremecourt/text/328/293.

2. Agrawal, Neeraj. "SEC Chairman Clayton: Bitcoin Is Not a Security." CoinCenter.org, April 27, 2018.

3. Rapier, Graham. "Ethereum's Officially Not a Security—Here's Why It Matters for Other Coin Offerings." *Business Insider*, June 15, 2018.

4. Parker, Geoffrey G. *Platform Revolution: How Networked Markets Are Transforming the Economy and How to Make Them Work for You*. New York: W.W. Norton, 2016.

Chapter 13: Quantitative Analysis Frameworks

1. Perez, Carlota. *Technological Revolutions and Financial Capital: The Dynamics of Bubbles and Golden Ages*. Northampton, MA: Edward Elgar Publishing, 2002.

2. Burniske, Chris, and Jack Tatar. *Cryptoassets: The Innovative Investor's Guide to Bitcoin and Beyond*. New York: McGraw-Hill, 2018.

3. Mahmudov, Murad, and David Puell. "Bitcoin Market-Value-to-Realized-Value (MVRV) Ratio: Introducing Realized Cap to BTC Market Cycle Analysis." Medium.com, October 1, 2018.

4. BarclayJames, "A Straightforward Guide to the Mayer Multiple." Medium.com, October 8, 2018.

5. Malone, Conor. "Bitcoin Price vs Cost of Mining." cryptoiscoming.com, June 28, 2018.

6. Lu, Kevin, and Coin Metrics Team. "Cryptoasset Valuation Research Primer, Part 1." *Coin Metrics' State of the Network*, February 11, 2020, p. 37. Weekly Feature.

7. Lu, Kevin, and Coin Metrics Team. "Cryptoasset Valuation Research Primer, Part 2." *Coin Metrics' State of the Network*, March 3, 2020, p. 40. Weekly Feature.

8. Burniske and Tatar, *Cryptoassets*.

9. Lu and Coin Metrics Team, "Cryptoasset Valuation Research Primer, Part 1."

10. PlanB, "Modeling Bitcoin Value with Scarcity." Medium.com, March 22, 2019.

11. Burniske and Tatar, *Cryptoassets*.

Chapter 14: Understanding Crypto Asset Classes

1. https://www.congress.gov/bill/116th-congress/house-bill/6154/text.

Chapter 15: Investment Themes

1. Imbert, Fred. "Yellen Says the Fed Doesn't Need to Buy Equities Now, But Congress Should Reconsider Allowing It." *CNBC Markets*, April 6, 2020.

2. Durden, Tyler. "30Y Sale Saved by the Fed's Bazooka as Record Tail Hints at Near Auction Failure." ZeroHedge, March 12, 2020. Reposting of an article from zerohedge.com. (Tyler Durden is a pseudonym/nom de plume.)

3. Mackenzie, Michael. "The Federal Reserve Has Gone Well Past the Point of 'QE Infinity.'" *Financial Times*, March 23, 2020.

4. U.S. Department of the Treasury. "Treasury and Federal Reserve Board Announce New and Expanded Lending Programs to Provide Up to $2.3 Trillion in Financing." Press Release, April 9, 2020.

5. Ammous, Saifedean. *The Bitcoin Standard: The Decentralized Alternative to Central Banking*. Hoboken, NJ: Wiley, 2018.

Further Reading and Resources

Books

Antonopoulos, Andreas M. (2016). *The Internet of Money: A Collection of Talks by Andreas M. Antonopoulos*. Merkle Bloom LLC.

Balbach, Anatol B., and Resler, David H. (1980). "Eurodollars and the U.S. Money Supply." Federal Reserve Bank of St. Louis, June/July.

Bitcoin Collective, Ajiboye, Timi, Buenaventura, Luis, et al. (2019). *The Little Bitcoin Book: Why Bitcoin Matters for Your Freedom, Finances, and Future*. Redwood City, CA: 21 Million Books.

Ferrara, Peter. (2013). "Rethinking Money: The Rise of Hayek's Private Competing Currencies." *Forbes*, March 1.

Ford, Martin. (2016). *Rise of the Robots: Technology and the Threat of a Jobless Future*. New York: Basic Books.

Friedman, Milton. (2002). *Capitalism and Freedom: Fortieth Anniversary Edition*. Chicago: The University of Chicago Press.

Hayek, Friedrich. (1990). *The Denationalisation of Money*. London: Institute of Economic Affairs.

Jackson, Andrew, and Dyson, Ben. (2012). *Modernising Money: Why Our Monetary System Is Broken and How It Can Be Fixed*. London: Positive Money.

Kelly, Brian. (2015). *The Bitcoin Big Bang: How Alternative Currencies Are About to Change the World*. Hoboken, NJ: Wiley.

Rickards, James. (2014). *The Death of Money: The Coming Collapse of the International Monetary System*. New York: Portfolio Books.

Selgin, George. (2017). *Money: Free and Unfree*. Washington, DC: Cato Institute.

Swensen, David F. (2000). *Pioneering Portfolio Management: An Unconventional Approach to Institutional Investment, Fully Revised and Updated.* New York: Free Press. Revised and updated 2009.

Taleb, Nassim Nicholas. (2018). *Skin in the Game: Hidden Asymmetries in Daily Life.* New York: Random House.

Timberlake, Richard. (2005). "Gold Standards and the Real Bills Doctrine in U.S. Monetary Policy." *Econ Journal Watch* 2 (2): 196–233.

Vigna, Paul, and Casey, Michael J. (2016). *The Age of Cryptocurrency: How Bitcoin and the Blockchain Are Challenging the Global Economic Order.* New York: Picador.

Weatherford, Jack. (1997). *The History of Money.* New York: Three Rivers Press.

Wolf, Martin. (2010). "The Fed Is Right to Turn on the Tap." *Financial Times*, November 9.

News Sites

Coin Telegraph
Coin Desk
Crypto Slate
Crypto News

Articles and Blogs

Medium

PlanB. (2019). "Modeling Bitcoin Value with Scarcity." Medium, March 22.

PlanB. (2020). "Bitcoin Stock-to-Flow Cross Asset Model." Medium, April 27.

Reddit – Bitcoin Reddit

Rimol, Meghan. (2019). "Gartner Top 10 Trends Impacting Infrastructure & Operations for 2020." Smarter With Gartner, December 10.

YouTube

Hacker Noon

Sumanov, Vasily. (2020). "Future of VC in the Web3.0 era: A Race to Investing in DAOs." Hacker Noon, May 18.

Services

Delphi Digital
CoinMetrics
The Block
Messari

Crypto Funds Blogs and Newsletters

A16z
Multicoin
BlockTower
Tradecraft Capital
Blockchain Capital
Ikigai Asset Management

Appendix

Location	Start Date	End Date	Month With Highest Inflation Rate	Highest Monthly Inflation Rate	Equivalent Daily Inflation Rate	Time Required for Prices to Double	Currency	Type of Price Index
Hungary	Aug. 1945	Jul. 1946	Jul. 1946	$4.19 \times 10\%$	207%	15.0 hours	Pengő	Consumer
Zimbabwe	Mar. 2007	Mid-Nov. 2008	Mid-Nov. 2008	$7.96 \times 10\%$	98.0%	24.7 hours	Dollar	Implied Exchange Rate
Yugoslavia	Apr. 1992	Jan. 1994	Jan. 1994	313,000,000%	64.6%	1.41 days	Dinar	Consumer
Republika Srpska	Apr. 1992	Jan. 1994	Jan. 1994	297,000,000%	64.3%	1.41 days	Dinar	Consumer
Germany	Aug. 1922	Dec. 1923	Oct. 1923	29,500%	20.9%	3.70 days	Papiermark	Wholesale
Greece	May 1941	Dec. 1945	Oct. 1944	13,800%	17.9%	4.27 days	Drachma	Exchange Rate
China	Oct. 1947	Mid-May 1949	Apr. 1949	5,070%	14.1%	5.34 days	Yuan	Wholesale for Shanghai
Free City of Danzig	Aug. 1922	Mid-Oct. 1923	Sep. 1923	2,440%	11.4%	6.52 days	German Papiermark	Exchange Rate
Armenia	Oct. 1993	Dec. 1994	Nov. 1993	438%	5.77%	12.5 days	Dram & Russian Ruble	Consumer
Turkmenistan	Jan. 1992	Nov. 1993	Nov. 1993	429%	5.71%	12.7 days	Manat	Consumer
Taiwan	Aug. 1945	Sep. 1945	Aug. 1945	399%	5.50%	13.1 days	Yen	Wholesale for Taipei
Peru	Jul. 1990	Aug. 1990	Aug. 1990	397%	5.49%	13.1 days	Inti	Consumer
Bosnia and Herzegovina	Apr. 1992	Jun. 1993	Jun. 1992	322%	4.92%	14.6 days	Dinar	Consumer
Venezuela	Nov. 2016	Feb. 2019	Jan. 2019	315%	4.86%	14.8 days	Bolivar	Exchange Rate

Location	Start Date	End Date	Month With Highest Inflation Rate	Highest Monthly Inflation Rate	Equivalent Daily Inflation Rate	Time Required for Prices to Double	Currency	Type of Price Index
France	May 1795	Nov. 1796	Mid-Aug. 1796	304%	4.77%	15.1 days	Mandat	Exchange Rate
China	Jul. 1943	Aug. 1945	Jun. 1945	302%	4.75%	15.2 days	Yuan	Wholesale for Shanghai
Ukraine	Jan. 1992	Nov. 1994	Jan. 1992	285%	4.60%	15.6 days	Russian Ruble	Consumer
Poland	Jan. 1923	Jan. 1924	Oct. 1923	275%	4.50%	16.0 days	Marka	Wholesale
Nicaragua	Jun. 1986	Mar. 1991	Mar. 1991	261%	4.37%	16.4 days	Córdoba	Consumer
Congo (Zaire)	Nov. 1993	Sep. 1994	Nov. 1993	250%	4.26%	16.8 days	Zaire	Consumer
Russia	Jan. 1992	Jan. 1992	Jan. 1992	245%	4.22%	17.0 days	Ruble	Consumer
Bulgaria	Feb. 1997	Feb. 1997	Feb. 1997	242%	4.19%	17.1 days	Lev	Consumer
Moldova	Jan. 1992	Dec. 1993	Jan. 1992	240%	4.16%	17.2 days	Russian Ruble	Consumer
Russia/USSR	Jan. 1922	Feb. 1924	Feb. 1924	212%	3.86%	18.5 days	Ruble	Consumer
Georgia	Sep. 1993	Sep. 1994	Sep. 1994	211%	3.86%	18.6 days	Coupon	Consumer
Tajikistan	Jan. 1992	Oct. 1993	Jan. 1992	201%	3.74%	19.1 days	Russian Ruble	Consumer
Georgia	Mar. 1992	Apr. 1992	Mar. 1992	198%	3.70%	19.3 days	Russian Ruble	Consumer
Argentina	May 1989	Mar. 1990	Jul. 1989	197%	3.69%	19.4 days	Austral	Consumer
Zimbabwe	Sep. 2017	Oct. 2017	Oct. 2017	185%	3.56%	20.1 days	"New Zim Dollar"	Implied Exchange Rate
Bolivia	Apr. 1984	Sep. 1985	Feb. 1985	183%	3.53%	20.3 days	Boliviano	Consumer
Belarus	Jan. 1992	Feb. 1992	Jan. 1992	159%	3.22%	22.2 days	Russian Ruble	Consumer
Kyrgyzstan	Jan. 1992	Jan. 1992	Jan. 1992	157%	3.20%	22.3 days	Russian Ruble	Consumer
Kazakhstan	Jan. 1992	Jan. 1992	Jan. 1992	141%	2.97%	24.0 days	Russian Ruble	Consumer

Location	Start Date	End Date	Month With Highest Inflation Rate	Highest Monthly Inflation Rate	Equivalent Daily Inflation Rate	Time Required for Prices to Double	Currency	Type of Price Index
Austria	Oct. 1921	Sep. 1922	Aug. 1922	129%	2.80%	25.5 days	Crown	Consumer
Bulgaria	Feb. 1991	Mar. 1991	Feb. 1991	123%	2.71%	26.3 days	Lev	Consumer
Uzbekistan	Jan. 1992	Feb. 1992	Jan. 1992	118%	2.64%	27.0 days	Russian Ruble	Consumer
Azerbaijan	Jan. 1992	Dec. 1994	Jan. 1992	118%	2.63%	27.0 days	Russian Ruble	Consumer
Congo (Zaire)	Oct. 1991	Sep. 1992	Nov. 1991	114%	2.57%	27.7 days	Zaïre	Consumer
Peru	Sep. 1988	Sep. 1988	Sep. 1988	114%	2.57%	27.7 days	Inti	Consumer
Taiwan	Oct. 1948	May 1949	Oct. 1948	108%	2.46%	28.9 days	Taipi	Wholesale for Taipei
Hungary	Mar. 1923	Feb. 1924	Jul. 1923	97.9%	2.30%	30.9 days	Crown	Consumer
Chile	Oct. 1973	Oct. 1973	Oct. 1973	87.6%	2.12%	33.5 days	Escudo	Consumer
Estonia	Jan. 1992	Feb. 1992	Jan. 1992	87.2%	2.11%	33.6 days	Russian Ruble	Consumer
Angola	Dec. 1994	Jan. 1997	May 1996	84.1%	2.06%	34.5 days	Kwanza	Consumer
Brazil	Dec. 1989	Mar. 1990	Mar. 1990	82.4%	2.02%	35.1 days	Cruzado& Cruzeiro	Consumer
Democratic Republic of Congo	Aug. 1998	Aug. 1998	Aug. 1998	78.5%	1.95%	36.4 days	Franc	Consumer
Poland	Oct. 1989	Jan. 1990	Jan. 1990	77.3%	1.93%	36.8 days	Zloty	Consumer
Armenia	Jan. 1992	Feb. 1992	Jan. 1992	73.1%	1.85%	38.4 days	Russian Ruble	Wholesale
General Government (Poland)	Jan. 1940	Jan. 1940	Jan. 1940	71.4%	1.81%	39.1 days	Zloty	Consumer
Tajikistan	Oct. 1995	Nov. 1995	Nov. 1995	65.2%	1.69%	42.0 days	Tajikistani Ruble	Wholesale

Location	Start Date	End Date	Month With Highest Inflation Rate	Highest Monthly Inflation Rate	Equivalent Daily Inflation Rate	Time Required for Prices to Double	Currency	Type of Price Index
Latvia	Jan. 1992	Jan. 1992	Jan. 1992	64.4%	1.67%	42.4 days	Russian Ruble	Consumer
Turkmenistan	Nov. 1995	Jan. 1996	Jan. 1996	62.5%	1.63%	43.4 days	Manat	Consumer
Philippines	Jan. 1944	Dec. 1944	Jan. 1944	60.0%	1.58%	44.9 days	Japanese War Notes	Consumer
Yugoslavia	Sep. 1989	Dec. 1989	Dec. 1989	59.7%	1.57%	45.1 days	Dinar	Consumer
Germany	Jan. 1920	Jan. 1920	Jan. 1920	56.9%	1.51%	46.8 days	Papiermark	Wholesale
Kazakhstan	Nov. 1993	Nov. 1993	Nov. 1993	55.5%	1.48%	47.8 days	Tenge& Russian Ruble	Consumer
General Government (Poland)	Aug. 1944	Aug. 1944	Aug. 1944	54.4%	1.46%	48.6 days	Zloty	Consumer
Lithuania	Jan. 1992	Jan. 1992	Jan. 1992	54.0%	1.45%	48.8 days	Russian Ruble	Consumer
Belarus	Aug. 1994	Aug. 1994	Aug. 1994	53.4%	1.44%	49.3 days	Belarusian Ruble	Consumer
Taiwan	Feb. 1947	Feb. 1947	Feb. 1947	50.8%	1.38%	51.4 days	Taipi	Wholesale for Taipei

Index

investments (*Continued*)
  risk (reduction), bearer instruments
    (impact), 171
  strategies, 174–5
    changes, 142
  system
    building, 223
    summary, 237–8
  themes, 209
  truth/fallacies, 36
Irruption phase, 31
iShares Emerging Market Stock Index,
  decrease, 92
issuance (USD), production metric, 186

J

Japan
  deflationary period, 71
  Lost Decade, 210
  QE, 62
job safety, business start (safety comparison), 36
job security, stability, 3

K

Kelton, Stephanie, 67
Keynes, John Maynard, 75
Kling, Travis, 207
knowledge Doubling Curve, 125–6, 126f
Know Your Customer (KYC), 164
  paperwork, 163
  processes, 84
Kondratieff cycle (K-wave), 28, 29f
  chart, 120f
  phases/seasons, 28–31
Kondratieff, Nikolai, 27, 120–1
Krugman, Paul, 67

L

Law, John, 52–4, 124
ledger, definition, 90
LedgerX, 174
Lee, Charlie, 106
Lee, Tom, 98, 207
Lehman Brothers, fall, 36
lending (increase), digital money
  (impact), 214
lending service, usage, 240
lending token mechanic, 194

leveraging, definition, 17
Libra (Facebook currency), 76, 78
Lietaer, Bernard, 74
liquidity
  constraints (risk management con-
    cept), 229–30
  coverage ratio, 188
  mining, 215–16
  premium value, 169
Litecoin, 106, 112, 159, 167
long-biased portfolio, 238
long-only portfolio, 238
long-term debt cycle, 20–1, 27
  current status, 22–3
long-term relative valuation ratios,
  182–3
long-term valuation ratios, 181
long-wave economic cycle, 27, 117
  Age of the Internet, 31–3
  analysis, 79
  building, 31
  history, 122–3
  technological revolutions, impact, 169
Lu, Kevin, 189

M

macro model, 239
Mahmudov, Murad, 47
MakerDAO, 193, 206, 217, 222
  divestment, 241
mandatory spending, increase (CBO
  estimate), 10
market
  capitalization, 186
  cycles
    explanation, 23
    movement, 34
  dynamics, 165–6
  opportunity, 231
  timing, consideration, 225
market value by realized value (MVRV)
  ratio, 181, 236
Markowitz, Harry, 224
Maturity phase, 31, 127, 190
Mayer Multiple ratio, 181, 187
Mayer, Trace, 99, 187
McCormack, Peter, 89
mean difficulty (production metric), 186
Medicare entitlements, 92